∽ INTO PRINT

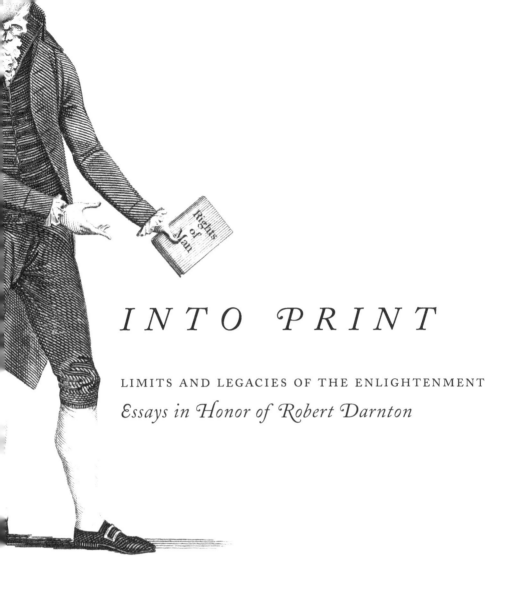

INTO PRINT

LIMITS AND LEGACIES OF THE ENLIGHTENMENT

Essays in Honor of Robert Darnton

EDITED BY

CHARLES WALTON

THE PENNSYLVANIA STATE UNIVERSITY PRESS
UNIVERSITY PARK, PENNSYLVANIA

Library of Congress Cataloging-in-Publication Data

Into print : limits and legacies of the Enlightenment :
essays in honor of Robert Darnton / edited by Charles Walton.
    p.   cm.—(The Penn State series in the history of the book ; 15)
Includes bibliographical references and index.
Summary: "A collection of essays examining how print culture
shaped the legacy of the Enlightenment. Explores the challenges,
contradictions, and dilemmas modern European societies have
encountered since the eighteenth century in trying to define,
spread, and realize Enlightenment ideas and values"—
provided by publisher.
ISBN 978-0-271-05012-6 (acid-free paper)
ISBN 978-0-271-05072-0 (pbk. : alk. paper)
    1. Book industries and trade—France—History—18th century.
    2. Book industries and trade—Europe—History—18th century.
    3. Books and reading—France—History—18th century.
    4. Books and reading—Europe—History—18th century.
    5. France—Intellectual life—18th century.
    6. Europe—Intellectual life—18th century.
    7. Enlightenment—Influence.
    I. Walton, G. Charles (George Charles), 1966– .
    II. Darnton, Robert.

Z305.158 2011
381'.45002094409033—dc23
2011020753

The Pennsylvania State University Press is a member of
the Association of American University Presses.

It is the policy of The Pennsylvania State University Press
to use acid-free paper. Publications on uncoated stock
satisfy the minimum requirements of American National
Standard for Information Sciences—Permanence of Paper
for Printed Library Material, ANSI Z39.48–1992.

CONTENTS

PREFACE AND ACKNOWLEDGMENTS

Charles Walton

In a pathbreaking essay appearing in the *Journal of Modern History* in 1971, Robert Darnton sketched out a new approach to the historical study of the Enlightenment. For him, it was not enough to "scale the peaks" of eighteenth-century philosophy, as the followers of Ernst Cassirer and Arthur O. Lovejoy were doing in their pursuit of new patterns of intellectual coherence.[1] Nor was it sufficient to inventory book collections according to social class, as the followers of Daniel Mornet were doing in France. Instead, Darnton called for examining how texts were produced, how they circulated, and how contemporaries responded to them. The "social history of ideas," as he saw it, called for analyzing the dynamic interaction between texts and social contexts, without reducing one to the other.[2] It sought to recover the "lived experience of literature," he later explained, by "follow[ing] thought through the entire fabric of society."[3] This approach, he believed, would open up new perspectives on the Enlightenment, showing how ideas figured concretely in the great social and political transformations of eighteenth-century France.

Over the past four decades, the social history of ideas has exploded into a veritable subdiscipline. Its influence, which now extends beyond the field of eighteenth-century France, owes much to its theoretical and methodological openness. The "ad hoc combinations of Cassirer and Mornet" that Darnton initially envisaged in 1971 have been expanded on and refined.[4] Much interdisciplinary cross-fertilization has taken place. He himself has incorporated the critical perspectives of several pioneering scholars in other fields, such as D. F. McKenzie (the sociology of texts), Pierre Bourdieu (sociological fields of cultural production), Erving Goffman (frame analysis), and Clifford Geertz (ethnographic "thick description"). Yet, in drawing on theory, Darnton has always remained attentive to disciplinary boundaries, to what the historian's craft specifically entails. While theory can point historians toward new sets of sources and help them formulate new questions, it can also, when applied heavy-handedly, run roughshod over historical specificities. In the final analysis, Darnton draws on cultural theories much like eighteenth-century peasants drew on the tropes, jokes, and symbols available to them in folktales, which he so memorably studied: they are "good to think with."[5]

Darnton has developed a distinctive approach to the study of cultural history. Like other "revisionist" historians of eighteenth-century France in the 1960s and 1970s, he rejected the Marxist tendency to view culture as determined by socioeconomic structures. For him, culture itself was constitutive of social and political life. But he parted ways with historians who limited culture to thought and language (i.e., "discourse"). Grasping the historical significance of cultural meanings, he believed, requires analyzing linguistic forces (epistemologies, ideas, opinions, attitudes, symbols, narrative frames) and extralinguistic ones (interests, social conditions, institutions, materiality, circumstances). It involves uncovering the relationships among all these factors without imposing an all-embracing scheme of interpretation. As Roger Chartier remarks below, Darnton's approach has been artisanal rather than systematic.

The treatment of texts and social contexts as distinct but dynamically interrelated phenomena runs through nearly all of Darnton's work. When historians began taking linguistic and semiotic turns in the 1980s—turns he contributed to—he nevertheless continued incorporating social factors into his analysis. In *The Great Cat Massacre*, arguably his boldest foray into semiotics, he treated eighteenth-century culture not as a coherent semiotic whole, but rather as clusters of meaning inflected by nonlinguistic forces, especially social conditions. In teasing out cosmologies from the symbols and tropes of peasant tales, he related those "worldviews" to the facts of rural life in France and Germany: hunger, violence, and social hierarchy. (Still, it is important to note that he did not *reduce* those cosmologies to socioeconomic conditions; indeed, the different ways that French and German peasants recounted the same tales suggest that cultural frames have a certain degree of autonomy.) Similarly, when Parisian journeymen in the rue Saint-Séverin laughed themselves silly executing the cat of their master's wife in the 1730s, they gave vent to rising social resentments permeating eighteenth-century print shops, expressing them in a carnival-like idiom of inversion that was becoming increasingly repulsive to bourgeois masters such as theirs. Even at his most semiotic, then, Darnton never lost sight of the social.

But social conditions are not the only nonlinguistic factors Darnton has considered in analyzing the historical significance of texts and meanings. He has also paid attention to the material, commercial, and political forces. These forces were analyzed extensively in *The Business of Enlightenment*. Tracing the

Encyclopédie méthodique from its initial success as a subscription-based multi-volume project in the 1770s to its financial collapse in the Revolution, Darnton aimed to show how the Enlightenment had penetrated late eighteenth-century French society, affecting a wide range of institutions: the book trade, the stock market, the guilds, and the royal administration. He discovered historical ironies that a straightforward history of ideas would have missed, such as the fact that the *Encyclopédie méthodique*'s publisher, Charles Joseph Panckoucke, had become attached to the very regime his publication was throwing into question: that of absolutism, privileges, and the guilds. Darnton remained prudent in advancing an overarching thesis. He argued neither that "encyclopedism" was the Revolution's foremost cause, nor that it spawned Jacobinism. He made the more measured claim that it was an "ism," one symptomatic of a "widespread disposition to question the ideological basis of the Old Regime."[6] Although the *Encyclopédie méthodique* reinforced this critical disposition among the many lawyers, officeholders, and local notables who subscribed to it—that is, the very people who would lead the Revolution—Darnton left room in his interpretation for other explanatory factors. "If other forces had not destroyed the Old Regime," he speculated, "encyclopedism might have been assimilated in France, and the kingdom might have ridden out the Enlightenment."[7] To be sure, Darnton is not principally a narrative historian, for whom events and circumstances are key to interpreting history. Culture, not contingency, has been his central concern. Still, the place he has accorded to circumstances in much of his work is significant. It bespeaks the judicious way he limits the explanatory reach of his cultural analysis, leaving room for other explanations. Artisanal and unsystematic, Darnton's approach has the great merit of being open and non-reductionist.

The Forbidden Best-Sellers of Pre-Revolutionary France arguably represents Darnton's most wide-ranging and sophisticated treatment of the linguistic and nonlinguistic factors producing historical change. It goes further than *The Business of Enlightenment* in advancing a causal argument for the Old Regime's collapse. In it, Darnton weaves together analyses of epistemology, slander, pornography, history, public opinion, and ideology with analyses of markets, books (as physical objects), communication networks, institutions, and circumstances, presenting a highly textured tapestry of the forces undermining the regime's legitimacy. He sketches the evolution of the early modern genre of *libelles* from seventeenth-century *frondeur* tracts to eighteenth-century best-selling books. Combining Enlightenment epistemology with anecdotes about sex scandals at the court and in the church, these illegal books repeatedly told the story of how the regime had degenerated into corruption and despotism. But according to Darnton, it was the commercial value and material heft of these books, not only their content, that made them so politically potent. For unlike the ephemeral *frondeur* pamphlets of the seventeenth century, with their fitful bursts of irreverence, eighteenth-century *libelles* became collector's items. Their widespread diffusion and long shelf life amplified and prolonged their messages. Often written as histories of the regime, they provided contemporaries with a master narrative that helped them make sense of the complex crises of the late 1780s. Once again, Darnton was careful in how far he pushed his thesis. He did not claim that bad books were the foremost cause of Revolution. Despite the title of the third section of *The Forbidden Best-Sellers* ("Do Books Cause Revolutions?"), his thesis is more nuanced than a simple "yes." He argued that these illegal best-selling books had weakened the monarchy's ability to command respect, thereby impairing its ability to control the political situation once crisis struck. The crisis itself, he clearly stated, had a multitude of causes: economic, fiscal, and circumstantial.[8] Although he did not elaborate on those other causes, he left room for them, and he took issue with historians who, in attributing the Revolution's subsequent slide into the Terror to the discourse of 1789, left no room for circumstances at all: "I think there is a great deal to be said for the 'thesis of circumstances,' unfashionable as it is."[9] His criticism of reductive, discourse-based explanations and his attention to extralinguistic factors do not amount to a blanket rejection of the value of analyzing texts. "The social history of ideas," he clarified in responding to his critics, "leaves plenty of room for philosophical exegesis based on close reading of texts."[10] Indeed, he has analyzed canonical texts in several of his essays. But such exegesis can take us only so far in understanding the period: "The Enlightenment was more than a set of propositions. It was a movement, an attempt to change minds and reform institutions."[11]

Darnton has both broadened and narrowed our understanding of the Enlightenment. He began by broadening it. Drawing attention to noncanonical texts, book-purchasing patterns, communication networks, and reader reception, he opened up new domains of historical inquiry, inspiring at least two generations of scholarship. More recently, though, he has insisted on narrowing what we refer to as "the Enlightenment." Troubled by the late and post–Cold War tendency to conflate the Enlightenment with all Western civilization (and, hence, to blame it for all of modernity's ills and horrors), he has called for restoring it to its proper proportions as an eighteenth-century "movement, cause, and campaign."[12] "Shrinking the Enlightenment down to its true size," as he put it, and separating it from nineteenth-century imperialism and twentieth-century totalitarianisms, might seem to run the risk of making it too remote and therefore irrelevant for us today. Darnton does not think so. To the contrary, he believes that separating the eighteenth-century Enlightenment from what came later forces us to be rigorous in distinguishing its philosophical legacy from other historical processes. And far from making the Enlightenment irrelevant, a narrower, more historical approach to its study allows us to unburden it of modern accretions and anachronistic freight; further, it allows us to appreciate the movement not only for its philosophical content (reason, toleration, happiness, skepticism, individualism, civil liberty, cosmopolitanism), but also for the great courage of those who championed its cause. If history shows us that the Enlightenment *in practice* was not the "heavenly city" that historians once thought—and Darnton himself has exposed its seamier side—this does not mean we must repudiate it, root and branch.[13]

Darnton, in any case, has felt no need to do so. He acknowledges the inspiration he draws from the Enlightenment's philosophical legacy, which has fueled a number of his *engagements*. His public interventions over the years have demonstrated his deep commitment to civil liberties and human rights, particularly the freedom of information and expression. Like the philosophes of the eighteenth century, he believes in the beneficial effects of freely circulated knowledge, and he has taken up the cudgels to defend it from forces threatening its production and diffusion.[14] Recently, he has enlightened the public about the potential dangers of Google's quasi-monopolistic control over digitized books. While recognizing the great advantages to having centuries of books available online, he worries that commercial interests may complicate access to them: "Yes, we must digitize. But more important, we must democratize."[15] His concern for realizing the democratic potential of print spurred his efforts, as president of the American Historical Association in 1999, to advance the cause of online publishing. He later helped found the Gutenberg e-Prize and coordinated with Columbia University Press to publish winning manuscripts as peer-reviewed online monographs. In addition to expanding the possibilities for presenting scholarly knowledge by exploiting new technologies, Darnton's purpose was to promote its diffusion at a time of contraction in academic publishing. He expressed his commitment to improving the production and spread of knowledge in his 2007 decision to accept the directorship of Harvard University Library. He explained, "Having, as a historian, studied the world of books in the distant past, I now have an opportunity to do something for the cause of books and book learning in the present, and I want to help find a way in which the new and the old media can reinforce each other, strengthening and transforming the world of learning."[16] He has thus gone from writing the history of the book to making the history of the book.

Darnton's professional and public actions reflect his desire to perpetuate one of the Enlightenment's most noble aims, namely, to inspire critical discussion and mobilize knowledge for the sake of progress, democratic empowerment, and human fulfillment. His historical writing has also contributed to these ends, for it has succeeded in making history meaningful and accessible to nonspecialists. I recall the fascination with which I read *The Great Cat Massacre* in my first undergraduate history course at the University of California, Berkeley. Years later, I assigned the book in my first undergraduate lecture course and witnessed the same fascination in my students. "I have never thought of folktales in this way before," one of them beamed, lights flashing in his eyes. Indeed, sparking readers' interest in the past is Darnton's specialty. Without sacrificing subtleties or succumbing to anachronism, he renders history meaningful and relevant. He makes it, in other words, "good to think with," whether we are trying to understand the violent humor of other cultures or trying to think through the risks and benefits of creating the world's largest online library.

The contributors of the main essays in this volume, all former doctoral students of Darnton, offer them as a tribute to him and as an expression of thanks for the inspiration and guidance, the measure and wisdom, he has offered us. Our overarching concern, print culture, has been at the heart of our adviser's research throughout his career, from his University of Oxford dissertation "Trends in Radical Propaganda on the Eve of the French Revolution, 1782–1788" (1964) through to his most recent study, *Poetry and the Police: Communication Networks in Eighteenth-Century Paris.*[17] Our essays touch on many of his concerns: writers, books, news, communication networks, reading practices, markets, states, politics, revolution, textual hybridity, social consciousness, Enlightenment universalism, and cultural difference. Our collection's subtitle, "Limits and Legacies of the Enlightenment," ties these themes together, capturing, we believe, what the social history of ideas is capable of revealing: By investigating the production, circulation, and reception of ideas, we can ascertain how the Enlightenment was delimited, or took shape, through practice and how it was reshaped over time.

Our collection begins with a transcription of Roger Chartier's keynote address, delivered at the conference in honor of Darnton at Princeton University in 2006. It reflects the lively, collegial spirit with which these two pioneers of cultural history have engaged each other for decades. Chartier highlights Darnton's chief contributions to the historical study of print culture, and those contributions inform the approach adopted throughout this volume. The essays are grouped according to themes that have been prominent in Darnton's work.[18] Our first section, "Making News," explores the social, cultural, and political forces affecting the diffusion and reception of news in the eighteenth and twentieth centuries. Will Slauter opens this section with "A Trojan Horse in Parliament: International Publicity in the Age of the American Revolution." He examines the *Courier de l'Europe*, a French-language, London-based newspaper covering parliamentary speeches in the 1770s and 1780s. He shows "what happened when words pronounced in a specific moment of national debate, recorded and printed according to local conventions, were republished for readers speaking different languages and obeying different rulers." The newspaper's poor, decontextualized translations of passages lifted from British newspapers led to misunderstandings that had significant political and diplomatic ramifications. Slauter exposes the historical limits to transnational communication; for despite the *Courier's* attempt to generate a cosmopolitan, or at least European, public opinion, its "cut and paste" methods distorted the context of original speeches and failed to overcome the particular cultural frames within which reading publics made sense of the *Courier's* articles. In her essay "'The Bastard Child of a Noble House': *Détective* and Middle-Class Culture in Interwar France," Sarah Maza takes us into the French publishing world of the 1920s and 1930s. She examines the sensational weekly newsmagazine *Détective*, France's first modern periodical devoted to crime, issued by the distinguished publishing house Gallimard. She shows how Gallimard, in seeking a greater readership market, created a hybrid genre of literature that spoke to a new, upwardly mobile middle class in search of its identity. The newspaper reassured readers of whom they were *not*, namely, the characters depicted in the magazine's leading stories: "cruel foreigners, urban riffraff, violent and greedy rurals." At the same time, the magazine provided this class with respectability. It carried contributions by distinguished writers, filled its pages with advertisements for highbrow books, and could boast the readership of some leading minds of the day, such as Jean-Paul Sartre, Simone de Beauvoir, and the Surrealists. Although Maza does not deal with the eighteenth-century Enlightenment, her focus on cultural hybridity in print—the fusion of high- and lowbrow texts—is reminiscent of Darnton's work on eighteenth-century print culture. Unlike eighteenth-century folktales, libels, and pornography, however, *Détective*, Maza suggests, helped forge a middle-class consciousness.

Our second section, "Print, Paper, Markets, and States," examines the various ways print and the papermaking industry figured in the expansion of markets and state power in eighteenth-century Europe. In his "Who Were the Booksellers and Printers of Eighteenth-Century France?," Thierry Rigogne discusses the rise of a new commercial institution, the retail bookseller. Unlike traditional printer-booksellers (the functions overlapped)—whose numbers declined over the course of the eighteenth century due to increased guild regulations and government consolidation of the print industry—retail booksellers, who operated with little guild or government interference, proliferated. Whether they sold books written by philosophes or their adversaries, these retail booksellers, Rigogne argues, ultimately fulfilled "the Enlightenment's most exalted mission: to promote the broadest possible diffusion of all ideas." In his "Making the Fair Trader: Papermaking, the Excise, and the English State, 1700–1815," Leonard Rosenband investigates struggles in late eighteenth-century England over defining "legitimate" interests in the paper trade, not only between workers and manufacturers but also between those two groups and the state. Debates over what "fair trade" meant, Rosenband argues, became mired in conflicts over workers' pay, company profits, and state revenues. He shows that, ironically, it was the British state, and not the paper manufactures, that advanced a Smithian conception of "fair trade" in its efforts to extract tax revenues. Rosenband underscores the interplay and tensions between interests and ideas in debates over regulating the papermaking industry. Renato Pasta concludes this section with his "Commerce with Books: Reading Practices and Book Diffusion at the Habsburg Court in Florence (1765–1790)." Examining the book-collecting strategies of the Grand Duke of Tuscany in Florence, Pasta shows how international networks of courtiers and freemasons influenced the grand duke's library holdings, which exhibited a great deal of eclecticism and cosmopolitanism, not to mention a predilection for "bad books." But if some of the collection bespoke an interest in progressive and radical Enlightenment thought, most of it reflected concerns about maintaining social and political hierarchies. The Enlightenment may have penetrated the court in Florence, but it was, overall, reformist rather than radical or revolutionary.

Our third thematic section, "Police and Opinion" begins with Tabetha Ewing's "Invasion of Lorient: Rumor, Public Opinion, and Foreign Politics in 1740s Paris." Ewing examines communication networks and police surveillance of public opinion in France in the wake of the failed British invasion of the French city of Lorient during the War of the Austrian Succession. She analyzes the political and social forces that shaped how news about the event was framed

and diffused, from the court in Versailles to cafés in Paris. She argues that foreign affairs constituted a prime topic of discussion through which a self-aware
public opinion came into being. Ewing also shows that the police worried about
the influence of this critical force, which they referred to specifically as "public opinion." Her analysis of police reports reveals that the public often couched
its opinions in official rhetoric, assuming the voice of legitimate political
authority. And rather than expressing the views of rational individuals, the
public opinion being worked out in Paris was often arrived at through vocal,
collective consensus building. Thomas Luckett takes us to the eve of the Revolution with "Book Seizures and the Politics of Repression in Paris, 1787–
1789." Whereas other historians have claimed that the policing of the press was
relaxed in this period (the print boom has been taken as evidence of expanded
press freedom), Luckett shows that police seizures of pamphlets increased.
Rather than suppressing sedition, however, heightened repression, he argues,
"may actually have contributed to the forces driving France toward revolt."
Luckett debunks the myth of 1789 opening up a liberal phase of press freedom. To the contrary, despite a brief moment of relative freedom in summer
and early fall, police raids on print shops resumed by the end of that year.

Our fourth section, "Enlightenment in Revolution," examines how Enlightenment ideas, writers, and reading practices figured in the political mael-
strom after 1789. In "A Grub Street Hack Goes to War," David Bell traces the
career of Charles-Philippe Ronsin from a struggling prerevolutionary writer
to a mass-murdering *répresentant en mission* during the Terror. Bell discusses
the changing nature of ambition in this period and shows how military and
literary aspirations before 1789 mixed with political ones as the Revolution
offered new opportunities for ambitious young men. In her "Reading *in extremis*: Revolutionaries Respond to Rousseau," Carla Hesse carries the question
of Darnton's famous essay in *The Great Cat Massacre*—how readers responded
to Rousseau—into the Revolution. She shows how revolutionaries transformed the style of private, intimate reading, which Rousseau had promoted,
into public ritual. Whereas numerous scholars have explored the impact of
Rousseau's political thought on revolutionary politics, Hesse demonstrates that
Jacobin invocations of Rousseau were less about working out the fine points
of his "social contract" theory than they were about spreading his spirit and
sensibility. In my "*Les graines de la discorde*: Print, Public Spirit, and Free Market
Politics in the French Revolution," I examine how revolutionaries struggled
over determining what kinds of propaganda would best bolster the legitimacy
of the fledgling republic in 1792 and 1793. Analyzing surveillance reports by

itinerant government agents responsible for spreading propaganda, I identify three positions on how to stabilize the new regime: first, free markets accompanied by civic instruction; second, government regulation of staple markets and wealth redistribution; and third, demonization, or scapegoating, through libels. I show that sharp disagreements among revolutionaries over the first two options—moral discipline and free grain markets on the one hand, and market regulations and wealth redistribution on the other—led to increasing reliance on the third option, scapegoating through libels. These libels, I suggest, injected punitive, exclusionary dynamics into revolutionary politics, thereby contributing to the Terror.

Our last section, "Enlightenment Universalism and Cultural Difference," explores the vexed issue of the Enlightenment's relationship to Muslims and Jews, specifically, how the Enlightenment depicted Muslims and impinged on Jewish traditions. Jeffrey Freedman's "The Limits of Tolerance: Jews, the Enlightenment, and the Fear of Premature Burial" discusses the widespread anxiety in eighteenth-century Europe about premature burial, and describes the dilemmas that scientists and enlightened policy makers faced in trying (and failing) to persuade Jewish communities to delay burial beyond the twenty-four-hour limit imposed by Jewish tradition. According to Freedman, the protagonists of Enlightenment science came to the somber conclusion that reason alone would not suffice to persuade Jewish communities to change their customs and state coercion would therefore be necessary. In her "From Cosmopolitan Anticolonialism to Liberal Imperialism: French Intellectuals and Muslim North Africa in the Late Eighteenth and Early Nineteenth Centuries," Shanti Singham traces changes in the textual treatment of Muslims, from the Abbé Raynal's eighteenth-century *Histoire des deux Indes* to Alexis de Tocqueville's nineteenth-century writings on Algeria. Contrary to Edward Said and his followers, who accuse the Enlightenment of Eurocentrism and racism, Singham finds cultural tolerance and sensitivity for Muslims expressed in underground and revolutionary texts. It was with the rise of liberalism and nationalism in the nineteenth century that such discourses gave way to those of intolerance and racism.

Taken together, these essays offer contrasting perspectives on the Enlightenment and its legacy. In taking print culture as a focal point for exploring how ideas and practice have intersected over time, they highlight the practical limits and ambivalent legacies of the vast body of ideas and values that we have come to associate with the Enlightenment. There has been much debate in recent decades about the Enlightenment's legacy. While some scholars have seen it as generative of imperialism, racism, sexism, and myriad forms of totalitarianism, others have stressed its positive heritage: democracy, human rights, and a critical epistemology capable of expanding domains of freedom and empowerment. The contributors to this collection seek to neither condemn nor defend the Enlightenment. Rather, we seek to understand its history. In the pages that follow, readers will encounter how print culture figured in the Enlightenment's achievements but also its excesses and dilemmas. The social history of ideas—the analysis of the textual and the non-textual—is precisely the kind of critical engagement with the Enlightenment that can help us avoid the twin dangers of either accepting its legacy uncritically (with all the risks associated with blind faith) or rejecting it out of hand (with the risk of lapsing into ethical paralysis). The social history of ideas can provide perspectives that can help us make decisions about the moral and intellectual legacy we want to bequeath, not to mention the kinds of actions and institutions necessary to protect that legacy from distortions, manipulation, and unintended consequences. A well-contextualized history of the Enlightenment can help us choose how we draw from its legacy to get through tough times or, as Darnton puts it, to establish "an intellectual stance that will serve when lines are drawn and one's back is to the wall."[19]

These essays grew out of a conference in honor of Robert Darnton held at Princeton University on April 28 and 29, 2006. The contributors to this volume would like to thank the university's Department of History and the Shelby Cullom Davis Center for Historical Studies for hosting and supporting this event. We also extend our gratitude to the special guests of this conference, who provided useful comments that have helped us transform these papers into this collection of essays: Roger Chartier, Natalie Zemon Davis, Michael Fried, Anthony Grafton, Colin Jones, Daniel Roche, Jerrold Seigel, and Isser Woloch. Although they were not present at this conference, I would like to thank John Merriman and Francesca Trivellato for their helpful comments on parts of this volume, as well as Tatiana Grigorenko and Alyssa Reichardt for their for her assistance in preparing the manuscript for production. The Florence Gould Foundation generously provided funding for both the conference and this publication. We also thank Penn State University Press for their enthusiastic support for this project and expertise in seeing it through to completion. Above all, we thank Robert Darnton for his guidance and inspiration over the years. We hope that our essays do justice to his career's devotion to the social history of ideas.

NOTES

1. Robert Darnton, "In Search of the Enlightenment: Recent Attempts to Create a Social History of Ideas," *Journal of Modern History* 43, no. 1 (March 1971): 113–32.

2. Darnton appropriated the term used (albeit in different ways) by both Peter Gay in the United States and the historians of *Livre et société* in France; see ibid., 113 (Gay) and 124 (the *Livre et société* group).

3. Robert Darnton, *The Kiss of Lamourette* (London: Faber and Faber, 1990), 212.

4. Darnton, "In Search of the Enlightenment," 132.

5. Darnton borrowed Claude Lévi-Strauss's famous phrase; see *The Great Cat Massacre, and Other Episodes in French Cultural History* (New York: Vintage, 1985), 4.

6. Robert Darnton, *The Business of Enlightenment: A Publishing History of the "Encyclopédie," 1775–1800* (Cambridge: Harvard University Press, 1979), 540.

7. Ibid., 540–41.

8. Robert Darnton, *The Forbidden Best-Sellers of Pre-Revolutionary France* (New York: W. W. Norton, 1995), 245.

9. Ibid., 177.

10. Robert Darnton, "Two Paths Through the Social History of Ideas," in *The Darnton Debate: Books and Revolution in the Eighteenth Century*, ed. Haydn T. Mason (Oxford: Voltaire Foundation, 1998), 280.

11. Ibid.

12. Carl L. Becker, *The Heavenly City of the Eighteenth-Century Philosophers* (New Haven: Yale University Press, 1932).

13. Robert Darnton, *George Washington's False Teeth: An Unconventional Guide to the Eighteenth Century* (New York: W. W. Norton, 2003), 4.

14. Robert Darnton, *The Case for Books: Past, Present, and Future* (New York: Public Affairs, 2009).

15. Robert Darnton, "Google and the Future of Books," *New York Review of Books*, February 12, 2009, http://www.nybooks.com/articles/22281.

16. "Robert Darnton Named Carl H. Pforzheimer University Professor and Director of the University Library," Harvard University Library: News, http://hul.harvard.edu/news/2007_0522 .html (accessed September 17, 2009).

17. Most of the essays in this collection quote liberally from foreign-language sources. Unless otherwise noted, all translations have been completed by the authors.

18. Robert Darnton, *Poetry and the Police: Communication Networks in Eighteenth-Century Paris* (Cambridge: Harvard University Press, 2010).

19. Darnton, *George Washington's False Teeth*, 19.

UN GARÇON PLEIN D'ESPRIT MAIS EXTRÊMEMENT DANGEREUX:
THE DARNTON SUBVERSION

Roger Chartier

It is not an easy task to discuss Robert Darnton's achievements. I was a bit foolish when I accepted Charles Walton's invitation to do so, and since my reckless acceptance, I have been torn between the pleasure and honor of such an assignment and the impossibility of the task.

My imprudence is all the more incomprehensible in that I had to confront the same challenge two years ago when I was asked to introduce Bob for the Rosenbach Lectures he gave at the University of Pennsylvania under the promising and mysterious title of "The Devil in the Holy Water." On that occasion, I claimed to have found in the Parisian archives (and immediately everyone who knows that I "hate" the archives, as Bob revealed in a recent interview, understood that I was making the story up) a report written by the police inspector Joseph d'Hémery, who was in charge, as you know, of watching the men of letters in eighteenth-century Paris.

The report begins as follows:

Nom: Darnton, Robert, author.
Age: A little more than sixty.
Pays: New York.
Signalement: Tall, thin, handsome, charming. He is as much at ease with
the *gens du monde* as with the *gens de lettres*.

These remarks opened the conference in honor of Robert Darnton held at Princeton University on April 28 and 29, 2006.

Demeure: Princeton, a small city in the countryside. But he routinely travels throughout the different kingdoms of Europe for the purpose of spreading his subversive ideas. He has spent some time in Berlin, where he keeps a diary of the overthrow that has affected the kingdom of Prussia.

Histoire: Very learned and taught by the best masters. He began his career as a journalist. He has written numerous books, published within and outside of his native country. Readers of many different backgrounds and languages read them. He knows better than anyone (and certainly better than our police) the hack writers, clandestine peddlers, and subversive booksellers who propagate the pamphlets and libels that in the present time mock all forms of authority. "C'est un garçon plein d'esprit mais extrêmement dangereux," whose aim is to subvert the old dogmas, the received ideas, and the established authorities. He must be watched with the greatest attention.

Of course, *bis repetita non placent*: I cannot use the same trick and Diderot's file to present Bob today. Deeply embarrassed, I have decided to return to the simplicity of the New England primer. Or, to put it another way, I have decided to write an alphabetic "Darnton for beginners." Let me begin with the letter *A*.

A as in Anthropology. Thanks to twenty-five years of coteaching by Bob and Clifford Geertz, no cats in the world are as famous as those hanged in Paris in the late 1730s by the apprentices and workers of Monsieur Vincent, who ran a printing shop on the rue Saint-Séverin. Only cocks fighting in Bali can compete with "la Grise" and her unfortunate companions for such a worldwide reputation. The massacred cats were honored by five articles in the *Journal of Modern History*, which raised fundamental issues about the relationships between symbolic anthropology and cultural history, between textual logic and practical sense, and between the universality of symbols and local knowledge. Bob's reply to his critics (myself, Jim Fernandez, and Dominick LaCapra, who enjoyed staging a great Darnton and Chartier massacre) is an important piece that begins on the C Floor of Princeton University's Firestone Library with an advertisement posted on the door of a student's carrel: "Fiji, $499"—a joke that graduate students certainly got but that would strike those unfamiliar with the context as strange. Flying back from the Pacific island (same as above) to the rue Saint-Séverin, Bob wrote an essay that proposed a challenging program of exploring "how anthropological theory can help in the analysis of a historical problem." Seduced by the rigor of the "ethnographic diagram" in the manner of Lévi-Strauss, he drew up a series of graphs contrasting culture and nature, the domestic and the wild, work and sex. He did not, however, give up what matters most in all his books: the flesh and blood, but also the heart and soul, of men and women of the past. If it is true that "structure frames stories," it is still more true for him that events (ritualistic or not) and stories acquire a human density and complexity because they link, he writes, "polysemic symbolism" and "polymorphic ritualism." Bob's perspective resembles, in many respects, the conceptual distinction between structures and strategies advanced by a scholar that Bob, Daniel Roche, and I so much admired: the sociologist Pierre Bourdieu.

Best sellers will be my *B*. From his first essays, which rescued hack writers, provincial booksellers, and clandestine peddlers from the archives of the Société typographique de Neuchâtel, to his two-volume summa published in 1995 (*The Forbidden Best-Sellers of Pre-Revolutionary France*), Bob sought to reconstruct a list of the books that were most often bought and (perhaps) read by French readers of the eighteenth century. For him, the statistics drawn from the registers of the Direction de la librairie or from the inventories of private libraries were entirely misleading—and the French historians who trusted them were completely wrong. The clandestine best sellers and pamphlets were much more important than the inert and insignificant steady sellers for understanding profound changes in representations of the monarchy, religion, and authority in the last thirty years of the Old Regime. Bob wrote, "This corrosion operated in two ways: at the level of ideas, the writings of Voltaire and d'Holbach openly denounced the falsities of the systems of orthodoxy that supported the church and the crown; at the level of representation, the pamphlets and scandal-mongering chronicles desacralized by throwing mud on the monarchy and all the values that structured its political rationality."

Such a diagnosis offered a fresh and provocative reappraisal of the origins—or, to put it better, conditions of possibility—for the radical rupture that occurred in 1789. Darnton's interpretation rejected both the traditional socioeconomic interpretation of the Revolution as too mechanistic and the purely discursive one as too idealistic. Among the bitter disputes around the French Revolution's bicentennial, Bob attempted (as did Daniel Roche and I) to propose a third way, arguing that if political discourses construct interests, positions, and even events, they are themselves limited by the linguistic, conceptual, and material resources available for their production, circulation, and appropriation. At the time, such attempts were not easy and, in France at least, did not catch on very well, perhaps because they challenged old and new historiographical orthodoxies. Still, they opened up the possibility of showing how representations, beliefs, and emotions have historically mediated between society and political action. Our approach also drew attention to the materiality of the texts—how "forms effect meaning," to quote a scholar and a friend whom Bob and I admired and now miss very much, the late Donald F. McKenzie.

Historian of best sellers, Bob is himself the author of historical best sellers. A map of the translations of his books (to which we must add the books that were originally published in languages other than English) would replicate the geography of the Enlightenment. Bob is first an author of the Aufklärung, with thirteen of his books appearing in German. The Lumières were a little less welcoming, with only eight books in French, though three of these were originally published or written in French (as opposed to being translated). A ninth work in French, written for a series of twenty-six half-hour television broadcasts, should be added to the list. If the German *Kultur* honored the bookish Darnton, who received the Gutenberg Prize in 2004, the Parisian *civilisation* opened its salons to the distinguished homme de lettres, who was the only author ever applauded on the set of Bernard Pivot's television show *Apostrophes*.

Darnton's Europe is not at all limited to the three linguistic pillars of the Enlightenment (French, German, and English). It extends to the north (three books in Swedish, one in Danish, six in Dutch), the east (like Diderot, Darnton is present in Russia with two translations, but he is also published in Hungarian, Estonian, and Lithuanian), and the south (eight books in Italian, six in Spanish, eight in Portuguese). In the case of the last two language groups, the European metropoles have been surpassed by their former colonies, since Bob's books have been published mainly in Brazil, Mexico, and Argentina. My Braudelian journey does not end with Europe or the Atlantic world. It must also sail eastward all the way to Japan (six books), China (two), and Korea (two). Last but not least, a forthcoming publication in Hebrew of *The Great Cat Massacre* will be the fifteenth translation of this book, Darnton's absolute best seller.

After such a list, it naturally follows that Comparison will be my *C*. In an article appearing in *Publishing History* in 1987, Bob proposed an ambitious agenda for a comparative history of the book. He began by discussing the French *histoire du livre* and the German *Geschichte des Buchwesens*, but concluded by broadening the field of comparison: "The questions and comparisons could be multiplied indefinitely. By adding new countries, new insights could emerge. France can be compared best with England. . . . Similarly it might be best to compare Germany with Italy, a linguistic and cultural unit that was fragmented politically and divided economically along lines that determined the traffic in books."

In his own research, Bob explored the eighth topic on his agenda, censorship, and compared three cases: eighteenth-century France, nineteenth-century colonial India, and twentieth-century East Germany. The result was a series of lectures (among them one delivered in 1994 as part of the Oxford Amnesty Lecture Series) and several articles on British India that all suggested the necessity of a profound reappraisal of the meaning of censorship—one that did not, of course, imply any sympathy for the destruction of books and the suppression of ideas. In his 1987 article, Bob wrote, "Is it not misleading to think of censorship entirely in negative terms? The *approbations* in French books frequently show that the censor conveyed a royal stamp of approval for a work, along with compliments about its style and contents and even suggestions about how it should be approached by the reader." The analysis of printed *aprobaciones* in the books published in golden age Spain and the reports written by the censors for the *Real Mesa Censória* in the Portugal of Pombal entirely confirm such a diagnosis. It was the same idea that led Bob to describe censorship in nineteenth-century India as attempting to establish a liberal model of imperialism and, after the year he spent in Berlin in 1989–90 and several interviews with former censors of the ex-GDR, to affirm that his interlocutors "thought they were engaged in social engineering."

Comparative history is often more praised or talked about than really practiced and written. Bob's comparative history of censorship shows that while the task is difficult, it is not impossible, and, in any case, it is necessary if we want to locate the history of books within the new paradigm of interconnected histories.

Debate is my *D*. Very few historians have inspired an entire book devoted to discussing their approaches and conclusions. For Darnton, this came about in 1998 with the publication of *The Darnton Debate*, edited by Haydn T. Mason and published by the Voltaire Foundation. Fundamental issues are at stake in this volume, whose subtitle is *Books and Revolution in the Eighteenth Century*. To select just a few: Were the authors of pamphlets, libels, and scandalous chronicles angry hack writers expressing their frustration? Or did they write at the behest of their patrons (ministers, aristocrats, bankers), who commissioned such works as powerful instruments for their own political or financial strategies? Did the publishers of subversive and clandestine literature print these items because they made for handsome profits? Or should we believe in their ideological commitments? And last but not least, do books make revolutions? Can we suppose that the wide circulation of texts exposing the despotic corruption of the monarchy and the depraved mores of the court engendered a radical transformation of thoughts and representations, detaching readers from old loyalties? Or do we recognize that the same text can be understood in multiple ways, not all of them subversive, and that the symbolic and affective disinvestment that transformed relations with authority was produced by emotions and thoughts that owed nothing to reading radical philosophers and scandalous pamphlets?

Bob frequently debated such issues, and even when the polemic was harsh or unfair, I think he enjoyed it. I became convinced of this when I read an interview he gave in 2002 to the German historical online journal *Zeitenblicke.* In the first sentence of the conversation, Bob declares, "I like contradictions," and he continues, "In my first attempts to write history, I tried to smooth things out so that everything fit neatly into my argument. Now I favor arguments that bring out contradictions and that take account of the paradoxes and tensions built into human experience." All the objections that have been articulated as challenges to his views were, in fact, questions that he addressed to himself, from his first essays on the "low-life of literature," the "*Encyclopédie* wars," or "the origins of modern reading" to his major books on *The Literary Underground of the Old Regime, The Business of Enlightenment*, and *The Forbidden Best-Sellers of Pre-Revolutionary France.*

For Bob, academic and scholarly discussions cannot be separated from interventions in the public sphere. He likes newspapers and was even a reporter himself. He has written more than thirty long articles for the *New York Review of Books* since the first one was published in the April 5, 1973, issue. In the United States, he has contributed to the *New Republic*, the *Chronicle of Higher Education*, and *Daedalus.* In Germany, he has published articles in the *Frankfurter Allgemeine Zeitung*, and in France, in the *Lettre Internationale.* In Brazil, he wrote a column for the *Folha de São Paulo* for several years. At a time when we often deplore the separation between the university and the broader community, between scholarly knowledge and civic discussion, Bob is an example of a "public intellectual" who spends time elucidating recent scholarship to readers beyond the academy, helping young scholars (as was the case with the East-West Seminar he created during his presidency of the International Society for Eighteenth-Century Studies) and taking positions in important debates. The future of the book is one of those issues on which Bob has taken a stand.

This is why E-book will be my *E*. Bob is surely one of the first historians who understood the profound transformations that electronic media could bring to the process of writing, publishing, and reading historical books and articles. His famous piece published in the *New York Review of Books* on March 18, 1999, was the starting point for a twofold proposition: On the one hand, to consider electronic publishing as a possible answer to the crisis within academia concerning the publication of monographs (since the acquisition budgets of libraries are devoured by the enormous cost of scientific periodicals). And on the other hand, to consider it as a way to invent a new book form, "structured in layers arranged like a pyramid," including such elements as discussion of the argument, the documentation used by the historian, theoretical or historiographical appendices, suggestions for teaching, and exchanges among the author, editor, and readers.

In his article titled "The New Age of the Book," Bob was among the first to identify the transformation of cognitive operations implied by the use of digital media. For the author, historian or not, electronic textuality enables the development of an argument following a logic that is no longer necessarily linear or deductive, as is the logic imposed by the inscription of a text onto a page. For the reader, the validation or the refutation of an argument can henceforth occur by consulting texts (but also images, recorded speeches, or musical compositions) that are the very object of the study, provided, of course, that they are accessible in digital form. Here we have a fundamental epistemological mutation that profoundly transforms the techniques of proof and the modalities of the construction and validation of the discourse on knowledge. The three classic modalities of proof (note, reference, and citation) are utterly modified from the moment the reader is able to read the books read by the historian and to consult directly the documents he or she has analyzed.

Unlike many scholars who talk about electronic publishing but do not practice it, Bob pleads the case *par le fait et l'exemple*. When he was president of the American Historical Association in 1999, he published the first online article of the *American Historical Review*. Revealing the role of songs and conversations in the construction of Parisian public opinion in the mid-eighteenth century, the electronic version of the essay allows the "reader" to wander through a map of Paris, stopping by twenty-nine cafés in order to read the transcripts of gossip and conversations reported from each of them by police spies. He or she can read the lyrics of the songs of the chansonniers kept in the Parisian archives, and listen to the songs themselves, recorded by the French singer Hélène Delavault. As Bob commented, "By listening to her renditions of the most popular songs, the readers of the e-article could get a sense of how Parisians took in the daily news as it was sung in the streets."

In 2001, seeking to legitimize electronic publishing in the eyes of the profession and to strengthen the Gutenberg e-project he launched as president of the AHA, Bob published an electronic book available on the net, titled *Jacques-Pierre Brissot: His Career and Correspondence (1779–1787)*. It was something of a *retour aux sources*, since the second scholarly article published by Bob was devoted to Brissot as a police spy (it appeared in 1968 in the *Journal of Modern History*), and since Brissot was the man who, in 1965, led Bob to the fabulous treasure constituted by the archives of the Société typographique de Neuchâtel. The electronic database that accompanies the essay "Jacques-Pierre Brissot and the Société typographique de Neuchâtel (1779–1787)," published in the *Studies on Voltaire and the Eighteenth Century* in 2001, includes transcripts of 163 letters between Brissot and the STN. Bob concludes his essay with the following remarks:

> This material, along with a draft biography of Brissot, has been sitting in my files since 1968. I decided not to publish it at that point, because I had not completed research on Brissot's role in the Revolution. But then I began to pursue related themes, which seemed more urgent and which led to other fields of inquiry, notably in the new discipline now known as *histoire du livre* or history of the book. At present, however, the new possibilities of publishing created by the Internet have convinced me that I should make these letters accessible to other scholars. . . . If I complete the work in which I am now absorbed, I hope to return to Brissot. Meanwhile, others are invited to continue where I left off and to extend it in whatever direction may seem most promising to them.

As you can see, thanks to scholars like Bob, the friendly and collaborative ethics of the republic of letters have not vanished.

In an interview given to the Estonian online magazine *Eurozine* in 2004, Bob promised still more: "My own work includes an attempt to produce a large-scale electronic book on the subject of publishing and the book trade in eighteenth-century France and Switzerland. It will include a vast amount of archival and visual material, and readers will be able to use it in many ways. I expect them to read it as a conventional narrative, horizontally, so to speak. But they also will be able to read it vertically—that is, to click down through successive layers of mini-monographs and data."

Who could be surprised if my *F* goes to France? French history was the alpha and perhaps it will be the omega of Bob's intellectual trajectory. The Enlightenment in France and its relation to the Revolution were the topics of his Ph.D., completed under Robert Shackleton's supervision during the years he spent at Oxford as a Rhodes Scholar. It was also the French Enlightenment that gave him the topic of the work he undertook on Brissot when he was a member of the Society of Fellows at Harvard, which led him, in fact, "to read just about every one of the 50,000 letters" of the STN.

Between Oxford and Harvard, Bob worked for several months as a reporter for the *New York Times*, covering armed robberies and murders. But, and I quote him in the same interview, "after many weeks in the pressroom at police headquarters, the game of cops-and-robbers turned stale. All the stories began to look the same, and I yearned to return to the archives. I used to go into police headquarters with Burckhardt's *Civilization of the Renaissance* hidden inside a copy of *Playboy* so that the other reporters would not suspect my secret high-brow tendencies." In fact, considering the attention he paid in the following years to *Thérèse philosophe*, *Vénus dans le cloître*, and *L'éducation de Laure*, it seems that, in the end, *Playboy* had more influence on his work than did Burckhardt.

But let us return to France. It is a wonderful paradox that Bob was simultaneously one of the most active fellow travelers of French historiography (and particularly of the Annales school) and one the most biting critics of the quantitative *histoire des mentalités*. Everyone remembers the severe verdict he pronounced in the conclusion of *The Great Cat Massacre*, condemning French historiography for its "overcommitment to the quantification of culture and its undervaluation of the symbolic element in social intercourse." His judgment was sharp: "Cultural objects . . . need to be read, not counted." That's why French cultural historians have started to read books published since 1984—and they still have many more to read. But when they discovered that Bob's *The Forbidden Best-Sellers of Pre-Revolutionary France* was full of statistics, they realized that their punishment and penance was perhaps coming to an end.

These remarks are only jokes aimed at bringing back the good old days of our polemics. More seriously, it must be said that Bob's work has been essential to many French historians. The seminars and lectures he gave at the École des hautes études en sciences sociales and at the Collège de France, the translations of his books, and his public presence on French television have had, and still have, a considerable impact on France's understanding of its own past, among both scholars and members of the general public. The French government, which sometimes shows good judgment, recognized these achievements by welcoming Bob into both the Ordre des Arts et des Lettres and the Ordre National de la Légion d'Honneur. The University of Bordeaux bestowed an honorary doctorate on him in 2005, and the University of Paris-Sorbonne followed suit a year later.

Can we imagine a better *G* than Gutenberg? Bob named the AHA-sponsored electronic book project Gutenberg-e, stressing that "old books and e-books are not enemies," and that the latter contributed "to [the expansion of] Gutenberg's everlasting galaxy." And when he received the prestigious Gutenberg Prize in 2004 from the city of Mainz, Bob affirmed that "Gutenberg's invention released the most progressive force of modern history—the printed word and its power to liberate humanity from ignorance and oppression."

Such a strong statement defines, in the most encompassing manner, the fundamental project that has been present in all his work, from his first articles on Marat and Brissot, to current projects that will undoubtedly result in forthcoming books. In a very interesting conversation with Maria Lúcia Pallares-Burke, published in a book she edited under the title of *The New History: Confessions and Conversations* (where you can also encounter Natalie Zemon Davis and Daniel Roche), Bob declared that what he seeks as a historian is "to understand the power of print and the printed word—or just any words, including the spoken and sung word, but basically the printed word—as a force in history. And that means incorporating it into a very broad sort of social and cultural history, instead of simply treating the history of the book as something for erudition." In the same interview, Bob generously associates me with such a project, stressing the common ground we share that has allowed us to keep up a "friendly running argument"—and not a "battle" or "war," as some have imagined—for so many years.

Bob likes to contrast the dirty work of archival research with ideas that are perhaps bright but not sustained by any evidence. He delights in the artisanal dimension of the historical craft more than theoretical approaches to history. In another interview, published in 2003 in a book titled *Être dix-huitièmiste*, he declared, "I confess that I remain skeptical about theory. It can provide a fresh perspective or a new way of cutting into material, but in the end a historian is an artisan." As the son of an artisan, I fully agree with this. Unfortunately, Bob upgraded me to the position of "essayist," generously adding, "And why not? That is an excellent type of historian to be." I am not sure that I am any more pleased by this distinctive "essayist" label than he was when he read some of the essays of *The Darnton Debate*. After all, artisans do not always work with the same materials and the same tools. But that is for another running argument.

What remains true is Bob's extraordinary talent for resurrecting dead souls, for giving a name to the anonymous, and for understanding how people made sense of the world. He knows better than anyone how to convey to readers the emotion of the encounter with human beings of the past who, like us, loved, suffered, and hoped. Who can forget those extraordinary pages in *The Business of Enlightenment* where Bob identified, thanks to the STN wage book, the pressman who left a thumbprint on one of the sheets of the *Encyclopédie* he printed. His name was Bonnemain—"a singularly inappropriate nickname," wrote Bob—a dark-haired Norman who, despite his awful reputation among the master printers, remained at his press in Neuchâtel for two years. Thanks to Bob's sensitivity and work, Bonnemain joins us from the past and, for a while, is our contemporary.

My primer is not finished, but it is time to conclude. I leave to your imagination, memories, and feelings the task of completing this alphabetic "Darnton for beginners"—or "for followers." It was a pleasure and an honor for me to offer these first seven letters to my first American friend, who has been and continues to be a wonderful companion through the many intellectual journeys we have taken together since I met him in Paris on a beautiful day in 1971.

PART 1

MAKING NEWS

℘ ONE

A TROJAN HORSE IN PARLIAMENT:
INTERNATIONAL PUBLICITY IN THE AGE OF THE
AMERICAN REVOLUTION

Will Slauter

In the late summer of 1778, with France and Britain openly at war, the editor of the *Courier de l'Europe* defended his right to publish a French-language newspaper in London. An English reader had recently accused the editor, Antoine-Joseph de Serres de La Tour, of being a spy and claimed that Parliament was considering a bill that would stop foreigners from "publishing libels written in their own language."[1] These words invoked the notorious group of French *libellistes* operating in London, but on this occasion, Serres de La Tour was not being accused of either scandalizing the French monarchy or attempting to blackmail it.[2] The problem was that being based in London gave the French editor access to the latest news and commentary about the war, which he translated for the enjoyment of Britain's enemies across the channel. Even before the outbreak of war, another reader remarked that the *Courier de l'Europe* was "as strange inside our walls as the wooden horse was in Troy."[3] Jacques-Pierre Brissot, the revolutionary who began his journalistic career at the *Courier*, also found it surprising that a Frenchman could go to London and publish a newspaper that made British political and military designs known to France. The *Courier*, he said, was worth a hundred spies.[4]

What exactly made the *Courier de l'Europe* a Trojan horse? The answer was spoken dozens of times in the houses of Parliament, and duly noted in Serres de La Tour's accounts of the proceedings. Stressing the danger of admitting "strangers" to observe the debates, a number of orators worried about the consequences of making parliamentary debates available to an international public. The Earl of Sandwich, First Lord of the Admiralty, emphasized the danger of "producing information which could be transmitted abroad," and insisted that "foreign powers" had sent "emissaries" to record the proceedings.[5] French versions of the debates could exaggerate the sense of xenophobia, as when the *Courier* translated "strangers," the term for members of the public who observed from the "Strangers' Gallery," as "étrangers," which also meant foreigners. The *Gazette de Leyde* likewise quoted Prime Minister Lord North as wanting to exclude "témoins étrangers" (foreign witnesses).[6]

Yet Serres de La Tour rarely attended the debates himself. Avoiding the uncomfortable and noisy conditions of the Strangers' Gallery, he worked alone in his Brompton office, surrounded by piles of English newspapers.[7] The London press overflowed with critiques of ministerial policies and exposés on the costs of continuing the war with the American colonies.[8] To annoy British authorities, all the editor had to do was translate such material and export it to France. Complaining about the "misrepresentations" of French and Dutch gazettes, a British agent in Regensburg conceded that the problem began with "the licentiousness of our own publick writings and speakers, translated with augmentations and improvements into all foreign languages."[9] Lord North similarly complained that the accounts of the parliamentary opposition were sent everywhere (not least to America), and he justified closed-door deliberations on the grounds that printed versions of the debates tended to exacerbate the conflict with the colonies. North's fears about the corrosive power of publicity seemed confirmed in 1784 when Philip Yorke, then a young member of Parliament, concluded that "the publication of the debates and opposition speeches have lost America."[10]

One of the most important ways in which the newspaper acted as a medium of diplomacy in the late eighteenth century was by transforming speeches in Parliament into printed texts for readers *outside* Britain. In his classic study of the bourgeois public sphere, Jürgen Habermas stressed how the publication of parliamentary proceedings enabled members of the public to follow political developments and scrutinize decision makers even if they did not yet have the right to vote. Such publicity transformed Parliament from an assembly of estates into a modern representative government.[11] What about the international dimensions of publicity? What happened when words pronounced in a specific moment of national debate, recorded and printed according to local conventions, were republished for readers speaking different languages and obeying different rulers? How did the process of translating and editing the debates for an international public alter their meaning and significance?

Printed accounts of Parliament had flourished during the English Civil War, only to recede from view with the prohibition of news books in 1649. Yet the spread of news by word of mouth and the circulation of manuscript versions ensured that parliamentary business could never be kept entirely secret.[12] In the 1730s, the monthly magazines again began printing accounts of proceedings, but it was only starting in the 1770s that London newspapers provided daily coverage of the debates while Parliament was in session. After a struggle with several London printers in 1771, the House of Commons and then the House of Lords gave up their privileges of secrecy, and by the outbreak of the American Revolution, the debates had become the most important source of content in most London newspapers.[13]

They also became one of London's most curious exports. The French ambassador in London sent home versions of the debates drawn up by a defrocked Jesuit and double agent named Pierre Roubaud. After Roubaud was fired in the fall of 1777, the embassy prepared translations of the debates from London newspapers, which were read by ministers in Versailles and then edited for publication in the *Gazette de France*.[14] French-language gazettes printed in Amsterdam, Leiden, Utrecht, and Avignon also drew on the London press to provide their readers with parliamentary news, as did the *Affaires de l'Angleterre et de l'Amérique*, a periodical secretly published within the French Ministry of Foreign Affairs.[15] The *Courier de l'Europe* had particularly long and detailed accounts, and it became the trusted source for many in France.[16]

The printed translations of the 1770s caused diplomacy and publicity to interact in new ways. The accounts in the London press, picked up by newspapers around the Atlantic world and translated into all European languages, caused alarm among British officials worried about what we would now call national security. The Earl of Sandwich argued that an inquiry into the "state of the nation" (demanded by the parliamentary opposition) would "reveal to foreign powers the weakness of the British navy, or at least inform them that Parliament suspected the reality of that weakness." The Earl of Suffolk, a secretary of state for foreign affairs, similarly asked (in the *Courier*'s translation), "Why say to America, why say to rival nations that these facts are observed and recognized by the national assembly: isn't this to reveal to the universe that we are not in a position to do justice to ourselves?"[17] More dramatically, another orator claimed that a "public acknowledgement" of Britain's military weaknesses would provide "a direct invitation to the different branches of the House of Bourbon to attempt an immediate invasion of this kingdom."[18]

After the announcement of the Franco-American treaty in March 1778,

British officials searched in vain for a means to remove the Trojan horse. Unable to prohibit publication outright, they used a general goods embargo to seize the newspaper at Dover customs and thereby stop it from leaving the country. This strategy did not work, however, because the *Courier* had powerful protectors in France, including the minister of foreign affairs, Charles Gravier, comte de Vergennes. By mid-April, thanks to the intervention of the playwright and arms dealer Pierre-Augustin Caron de Beaumarchais, the *Courier*'s owner, Samuel Swinton, had met with Vergennes, who approved Swinton's plan to have English smugglers bring a copy of each issue across the channel to be reprinted at Boulogne-sur-Mer. To supervise the reprinting, Swinton hired the young Brissot.[19] The operation at Boulogne grew quickly and provided a steady flow of news from America via England into France and the rest of the Continent. As Beaumarchais explained to the U.S. Congress in 1783, "A single public paper was able to freely provide the French with accurate notions of your rights and old England's wrongs toward you. This was the *Courier de l'Europe*."[20]

As King Louis XVI and his ministers kept track of the American Revolution and attempted to gauge British intentions toward France, the translations found in the *Courier* supplemented, and sometimes contradicted, the official record of Parliament communicated through diplomatic channels.[21] As an example of how a newspaper like the *Courier* could intervene in diplomacy, consider what happened when the British ambassador, Viscount Stormont, visited Louis XVI's first minister, the comte de Maurepas, on November 25, 1777. Hoping to alleviate the growing tension between the two countries, Stormont gave Maurepas a copy of the speech delivered by George III at the opening of Parliament five days earlier. According to Stormont, Maurepas read the speech "as if new to Him, tho' I have since learnt that He had read it before; when He was reading it He said frequently, *c'est bien sage; c'est bien vu*, inquired into the particulars of the Debate, and expressed great satisfaction that the Sessions opened with so much éclat, and with such a decided superiority, as He said must give pleasure to all Lovers of Peace, who must wish success, stability, and Permanency to the present English Ministry."[22]

Maurepas's reaction enabled Stormont to write home with good news. Not only were George III's pacific intentions "universally admired" in France, but another speech by the Earl of Sandwich on the strength of the British navy had also made "a strong impression" in Versailles.[23] Yet Stormont's valiant efforts to promote a particular reading of this parliamentary session would ultimately fail. Unlike the king's address, which was drafted in committee and prepared for publication, most parliamentary speeches were improvised, and the printed text of a given speech varied from one newspaper to the next.[24] Vergennes, the minister of foreign affairs, relied on the *Courier de l'Europe*, and the version of Sandwich's speech he found there inspired a very different reaction from the one that Maurepas offered Stormont.

Sandwich's speech, as reported by the *Courier*, was long and complex, but Vergennes focused on a single passage in which Sandwich suggested that France's secret aid to the Americans would eventually lead Britain to retaliate. In a letter to his ambassador in Spain, Vergennes quoted this line from Sandwich's speech: "The time may come when we can obtain a full reparation for the insults that we may have received from France and Spain."[25] In light of this remark, Vergennes discounted George III's pacific language as "a lure designed to put us to sleep and make it easier to surprise us." Sandwich's words, on the other hand, revealed the "secret dispositions of the British council" to make war on the Bourbon powers. Vergennes remarked with satisfaction that Sandwich's speech had caused a stir in Versailles, and he asked his agents in foreign courts to monitor its effects abroad. At least two ambassadors wrote back echoing Vergennes's stated fear that Britain would reconcile with America and then attack France and Spain.[26] The Austrian chancellor, Wenzel Anton von Kaunitz, had a different view: he thought that the "party spirit" in Britain had carried Sandwich away and his words would remain an empty threat.[27]

Vergennes attached great importance to Sandwich's words. As he suggested to his ambassador in Spain, this speech—or rather the printed translation of it—could prove very useful for French diplomacy: "Let us engrave this deadly oracle in indelible characters, not to precipitate our resolutions, but to put us in a position to make one when our respective circumstances permit it."[28] Sandwich's speech would indeed be added to a list of grievances in an internal memo urging the French king to join the American war against Britain: "That a Suffolk, a Fox, or a Barré would vomit injurious sarcasms against France should not surprise us. It's the English custom, and a proven means to please the crowd and make one's reputation. But that a minister of state would dare in full Parliament to exhale threats and express himself in contemptuous terms against two powers such as France and Spain, is the height of indiscretion and arrogance."[29]

Describing the way that British politicians would "exhale threats" and "vomit injurious sarcasms" against France and Spain, the memo invoked the oral origins of the insult that Vergennes found in print. The London press transformed these spoken utterances into printed texts that could be read and cited, and the translations made by European gazettes enabled foreign powers like France and Spain to see how British politicians portrayed them before an international public. Insults and threats uttered in Westminster now reverberated throughout Europe, invoking claims of national honor and the *droit des gens*. As Vergennes put it, "If the deadly oracle that Lord Sandwich let slip, which expresses so well the secret dispositions of the British Council, does not serve us as a guide, then I see nothing else that could."[30]

Vergennes was just a few weeks away from concluding a treaty with the Americans. The French decision to go to war, and the timing of that decision, depended on a number of factors, including the ambition to restore French prestige after the nation's defeat in the Seven Years' War, the desire to make commercial gains vis-à-vis England, and the rebuilding of the navy.[31] But when it came time to justify the decision in writing, Vergennes and Louis XVI turned to the textual evidence they found in the newspaper. The fear that Britain would reconcile with America and then attack France and Spain had many sources, not least the repeated urgings of Beaumarchais, but it was ultimately the debates in Parliament that the king and his minister cited as the evidence that led them to act when they did.[32]

Given that parliamentary debates were read and discussed at the highest levels of the French monarchy, the form in which they appeared clearly mattered. In fact, Vergennes asked his ambassador in London to investigate whether Sandwich had actually pronounced the words attributed to him in the *Courier de l'Europe*, conceding the possibility that the version he had read might have been inaccurate.[33] As it turns out, the *Courier* had translated from the *Gazetteer*, which was the only London newspaper to report the phrase that bothered Vergennes. In other versions, Sandwich was reported as saying that although private individuals in France might be aiding the Americans, starting a war with the Bourbon powers on this basis would be unwise.[34] Vergennes, following the *Courier*, had "engraved" Sandwich's words in "indelible characters," but they were not necessarily the words he had pronounced. Although it was based on an aberrant English version, the *Courier*'s translation became the definitive one on the Continent, gaining credibility as it reappeared word for word in Amsterdam, Utrecht, and Avignon.[35]

When accused of misrepresentation, Serres de La Tour shifted the blame to the English newspapers from which he translated. On the same day as Sandwich's presumed insult, the Earl of Suffolk was reported to have said that French soldiers were inferior to German ones. Suffolk's words echoed throughout Europe and boomeranged back to London: The king of France got upset, the king of Prussia became intrigued, a French officer sent a challenge to Suffolk, and Parisians wagered on the duel.[36] Suffolk disavowed the speech before the French ambassador and demanded a retraction from the *Courier de l'Europe*. But the editor responded by citing the English newspaper from which he had "faithfully translated" (the *Gazetteer*). Pointing out that the *Gazetteer*'s version also appeared "word for word" in John Almon's *Parliamentary Register*, the editor thought that the English papers, not the *Courier de l'Europe*, should publish the retraction.[37]

Shifting the blame made sense in the journalistic culture of London, where most newspaper material remained anonymous and editors copied freely from one another. Almost every London newspaper covered the debates, but there were few original versions. Many of the newspapers had no reporters, and even those who did borrowed from their competitors to round out their accounts. Because editors sometimes altered the phrasing or the order of paragraphs they copied, two accounts based on a common source could look quite different. In Robert Darnton's vivid account of the "early information society" of eighteenth-century Paris, coffeehouse gossip, satirical songs, and libelous pamphlets fed into one another, creating a number of different but related composite texts.[38] Likewise, the parliamentary debates evolved as they moved through different phases of publication, acquiring new meanings as they were recorded, copied, translated, and rewritten. Subtle and not-so-subtle modifications—the "augmentations" and "improvements" noticed by the British agent in Regensburg—could completely change the meaning of the original utterance. Just who had modified the text of a speech, and in exactly what way, was often impossible for readers to determine. But by comparing the different versions that have come down to us, we can reconstruct how the printed versions came to contain the words they did.

Consider the example of a speech delivered by the Earl of Shelburne in the spring of 1778. Not counting translations or later compilations, the speech appeared in at least eight London newspapers, whose accounts ranged from a few paragraphs to more than six columns in length. The *Morning Chronicle*, which printed a four-column summary the day after Shelburne spoke, warned the reader that it could only give a "hasty sketch" of the complicated speech that had lasted almost two hours. The account combined a third-person summary of the speaker's argument with phrases drawn from the speech itself. Thus we read, "He ridiculed the Inactivity of Administration with great force, and said, if they had not spirit enough to call forth the Men to resist France, that the Ladies would send back their feathers to Paris, and fight the French for us; that the Ladies, the Wives and Daughters of their Lordships, had true British Hearts in their Bosoms, and were superior to such Pusillanimity as the present Ministry had shewn." The point of Shelburne's speech, according to the summary, was to criticize the current ministry of Lord North as cowardly and effeminate, but the precise language that appeared in the newspaper ended up offending the French as well. According to the *Morning Chronicle*, Shelburne said, "The Ladies knew what sort of people the French were, and would soon convince them how little they dreaded danger from a race of people who had such small pretensions to manhood."[39]

Those who read the *Morning Post* instead of the *Morning Chronicle* that day found a much shorter version of Shelburne's speech, and one that did not contain the passage opposing English ladies and French men. Those who read the *St. James's Chronicle* enjoyed a combination of the two versions: the editor decided to spice up the summary he found in the *Morning Post* with the offensive paragraph from the *Morning Chronicle*.[40] Yet another version appeared in the *General Advertiser*, which complained that Shelburne's speech was so long-winded and confusing that it was nearly impossible to follow.[41] The *General Advertiser* nonetheless became the basis for the versions published by the *London Chronicle* and the *London Evening Post*. To round out its account, however, the *Evening Post* inserted the juicy paragraph from the *Morning Chronicle* opposing English women and French men, but dropped the line about the ladies sending their feathers back to Paris.[42]

An entirely different version appeared scattered over two issues of the *Gazetteer*. That paper's reporter interjected his own commentary between the lines of Shelburne's speech and transposed from a third-person narrative to a first-person discourse, giving the impression of a verbatim transcript. Moreover, the *Gazetteer* completely altered the meaning of the passage, so that the focus was now on the national weakness of France rather than the incompetence of the British ministry:

> I have a great esteem and value for several individuals in France, but though the people of [England] are much degenerated from what they were, I would have the noble Duke [of Richmond] consider, the sort of people we shall have to contend with, infinitely more degenerated than us, should a war ensue. Men who have lost all that love of glory, military prowess, and superior discipline, which was known to prevail during the reign of Louis the XIVth; I profess, I believe such is the spirit of our very women, that if the combat were left to them alone, they would be equal

to the task of driving the French out of this kingdom, should they attempt to invade us.[43]

The same components have been worked into a very different whole. Although the *Gazetteer*'s account diverged significantly from the others, it gained a semi-official status when copied into John Almon's *Parliamentary Register* and then into William Cobbett's *Parliamentary History*.[44] Moreover, it was this version, translated into French by the *Courier de l'Europe* and then copied word for word by the *Gazette d'Amsterdam*, that offended the French.[45] Although no single version of the speech was necessarily more accurate than any other, the order in which newspapers and gazettes copied and translated from one another meant that one version could eventually become definitive.

The unflattering remarks attributed to Shelburne in the *Courier de l'Europe* caught the attention of readers in France, and at least one of them wrote to Shelburne demanding an explanation. Shelburne in turn solicited help from the writer and translator André Morellet, with whom he had already been exchanging news and ideas. In a letter translated and circulated by Morellet, Shelburne explained how contemporary practices of journalism had inevitably disfigured his speech. He described the printers as "a very ordinary class of Men" who hired "a still lower class" to attend the debates. Rather than the political convictions of the reporters, Shelburne emphasized their ignorance and poor working conditions: "They are not allowed to take a Note—and at 12 o'clock at night these Beasts are to put together what they can recollect in the most vulgar language, for they know no other, and instantly print them for the newspapers, which are to be circulated the next morning by 8 o'clock. There are some exceptions where people correct for themselves or send an account of what they said, a Practice which I never have nor ever will condescend to—From our Paper[s] they pass to the *Courier de l'Europe* &c. &c."[46]

Reporters often complained that the gallery was noisy and uncomfortable, and that they could not hear certain speakers or even see well enough to identify who was speaking. Note taking was not allowed, at least officially.[47] Yet even William "Memory" Woodfall, who wrote the versions found in the *Morning Chronicle*, relied on more than the recall for which he became known. Some members submitted copies of their speeches to the newspapers, and reporters like Woodfall occasionally worked with individual speakers to improve their manuscripts for publication. As editor of the *London Evening Post* and the *Parliamentary Register*, John Almon received submissions from orators who wrote from memory after the fact, transforming their speeches into political essays. John Wilkes, on the other hand, supposedly sent some of his speeches to Woodfall before he even pronounced them.[48] The reporter for the *Gazetteer* claimed that he generally rejected such "*closet* speeches, written beforehand, or manufactured some days after," because they were usually submitted by third-rate speakers who should not be accorded space in newspaper summaries.[49] Although there is some contemporary evidence to suggest that a type of shorthand was practiced, no reporter claimed to be providing a verbatim transcript.[50] Woodfall himself described his account as "a mere skeleton of the arguments urged upon the occasion" and warned readers not to expect "the exact phraseology used by the speakers." As the reporter for the *Gazetteer* put it, "We prefer the *substance* and true parliamentary *impression* of what passed, to a mere lifeless, though perhaps faithful narrative, in which the generality of readers are left to find their way, and of course to *mistake* what was *said*, for really what was *transacted*."[51]

The attention of French readers to what was said rather than what happened would indeed cause misunderstanding. According to Shelburne's own reconstruction of the speech, the original context for his remark about English women was an anecdote from the Anglo-Dutch Wars of the late seventeenth century.[52] According to Shelburne, during the campaign of 1672, the fortress of Naarden had been entrusted to fourteen drunken soldiers, but disaster was averted because an attentive servant maid raised the drawbridge before the enemy arrived. Shelburne hoped that English servant maids had as much "spirit" as the Dutch, and concluded the anecdote "by referring those that heard me to their Wives and Daughters, who tho' they might have French caps I was sure had English Hearts, and would in such a case send back their feathers to Paris, and themselves withstand the Enemy."[53]

How do we account for divergent accounts of a single speech? Individual newspapers clearly favored certain speakers by giving them more space than their opponents and by praising their remarks. A reader accused the *Gazetteer* of partiality in describing members of the opposition as speaking "ably," "masterly," and "learnedly," and called for the editor to give equal attention to the ministerial party and "never thrust yourself, or your italics, where you are not called upon."[54] The *Gazetteer*'s editor was clearly taking sides, but politics entered into the accounts in more subtle ways as well. In a brilliant article about the reporting of parliamentary debates during the age of the French Revolution, Dror Wahrman showed how notions of the "middle class" that were attributed to a given speaker depended on which newspaper one read. Rather than assuming that these differences resulted from intentional censorship or bias, Wahrman envisioned the printed debates as "distinct reconstructions, which were mediated through rhetorical practices specific to each newspaper and dependent on its political convictions." The differences between accounts meant "there was no single image of parliament available to and shared by everyone. Instead, the public was confronted with a plurality of representations, in which diverging political languages were employed to address differently formulated concerns."[55]

In other words, London newspaper editors and their reader-contributors participated in national politics by reconstructing parliamentary debates according to their own priorities. Everyone involved in this process—speakers, reporters, and readers—understood that the debates existed in multiple versions. Readers could either choose a newspaper they liked or combine details from several in order to create their own composite account. A speaker who found that a particular newspaper misrepresented him could fight back by publishing his own version.

While projecting British politics onto the international stage, translations decontextualized the debates in important ways. By choosing a single account to translate, or by creating a new composite version from several of them, the *Courier* reduced the "plurality of representations" described by Wahrman into a single coherent version. Without easy access to other English newspapers, French readers remained ignorant of how the struggle between rival publications had shaped each individual account. They did not know, for example, that the offensive remarks by Sandwich, Suffolk, and Shelburne all originated in the *Gazetteer*, whose reporter envisioned parliamentary reporting as a patriotic endeavor. After the outbreak of war with France, the *Gazetteer's* reporter made his political agenda explicit to English readers: he sought peace with America so that "every *head*, *heart*, and *hand* . . . may be employed not only in the *defence* of the country, but in *retaliating* on the common enemy, and punishing the House of Bourbon, for its *perfidy* and *accursed ambition*."[56] When Suffolk accused the *Courier* of misrepresentation, Serres de La Tour explained that he had translated from the *Gazetteer* because it was the only paper to carry a version of Suffolk's speech.[57] The *Courier*, following the custom at the time, did not document its sources, and so none of this was clear to French readers confronting Suffolk's speech for the first time. Repackaging the debates for a French audience, the *Courier* obscured the motivations of the *Gazetteer's* reporter while unintentionally advancing his political goal—to stir up animosity between France and England.

Writing to complain about the *Courier's* version of Shelburne's speech, a

London reader argued that by translating a printed summary of a spoken debate, the *Courier* had strayed too far from the original utterance. According to this reader, if the French editor had actually heard the speech, he would have noticed that all the lords burst out laughing and that Shelburne himself chuckled as he spoke. While insisting that the vocal event could never be adequately documented in print, the same correspondent admitted that drawing from a number of newspapers enabled the *Courier* to give the debates "un ensemble, une rondeur," not available in English summaries.[58] Reading the proceedings was more comfortable than listening to the speeches in the gallery, and the printed form gave the debates a coherence that they lacked as improvised speeches. Meanwhile, the publication of proceedings influenced the orators themselves, who knew that they were speaking for a wider public of readers rather than just their immediate listeners.[59]

But speakers were used to addressing the English public rather than the French one. When read in Paris rather than London, a casual remark by a member of Parliament could be interpreted as the statement of a British representative speaking for the nation. The *Courier* encouraged this kind of reading when it transposed from the third person to the first person, giving the impression of a transcript rather than a summary. One could propose a number of reasons why the French minister of foreign affairs cited the *Courier de l'Europe*'s version of Sandwich's speech: perhaps he judged the newspaper to be reliable based on past experience; maybe he treated this version as definitive because it was read by his colleagues in Versailles and his counterparts abroad; perhaps he simply exploited it because it served his own interests. Although we do not know what Vergennes thought, we do know which version of the speech he read and how that version came into being. In the end, what mattered was not whether the *Courier de l'Europe* accurately reported Sandwich's words, but rather the meaning those words had for readers confronting them in different contexts.

The significance of international publicity depended on not only the circulation and readership of a given newspaper, but also the afterlife of its content. A political speech or military bulletin printed in the *Courier de l'Europe* reached not only the readers of that gazette (themselves scattered over a wide geographic area), but also readers of other gazettes that drew material from it. In the case of Sandwich's speech, the *Gazette d'Amsterdam*, the *Gazette d'Utrecht*, and the *Courrier d'Avignon* all copied the *Courier de l'Europe*'s translation verbatim.[60] What made the *Courier* a Trojan horse was not so much the political convictions of its editor as the paper's role of intermediary between the journalistic culture of London and the French-language gazettes on the Continent.

The abbé Morellet, whom Shelburne employed to repair the damage in France caused by his speech, understood that Shelburne had not meant to upset the French but rather to rally the British. Morellet did not necessarily agree that France suffered from a "lack of public spirit," but he believed that an "Englishman speaking to his nation" should be able to make such a remark without people in France getting upset about it.[61] Whatever Morellet may have wished, the reality was otherwise: the *Courier* transformed words uttered in a specific moment of national debate into a printed account for an international public. The notorious French journalist Simon-Nicolas-Henri Linguet, then living in London, worried that French readers would inevitably misread these debates: what the English saw as pure theater would be taken too seriously by those seated far from the stages of Westminster. Yet Linguet, unlike Morellet, recognized that if an English orator had the right to express his "own opinion" in Parliament, then a French reader also had the right to be offended by it.[62]

According to Linguet, if a speaker did not disavow the words printed in the newspaper, then a reader could assume he had actually said them. In a paradoxical but pragmatic solution, Linguet argued that the silence of the speaker was the only thing that guaranteed the authenticity of the printed text.[63] But "authentic" did not mean literal: the verbatim transcript, like the lead paragraph or the interview, has a history, and when we cite the political debates found in eighteenth-century sources, we need to consider how they came to take the form that they did.[64] The newspapers printed different versions of the same speech, and subsequent editions of proceedings (such as Almon's *Parliamentary Register* and Cobbett's *Parliamentary History*) drew on these divergent accounts without indicating which ones they were using. The reporters themselves denied the possibility of word-for-word transcripts, even if interested readers like Vergennes wanted to treat them as such.

The examples analyzed above suggest that misunderstanding was created not by self-interested politicians or irresponsible reporters, but by the practices of eighteenth-century journalism. The working conditions of the reporters, as well as their goal to give the "impression" of debates rather than a full transcript, ensured that these summaries owed much to the memory and imagination of the individual writers. In selecting passages to copy, summarize, or translate, editors made judgments that could be interpreted in political terms, but we should not forget that they looked everywhere for sources to fill their columns, including newspapers with different political affiliations. Members like Edmund Burke and John Wilkes, who submitted their speeches to the press, had the upper hand on those like Sandwich and Shelburne, who refused to "condescend" to this practice. The character and content of late eighteenth-century newspapers depended not only on the ideological convictions of printers and editors, but also on the way they copied, translated, and reworked one another's words. The interdependence of newspapers and the malleability of the texts they contained created a range of possibilities for the writers and readers who made use of these texts to advance their own goals.

Although Shelburne did not prepare his speeches for the London press, he felt obliged to correct the impressions they made abroad. In employing Morellet as his publicity agent, Shelburne was battling the growing international press. By the time of the American Revolution, the manuscript translations that Morellet distributed to a select audience were competing against the printed versions found in trusted sources like the *Gazette de Leyde* and the *Courrier d'Avignon* as well as those furnished by a formidable newcomer called the *Courier de l'Europe*. The wider circulation of printed translations made it more difficult for someone like Morellet—let alone the British ambassador—to control French readings of British politics.

NOTES

1. *Courier de l'Europe* (hereafter cited as *CE*), September 11, 1778, 164. On the *CE*, see Gunnar von Proschwitz and Mavis von Proschwitz, *Beaumarchais et le "Courier de l'Europe": Documents inédits ou peu connus*, 2 vols. (Oxford: Voltaire Foundation, 1990), which provided me with crucial references to parliamentary speeches denouncing "strangers" and "spies." See also Simon Burrows, "The *Courier de l'Europe* as an Agent of Cultural Transfer," in *Cultural Transfers: France and Britain in the Long Eighteenth Century*, ed. Ann Thomson, Simon Burrows, and Edmond Dziembowski (Oxford: Voltaire Foundation, 2010), 189–201.

2. See Simon Burrows, *Blackmail, Scandal, and Revolution: London's French "libellistes," 1758–92* (Manchester: Manchester University Press, 2006); and Robert Darnton, *The Devil in the Holy Water, or the Art of Slander from Louis XIV to Napoleon* (Philadelphia: University of Pennsylvania Press, 2009).

3. *CE*, January 23, 1778, 55.

4. Jacques Pierre Brissot de Warville, *Mémoires (1754–1793)*, ed. Claude Perroud (Paris: Picard et fils, [1911]), 1:137–40, 305–6.

5. *CE*, December 2, 1777, 421; *CE*, February 13, 1778, 101–2.

6. Proschwitz and Proschwitz, *Beaumarchais*, 46–49; *Gazette de Leyde* (hereafter cited as *GL*), suppl. to May 16, 1777, 3.

7. *CE*, September 11, 1778, 164; Brissot, *Mémoires*, 1:304–10. For one occasion on which he did attend Parliament, see *CE*, April 10, 1778, 227.

8. Solomon Lutnick, *The American Revolution and the British Press, 1775–1783* (Columbia: University of Missouri Press, 1967); Hannah Barker, *Newspapers, Politics, and Public Opinion in Late Eighteenth-Century England* (Oxford: Clarendon Press, 1998); Troy Bickham, *Making Headlines: The American Revolution as Seen Through the British Press* (DeKalb: Northern Illinois University Press, 2009).

9. Hugh Elliot to William Eden, Ratisbon (i.e., Regenburg), July 3, 1776, British Library (hereafter cited as BL), Add. 34,413, fol. 58–59.

10. North quoted in *GL*, suppl. to May 16, 1777, 3; and *CE*, May 2, 1777, 458. Yorke quoted in Jeremy Black, "Flying a Kite: The Political Impact of the Eighteenth-Century British Press," *Journal of Newspaper and Periodical History* 1, no. 2 (Spring 1984): 13.

11. Jürgen Habermas, *The Structural Transformation of the Public Sphere: An Inquiry into a Category of Bourgeois Society*, trans. Thomas Burger (Cambridge: Polity Press, 1989), 61–63, 83.

12. Harold Love, *Scribal Publication in Seventeenth-Century England* (Oxford: Clarendon Press, 1993); Joad Raymond, *The Invention of the Newspaper: English Newsbooks, 1641–1649* (Oxford: Clarendon Press, 1996).

13. Arthur Aspinall, "The Reporting and Publishing of the House of Commons' Debates, 1771–1834," in *Essays Presented to Sir Lewis Namier*, ed. Richard Pares and A. J. P. Taylor (London: Macmillan, 1956), 227–57; Peter Thomas, "The Beginning of Parliamentary Reporting in Newspapers, 1768–1774," *English Historical Review* 74, no. 293 (October 1959): 623–36.

14. For the embassy's arrangements with Roubaud, see Archives du Ministère des affaires étrangères (hereafter cited as MAE), CP-Angleterre, vol. 515, fols. 3–4v, 62v; vol. 519, fol. 33; vol. 525, fols. 266r–v.

15. Jack Censer, "English Politics in the *Courrier d'Avignon*," in *Press and Politics in Pre-revolutionary France*, ed. Jack Censer and Jeremy Popkin (Berkeley: University of California Press, 1987), 170–203; Jeremy Popkin, *News and Politics in the Age of Revolution: Jean Luzac's "Gazette de Leyde"* (Ithaca: Cornell University Press, 1989); Simon Burrows, "The Cosmopolitan Press, 1759–1815," in *Press, Politics, and the Public Sphere in Europe and North America, 1760–1820*, ed. Hannah Barker and Simon Burrows (New York: Cambridge University Press, 2002), 23–47.

16. Prominent readers included Vergennes, the duc de Croÿ, and the marquise du Deffand. According to Brissot, the paper had between three and four thousand subscribers within six months of its first issue of June 26, 1776. Charles Théveneau de Morande claimed the paper had six thousand subscribers at its peak; according to the duc de Croÿ, it reached seven thousand (Proschwitz and Proschwitz, *Beaumarchais*, 33).

17. *CE*, February 3, 1778, 77; *CE*, April 28, 1778, 270–72.

18. *Gazetteer and New Daily Advertiser* (hereafter cited as *GAZ*), February 4, 1778, p. 2, col. 3.

19. Proschwitz and Proschwitz, *Beaumarchais*, 58–74, 473–75; Brissot, *Mémoires*, 1:137–40.

20. Quoted in Gunnar von Proschwitz, "Vergennes, Beaumarchais et le *Courrier de l'Europe*," *Revue d'histoire diplomatique* 101, nos. 3–4 (1987): 369.

21. See John Hardman and Munro Price, eds., *Louis XVI and the Comte de Vergennes: Correspondence, 1774–1787* (Oxford: Voltaire Foundation, 1998), 208, 212–14, 229, 241, 268.

22. Stormont to Weymouth, Paris, November 26, 1777, National Archives, Kew (hereafter cited as PRO), SP 78/305, fols. 105–6v.

23. Stormont to Weymouth, Paris, December 3, 1777, PRO, SP 78/305, fols. 157–58.

24. On the drafting of the king's speech, see BL, Add. 34,414, fols. 309–10v, 337–44.

25. Vergennes to Montmorin, Versailles, December 3, 1777, quoted in Proschwitz and Proschwitz, *Beaumarchais*, 36. Vergennes's source was *CE*, November 25, 1777, 407–8, which was translated from *GAZ*, November 24, 1777, p. 2, col. 1: "*But a time may come,* when a *full reparation* may be obtained, for any injurious treatment we may have received from either France or Spain" (emphasis in English original).

26. La Vauguyon to Vergennes, The Hague, December 5, 1777, MAE, CP-Hollande, vol. 531, fols. 183v–84; Breteuil to Vergennes, Vienna, January 3, 1778, CP-Autriche, vol. 334, fol. 17v.

27. Breteuil to Vergennes, Vienna, January 3, 1778, MAE, CP-Autriche, vol. 334, fol. 18.

28. Vergennes to Montmorin, Versailles, December 3, 1777, MAE, CP-Espagne, vol. 586, fols. 135–36v; quoted in Proschwitz and Proschwitz, *Beaumarchais*, 36.

29. "Mémoire/Colonies/Decembre 1777," Archives Nationales, Marine B7, 458, unnumbered piece.

30. Quoted in Proschwitz and Proschwitz, *Beaumarchais*, 36.

31. See Edward S. Corwin, *French Policy and the American Alliance of 1778* (Princeton: Princeton University Press, 1916); Jonathan Dull, *The French Navy and American Independence: A Study of Arms and Diplomacy* (Princeton: Princeton University Press, 1975); Orville Murphy, *Charles Gravier,*

Comte de Vergennes: French Diplomacy in the Age of Revolution, 1719–1787 (Albany: SUNY Press, 1982); and Jonathan Dull, *A Diplomatic History of the American Revolution* (New Haven: Yale University Press, 1985).

32. Louis to Charles III, January 8, 1778; Louis to Charles III, March 9, 1778; and Vergennes to Louis, ca. January 3, 1780, in Hardman and Price, *Louis XVI and the Comte de Vergennes*, 255–56, 260, 277–83. On Beaumarchais's role, see Gunnar von Proschwitz, "Beaumarchais écrit au comte de Vergennes, ou l'art de persuader," in *Littérature et séduction: Mélanges en l'honneur de Laurent Versini*, ed. Roger Marchal and François Moureau (Paris: Klincksieck, 1997), 721–25.

33. Vergennes to Noailles, Versailles, December 6, 1777, MAE, CP-Angleterre, vol. 527, fols. 89–90.

34. Compare *GAZ*, November 24, 1777, p. 2, with *Morning Post* (hereafter cited as *MP*), November 21, 1777, 2; *Morning Chronicle* (hereafter cited as *MC*), November 21, 1777, 2; *London Chronicle* (hereafter cited as *LC*), November 20–22, 1777, 501; *London Evening Post* (hereafter cited as *LEP*), November 20–22, 1777, 2; and *General Evening Post*, November 22, 1777, 1.

35. *Gazette d'Amsterdam* (hereafter cited as *GA*), December 12, 1777; *Gazette d'Utrecht* (hereafter cited as *GU*), suppl. to December 12, 1777; *Courrier d'Avignon* (hereafter cited as *CA*), December 16, 1777, 402.

36. A. Francis Steuart, ed., *The Last Journals of Horace Walpole During the Reign of George III from 1771–1783* (London: Bodley Head, [1913]), 2:92; [Hugh Elliot] to William Eden, Berlin, January 12, 1778, BL, Add. 34,415, fols. 70–70b; Simon-Nicolas-Henri Linguet, *Annales politiques, civiles et littéraires du dix-huitième siècle* (hereafter cited as *Annales*) (Londres, 1777), 3:143–46, 199–206.

37. Proschwitz and Proschwitz, *Beaumarchais*, 53–55; *CE*, December 26, 1777, 477; *CE*, January 9, 1778, 20.

38. Robert Darnton, "An Early Information Society: News and the Media in Eighteenth-Century Paris," *American Historical Review* 105, no. 1 (February 2000): 1–35.

39. *MC*, April 9, 1778, p. 2, cols. 3–4.

40. *MP*, April 9, 1778, p. 2, cols. 1–2; *St. James's Chronicle*, April 7–9, 1778, p. 4, cols. 1–2.

41. *General Advertiser*, April 9, 1778, p. 2, col. 2.

42. *LC*, April 7–9, 1778, 343–44; *LEP*, April 7–9, 1778, p. 3, cols. 2–3.

43. *GAZ*, April 10, 1778, p. 2, col. 3.

44. *The Parliamentary Register; or, History of the Proceedings and Debates of the House of Lords* (London: Printed for John Almon, 1778), 10:382; William Cobbett, *Parliamentary History of England from the Earliest Period to the Year 1803* (London, 1803), 19:1038.

45. *CE*, April 14, 1778, 239; *GA*, suppl. to April 21, 1778.

46. William Petty, Earl of Shelburne, to Guy Claude, comte de Sarsfield (sent to Morellet to be translated), May 21, 1778, in Dorothy Medlin, Jean-Claude David, and Paul LeClerc, eds., *Lettres d'André Morellet* (Oxford: Voltaire Foundation, 1991), 1:382–84.

47. Aspinall, "Reporting and Publishing of the House of Commons' Debates," 234–39; Thomas, "Beginning of Parliamentary Reporting," 632–36.

48. See the exchange between Woodfall and William Eden in BL, Add. 34,453, fols. 141–42, 147–48v; the letter from Lord Bristol to Almon in BL, Add. 20,733, fol. 16; and Peter Thomas, *John Wilkes: A Friend to Liberty* (Oxford: Clarendon Press, 1996), 177.

49. *GAZ*, July 6, 1779, p. 1, col. 3.

50. See Johann von Archenholz, *A Picture of England* (Dublin, 1790), 42.

51. Woodfall quoted in Thomas, "Beginning of Parliamentary Reporting," 636; *GAZ*, February 13, 1778, p. 1, col. 4.

52. Compare Shelburne's version to his likely source, David Hume, *History of England* (London, 1767), 6:219.

53. Shelburne to Sarsfield, May 21, 1778, in Medlin, David, and LeClerc, *Lettres d'André Morellet*, 1:383–84.

54. *GAZ*, June 10, 1779, p. 2, cols. 3–4.

55. Dror Wahrman, "Virtual Representation: Parliamentary Reporting and Languages of Class in the 1790s," *Past and Present* 136 (August 1992): 85.

56. *GAZ*, July 6, 1779, p. 1, col. 3; p. 2, col. 1.

57. *CE*, December 26, 1777, 477

58. *CE*, May 2, 1778, 280.

59. Edmund Burke: "It is very unlucky that the reputation of a speaker in the House of Commons depends far less on what he says than on the account of it in the newspapers." Quoted in Aspinall, "Reporting and Publishing of the House of Commons' Debates," 243.

60. *GA*, December 12, 1777; *GU*, suppl. to December 12, 1777; *CA*, December 16, 1777, 402.

61. Morellet to Shelburne, [June 11, 1778], in Medlin, David, and LeClerc, *Lettres d'André Morellet*, 1:382.

62. *Annales*, 2:528–30, 3:204–5.

63. "Les harrangues qui se prononcent au Parlement n'étant pas écrits et souvent n'étant que le fruit du moment, n'ont d'authenticité que le silence des membres à qui on les attribue; quand ils ne réclament pas contre les propos qu'on leur prête, on peut croire qu'en effet ils les ont tenus" (*Annales*, 3:402).

64. On the lead paragraph and the interview, see Michael Schudson, *The Power of News* (Cambridge: Harvard University Press, 1995). On legislative reporting in eighteenth-century America, see Eric Slauter, *The State as a Work of Art: The Cultural Origins of the Constitution* (Chicago: University of Chicago Press, 2009), 22–24, 148–66. For France, see Patrick Brasart, *Paroles de la Révolution: Les assemblées parlementaires, 1789–1794* (Paris: Minerve, 1988), 169–89.

"THE BASTARD CHILD OF A NOBLE HOUSE":
DÉTECTIVE AND MIDDLE-CLASS CULTURE IN INTERWAR FRANCE

Sarah Maza

From his earliest writings on the "information ages" of the past and present, Robert Darnton has made the point that "news" is not found but made. Darnton's sparkling memoir of his years as a rookie journalist, first published in 1975 and significantly titled "Journalism: All the News That Fits We Print," describes the multiple forces that converge to turn an arbitrarily defined slice of experience into newsprint: newsroom hierarchies and rivalries, tensions and collusions between reporters and their sources, nebulous claims of an "imagined reader." "News" emerges from all these dynamics, more or less reliably collected and tailored by editors with specific publics in mind.[1]

Some of the memoir's most vivid pages evoke the dynamic of the newsroom at the *Newark Star-Ledger*, where Darnton worked in 1959 on the crime beat. Crime news was shaped by the relationship between the reporters and the local police force, molded by a predictable array of biases and prejudices, most of which are still in force today: if it concerns a debutante, the story is big; if it concerns a poor black family, it does not even make the news; and so on.[2] Amid jokes, obscenities, and endless games of poker interrupted by the collection of "squeal sheets" from the police, the rookie reporter learned which stories mattered, and which tales came up repeatedly, with variety found only in the details.

Darnton's account of his early years at the *Star-Ledger*, and even of his work a few years later at the *New York Times*, is not that different from the account of a journalist who worked between the wars for France's leading crime newspaper,

Détective. In 1931, Paul Bringuier contributed an article, also in memoir form, explaining to readers how he learned the trade. As a young man, he applied for a position on the crime beat at a leading newspaper, whose editor in chief delivered his usual discouraging speech: "You need an overpowering vocation, the energy of a brute to stay in the game. Talent? Doesn't matter. . . . You know how to write? Don't answer, I'm telling you that you don't. You got university degrees? Actually I don't give a damn, I only ask because of spelling." His new colleagues toss him a cigarette and explain that Paris is divided for the job into eight sections, with a reporter assigned to each one. His task is to make the rounds of a dozen police stations, trawling for news. If it's "dead dogs," you file four or five lines that most likely won't get published; for medium stuff, call the office, you may get to keep it; if the Papal Nuncio goes missing or a Hindu prince is murdered, everyone will be over in a flash. Young Bringuier makes his way to the first police station, where he's told that nothing's going on. As he starts to leave, a gendarme stops him and says, "Nothing. It's a manner of speaking. You want an eighty-year-old man who shot himself seven times in the head? Didn't die, by the way. Yes? The report's over there on the desk, that one there, you can copy it out. Do you play poker, by the way?"[3]

Bringuier eventually worked for *Détective,* a publication that still exists today as a lurid tabloid. Between the wars, however, *Détective* was a unique cultural phenomenon; once described as "the bastard child of a noble house," it was a stunning popular success.[4] This broad success was published by none other than the distinguished Gallimard publishing house, which had established itself after World War I as the symbol and arbiter of high literary quality.

Détective, I will argue here, represents a particularly intriguing cultural hybrid whose disparate contents offer insights into interwar lower-middle-class culture. Various pieces of evidence suggest that the magazine's readership was made up primarily of people moving from the working class into white-collar work, and that the publication's contents appealed especially to a modest but upwardly mobile social group. The crime news in *Détective,* as in the later contexts evoked by Darnton, was shaped by its own array of forces: the relationship between an elite publishing house and its reporters, who self-consciously styled themselves as renegades; the need for the prestigious house of Gallimard to make financial ends meet; and especially the cultural horizons and ambitions of France's new white-collar middle classes. My aim here is to show how, in the hands of a particular group of people, crime news was transformed into respectable entertainment for a broad swath of the interwar urban population, but aimed especially the newly educated and ambitious *classes moyennes.*

The other essays in this volume are concerned with the later eighteenth century, a time that is generally considered to have witnessed the appearance of the first "public sphere." The philosopher Jürgen Habermas famously argued that in the age of Enlightenment, private persons came together in the new institutions of the public sphere—reading rooms, salons, literary academies—to engage in discussions that subjected existing political institutions to critical scrutiny; and in doing so, they formed a republic of letters, the blueprint for post-monarchical liberal governments. The phenomena discussed in this essay, by contrast, take place at the other end of the process that Habermas terms the "structural transformation of the public sphere": the modern invasion of public life by commerce, diversion, and consumerism. Writing in the early 1960s, Habermas took a dim view of what he termed the "refeudalization" of a once-again passive public whose new masters were the captains of industry and wizards of advertising.[5] In recent years, scholars have taken issue with Habermas's uncritical lionizing of an eighteenth-century "rational" public that is implicitly male and upper class.[6] In the vein of those critiques, this essay offers an instance of a highly commercial publication that represented a dynamic fusion of high and low, a blend of literary elitism, sensational stories, and invitations to social mobility that would have been unthinkable in the eighteenth century.

Détective owed its existence to Gaston Gallimard, a brilliant and charming man of the world who had not done much of anything until age thirty. In 1911, Gallimard was recruited by the rarefied group of intellectuals around André Gide to launch a publication as a spin-off of their successful literary periodical, the *Nouvelle revue française*. The choice was a stroke of either luck or genius, since Gallimard turned out to possess both an excellent business sense and an extraordinary eye for literary quality. The upshot was a collaboration between the period's foremost writers and its best editor, which, while it made literary history, was also famously rocky. Tensions erupted at regular intervals between "Gaston" (as all of Paris knew him), who loved flashy actresses and long lunches and did not despise money, and the high-minded group around André Gide, Jean Schlumberger, Jean Paulhan, Bernard Groethuysen, and others, whom contemporaries variously lampooned as the "bonne société protestante" or the "Calvin follies." In 1919, Gallimard created his own publishing house and continued to promote books by his *NRF* colleagues, mutual distrust notwithstanding: each of the parties knew exactly how good the other was.[7]

By 1928, Gallimard had the most prestigious publishing list in France, but he was facing severe financial difficulties as Anglo-American paper overstocking, combined with the incipient international economic crisis, drove up production costs. He had launched several literary and artistic periodicals, which sold better than books, and added popular titles by the likes of Gaston Leroux to his list—to the disgust of Gide and his acolytes. Since he scorned neither the profit motive nor middlebrow culture, Gallimard was receptive to a proposal put to him by the writer Joseph Kessel and his less famous but enterprising brother Georges. Since readers obviously hungered for the crime stories (*faits divers*) that regularly gobbled up of the front page of mass-market dailies like *Le Petit Parisien* or *Le Journal*, why not, the Kessel brothers suggested, just drop the serious news and devote a whole weekly magazine to crime? Gallimard handed the start-up money to Georges Kessel, who promptly lost it all betting on horses at the Saint-Cloud racetrack. Along the way, he did manage to recruit two friends, Marcel Montarron and Marius Larique, despite their concern that their own reputations as hard-living investigative reporters might be compromised by an association with the effete folks at Gallimard. Somehow, under the wire and on borrowed money, the first issue got produced.[8]

It was a huge success. The first issue, dated November 1, 1928, with a cover story on "Chicago, Capital of Crime," reportedly sold 350,000 copies.[9] One year later, the editors crowed in an October 24, 1929, editorial that *Détective*'s readership had increased from 200,000 per issue in the initial weeks to 300,000 six months later and now stood at 600,000.[10] By 1931, the editors claimed that each issue was read by a million people.[11] The official press run in 1933 was 292,000, but there are indications that several people read a single physical issue; in 1936, an editorial still claimed sales of around 300,000 and a million readers.[12] As with celebrity magazines today, *Détective*'s editors banked heavily on the magazine's cover, which was always visually striking and promoted the week's most sensational story: life in women's prisons, torture in Japan, a man's last hours before execution, and so on.[13] At the time, the biggest daily newspapers had a circulation range of one to two million, and other successful weekly magazines, such as *Gringoire* and *Confidences*, came in at around half a million.[14]

Why did crime sell so well in the 1930s? A 1930 editorial in *Détective* boasted about the magazine's success and the irresistible rise of the crime rubric known as *faits divers*, which the publication was said to have "rehabilitated": "The *fait divers* is now the object of intellectual concern, no longer cast aside as unworthy of examination. . . . One of the masters of contemporary thought, Monsieur André Gide, long drawn to the *fait divers*, has recently signaled his interest by taking on the publication of a series of works that are incomparable documents drawn from real life."[15] Granted, one can find fascination with crime in any historical period, but the forms of and reasons for public interest in violence and transgression vary according to context. A popular tradition going back to the Old Regime endlessly retailed the exploits of larger-than-life criminals, "monsters" whose acts defied both society and the heavens: the bandits Cartouche and Mandrin, the sadist Gilles de Rais, the would-be regicide Damiens, the dandy Lacenaire, the poisoner Marie Lafarge, and the more recent murderers Soleilland and Landru.[16] The crime and punishment of such exceptional villains cathartically reaffirmed the cohesion of the social order by uniting the crowds of spectators, and later readers, to witness executions that symbolically cleansed both the criminals and the world at large from the taint of crime.[17] The nineteenth-century interest in the sociologically defined criminality of the "dangerous classes," which endured into the fin de siècle obsession with the Paris working-class gangs known as Apaches,[18] was very different.

These two traditions still flourished in the twentieth century and provided a great deal of fodder for *Détective*: the magazine included regular articles on the great criminals of the past, and much of its contents consisted of the exploration of urban criminal underworlds, ostensibly for high-minded sociological purposes. But in the early twentieth century, there were new reasons for interest in a different sort of crime. Intellectual figures like Gide and his colleagues at the *NRF*, as well as the sprawling surrealist group, took an interest in *faits divers*, the bizarre, unclassifiable crimes that were grist for the mill of daily newspapers. To the literary and artistic avant-garde, the sudden eruption of crime in a tranquil, "normal" milieu provided the only transcendent relief from the dreariness of ordinary morality, politics, daily life, and social relations.[19] "Ordinary crime" became an object of intellectual fascination, especially acts of violence with obscure motivations. Writers like Gide and François Mauriac rebelled against conventional norms of causality and ethics by creating characters who murdered for accidental or arbitrary reasons.[20] The surrealists and other major intellectual and literary figures became obsessed with the crime of Christine and Léa Papin, a pair of slow-witted maidservants in Le Mans who bludgeoned their mistress and her daughter to death with household objects in 1933, for no apparent reason.[21] This was the kind of act—an inexplicable explosion in the most banal of settings—that contemporary intellectuals found illuminating (Jean Genet recast the Papin crime in his most famous play, *Les Bonnes*).[22]

The *fait divers* appealed to middle- and lower-middle-class readers for fairly straightforward reasons: they offered a titillating entrée into the lives of peo-ple just like themselves, a blend of the familiar and the shocking, similar to what English murder mysteries offered readers at the time. But the genre also fascinated those artists and intellectuals of the 1920s and 1930s—the likes of Salvador Dalí, Max Ernst, Man Ray, or René Magritte—who teased disturb-ing beauty out of the reframing of ordinary things.[23] A publication like *Détec-tive*, focused on crime and daily life, fit perfectly at the intersection of elite and mass culture.

The magazine quickly built up its own lore around the myth of the crime reporter. The journalists at *Détective* cultivated their image as the enfants ter-ribles of the Gallimard house. They held shooting practice in the warehouse they were given for an office and even faked a William Tell scene when the Gallimard upper management came to visit. The reporter Paul Bringuier pulled a bottle off his own head with an invisible string when a colleague shot a blank at him, while the other guys fired real bullets into stacks of luxury editions of works by Charles Péguy and Paul Claudel.[24] The enterprise was very much seat-of-the pants, especially at the beginning. Before the magazine had its own photographers, the journalists purloined whatever shots they could out of agencies and archives and tried to fit them to their stories: "We were the rag-pickers of *faits divers*," wrote Marcel Montarron.[25] Neither was journal-istic rigor always up to the highest of standards. Covering a parricide case in a provincial town, Geo London filed a premature report about the crowd scream-ing for the murderess's blood when she crossed the town square; to his dis-may, when she did appear on the street, everyone was at home eating lunch, so the journalist interrupted his own meal to run outside and yell "À mort!"[26] Although most of the correspondents did actually exist and write their pieces, reports from the United States were signed by the entirely fictional "Roy Pinker."

Who were the readers who pounced on the latest report of child murder in the countryside or gay bars in Montmartre? The price of the publication was certainly not prohibitive. For most of the 1930s, *Détective* cost one and a half francs, an affordable weekly indulgence at a time when an unskilled worker made seventeen francs a day, an office worker around thirty-five, and a special-ized artisan anywhere from twenty-five to forty-five.[27] The July 10 through August 31 issues of the magazine published the names and addresses of 784 respondents to a contest called "The Thirteen Culprits," concocted by a pseu-donymous Georges Simenon. While the sample is not huge and may be var-iously skewed, it does suggest several things. The readership was heavily urban, though not overwhelmingly Parisian: at least 80 percent of the respondents lived in big or medium-sized cities in France and the French colonies. Within Paris, though the numbers for each arrondissement are very small, they do suggest a readership scattered all over the city: smaller numbers in the central "single-digit" arrondissements, higher numbers in the more popular outer circle of the 11th, 12th, 14th, 15th, 17th, 18th, 19th, and 20th.[28]

The magazine's advertisements offer more clues about its readership. Ads appeared every week for astrologers, tarot readers, and private detectives. Increasingly, these were outnumbered by ads for consumer goods: department store ads for furniture that could be bought on credit, such art deco bedrooms and faux-Renaissance dining rooms that would set a family back 1,200 francs or more; traditional household goods, such as linens and pan sets; and the spoils of modernity, like cameras, radio consoles, phonographs, and bicycles. All these items no doubt reflected the standard aspirations of modest urban consumers. Most revealing, however, are the increasingly frequent advertisements for educational and vocational self-improvement. The May 15, 1930, issue, for instance, carried a half-page advertisement for the *Nouvelle encyclopédie autodidactique illustrée*, which reminded readers, "It is known that the best positions go to those who have acquired in their schooling the components of the literary, scientific, and practical information of the specialized Grandes Écoles; TO KNOW is already TO SUCCEED." Later issues carried publicity for the Écoles Pigier, which offered (and still do) training for white-collar jobs, illustrated with vignettes of well-dressed men and women seated at desks. "You are young! You are ambitious! Succeed!," trumpeted an October 1930 advertisement for a private vocational school. In order to succeed, one might have to transform one's appearance—hence the numerous ads for diet products and tattoo-removal services.

All this suggests that while *Détective*'s readership was hardly uniform, the publication catered heavily to the fastest-growing group of workers in most cities in the 1930s: white-collar workers and those just making the transition into services and office work. The number of office employees in France grew from under a million in the late nineteenth century to about three million in the 1930s, almost twice as fast as the growth in manual and industrial workers. These new office workers participated more heavily than other groups in the consumer economy: they were more likely than other workers to have a single child, and they spent 10 percent less of their total budget on food. White-collar workers were of course better educated than others, and, in Paris at least, more geographically mobile. Women in particular moved around the city on

a daily basis, since many of them lived close to their families of origin in popular districts like the 12th or the 18th and commuted to work in the central
districts by metro or tramway.[29]

The magazine's origins as a cultural hybrid dovetailed nicely with the soci-
ocultural position and aspirations of such a readership. The editors seem to
have played up a middlebrow orientation that reminded readers of the publication's roots in the respectable Gallimard empire. *Détective* regularly carried ads for fiction by the likes of Gide, Pierre Drieu la Rochelle, and Erich
Maria Remarque, all published under the *NRF* label. Naturally, they also promoted books by members of their own team. *Détective*'s reporters and writers
were well-known authors who, in the tradition of the great Albert Londres,
specialized in socially redemptive investigations of chain gangs, prisons, and
criminal underworlds and often doubled as B-list fiction writers. Staff members and contributors like Paul Morand, Francis Carco, and the editor's brother
Joseph Kessel were names familiar to general readers long before the magazine was launched. On February 6, 1930, *Détective* announced a crime novel
by Morand, "a great writer known for the high quality of his works and the
purity of his language." The novel, *Les Ombres de Paris*, was touted as "a strikingly truthful and heart-rending tableau of the secret Paris of 1930." Morand
appeared in an accompanying photo looking overwhelmed by a large accordion strapped to his chest.[30]

Détective had pretensions to being much more than yellow journalism, and
we know that it attracted the attention of members of the intellectual elite.
Gide read the magazine, and his colleagues at *Détective* promoted his writings
on *faits divers*, such as his account of a famous case in Poitiers, of a woman
who was kept locked in a room by family members.[31] Jean-Paul Sartre and
Simone de Beauvoir read it in the early 1930s, using the periodical as a spring-
board for debates about abnormal psychology and bourgeois morality.[32] Beauvoir claimed (perhaps defensively) that the magazine "at that time frequently
attacked the police and the moral establishment."[33] Her comment is interesting since in December 1929, *La Révolution surréaliste* published an angry article
by Georges Sadoul accusing *Détective* of encouraging vigilantism, denuncia-
tions, and repression.[34] Sadoul's disapproval is hardly convincing, since the
surrealists, embattled against conventional aesthetics, Christian morality, and
the bourgeois family, found plenty of ammunition in *Détective*. The work of
André Breton and his friends draws copiously on the "great crimes" of the late
twenties and early thirties as reported in the magazine: the deed of the Papin
sisters, the crime of the teenage parricide Violette Nozière, and the murder by

the psychopathic young bourgeois Michel Henriot of his young wife in an isolated mansion in Brittany.[35]

In short, the magazine, true to its hybrid institutional origins, served as
something of a cultural crossroads. It offered intellectuals an opportunity for
cultural slumming; at the same time, feeding off popular interest in the *fait
divers*, it presented an aura of literary respectability attractive to the new salaried
middle classes of Paris and the provincial cities.

I am suggesting, then, that *Détective* found its main readership in the members of the social group that was discovered and exhaustively discussed in the
1930s, the new *classes moyennes*. The drive to define a middle class in the 1930s
partly resulted from a broad political dynamic linked to the decline of the Radical Party and the resulting scramble on the Left and Right to capture middle-
class voters. Politicians and social scientists suddenly discovered previously
unknown categories, such as the middling cadres, and in the later thirties especially, in the wake of successful working-class mobilization, middle-class unions
like the Union des Syndicats des Classes Moyennes began to mushroom.[36]

The major social scientists of the 1930s agreed that France's social dynamic
could no longer be captured by the opposition between capital and labor.
Something else was there: the *classes moyennes*. Émile Durkheim's most brilliant
disciple, the sociologist Maurice Halbwachs, tried to pin down the distinction between the *classes moyennes* and a bourgeoisie that was now theorized as
purely upper class. For Halbwachs, the essence of bourgeois existence, closely
akin to aristocratic life, was a dual immersion in both one's profession and a
wide nexus of familial and social relations. The bourgeois existed in large
part, like the aristocrat, within a dense horizontal network, which is what distinguished his culture from that of the middle-class man, for whom only his
identification with a profession and a company and his ambitions for his
immediate family's future mattered. Compared to the bourgeoisie, the middle class operates, Halbwachs observed, in a vacuum created by investment in
the workplace, the painstaking accumulation of a family *patrimoine*, and the
obsession with the next generation's superior educational achievement.[37]

While better-off manual workers undoubtedly read *Détective*, it is plausible, I think, to connect the magazine with the world of the urban white-collar
worker: single men and women or small families with typically one, maybe
two, children—people with some secondary or technical education but eager,
as the ads suggest, for further cultural and social promotion. To these sorts of
readers, *Détective* offered a broader purview, though often in the form of sen-
sationalism packaged as cultural enrichment. The very first issue opened with

an editorial that cast the magazine as a protean creature whose mission was expressed by the original meaning of "de-tecting": to remove the roof.[38] *Détective* was to be "partout et pour tous" (everywhere and for everyone): "*Détective* has no uniform, no official insignia, no identifying signs. The Universe ignores him, but he ignores nothing: the nights of Chicago, the dives of Singapore, every ghetto, Whitechapel, the secrets of salons, courts, and ministries."[39]

To those with no connections, *Détective* promised access to a wider world; to those with narrow training, it offered broad expertise. *Détective*, the editorial continued, will be a scientist, chemist, physicist, psychiatrist, jurist; it will be a historian familiar with every language, library, and archive; it will be a novelist, too. While trumpeting the publication's moral and educational goals, the editors also spoke to the essence of modern urban life, at once private and spectacular. With *Détective*, they wrote, "You will have your weekly film at home." The magazine's politics were ambiguous, no doubt deliberately so: most of the editorial staff was left of center, but *Détective* also published prominent right-wing writers like Léon Daudet. The publication courted reader involvement, inviting participation in games and surveys and inciting indignation over public safety issues and injustices. In sum, *Détective* addressed public issues in an ostensibly apolitical fashion. Its success in the early 1930s coincided with widespread alienation from the scandal-ridden morass of republican parliamentary politics.[40]

Détective's "weekly film at home" consisted of a varying mix of features that exposed the typical reader, a lower-middle-class urban worker, to sensationalized worlds from which they felt safely removed. The cover stories were most often *grands reportages*—long investigative reports of a social problem or milieu in France or abroad, or the week's biggest crime story. The rest of the magazine included, in addition to the weekly editorial, lesser crime stories, histories of famous criminals in the past that echoed the ancient traditions of chapbooks and canards, write-in contests, short crime fiction, and, increasingly as the years went on, astrology and letters from readers.[41]

Given the magazine's title, it is ironic that its contents, in which *grands reportages* dominated everything else, lionized not the detective, as in earlier generations, but the reporter. The emergence of the reporter-adventurer as a figure of popular interest and admiration in the early twentieth century was a cultural phenomenon with roots in the Anglo-American world, crystallized in France by Albert Londres's exposés of French penal colonies in the 1920s, and soon given enduring life via the figure of Hergé's teenage boy reporter Tintin.[42] From the late twenties to the late thirties, while one-third of the magazine's covers depicted specific crimes, two-thirds were devoted to investigations of police techniques, criminal underworlds, life in penal institutions, prostitution and other sex crimes, and crime overseas.[43]

The common thread, of course, was an appeal to voyeurism, thinly disguised as a pitch for cultural enrichment. In the first couple of years, the publication banked heavily on exotic sadomasochism via foreign "crimes and punishments" as regular cover stories, including pieces on punishments on convict ships bound for Australia, and crime and punishment in Afghanistan, the Antipodes, the Philippines, and China. In the January 24, 1929, issue, the article "Crime and Punishment in Afghanistan" detailed everything from foot flogging to ceremonial public strangulation, before piously concluding, "Barbaric customs, rituals one might imagine long abandoned, that is what I believed it my duty to reveal to the readers of this great magazine."[44] A couple of weeks later, Australian aboriginal culture was gruesomely detailed: child sacrifices, female slavery, ordeals in which the parties bludgeoned one another to death, and tribal leaders "one would not like to encounter without a Browning or a Winchester."[45] In China, an article ominously reported that, decapitations and crucifixions notwithstanding, "death is the least feared of punishments."[46]

By 1930, the magazine's focus, reflecting a broader trend in French culture, shifted to the United States, increasingly featured as the setting for exotic cruelty. Several articles with American bylines detailed the horrors of _la loi de lynch_ as a symptom of the essential violence of the American soul. In July 1930, for instance, readers were treated to the dreadful account of a Texas case in which a crowd mobbed the courtroom screaming for blood, and the African American defendant turned down the police's offer to set him free to run for his life, preferring a steel-plated lockup. He died when the crowd set fire to the prison, and his charred body was dragged in triumph behind a car.[47] In the hot American summer, another article commented, "You wait every day for the sinister cry to go up: 'Race riot!'"[48] The articles in _Détective_ echoed other best-selling commentaries of the age in pointing to the incomprehensible paradoxes of American culture, which was deemed all at once scientific, puritanical, and brutal: "No doubt they think it is far less evil to kill a black man than to play cards, drink whisky, or go to the theatre."[49] Even the United States' officially sanctioned criminal justice was, according to the magazine, riddled with cruelty, from brutal interrogations (known as _le grilling_) to the futuristic horror of the electric chair.[50] Americans might claim to be scientific and modern, but they were clearly, readers learned, far more bestial and primitive than were the French.

The wave of anti-Americanism crested by 1933; by that time, another country closer to home had become the leading avatar of violence in a Western context. *Détective* ran regular articles deploring the rise of the Nazis and of anti-Semitic violence in Germany. One of the first such pieces, titled "Nailed to the Swastika," detailed the savagery recently unleashed against communists and especially Jews: "Assassination, coercion, exile, theft, expropriation, it was all brought to bear at once."[51] (The reporter, Marius Larique, did call it wrong by explaining that of the three leaders of the Nazi Party, Goebbels was the most dangerous, Goering an anarchist intellectual, and Hitler "the most harmless . . . a sort of illuminated pervert."[52]) *Détective* repeatedly denounced the rise of anti-Semitism in Germany, though its writers remained within the bounds of contemporary prejudice.[53] Larique, expressing sympathy for German Jews, carefully added that while he had "Israelite" friends and great respect for their race, "I cannot stand them when they profess Jewishness, that is, when several of them are in the same place."[54]

Détective partook of the spectacular nature of emerging mass culture, offering readers graphic descriptions, abundantly illustrated by photographs, of exotic worlds and especially of foreign violence. Karen Halttunen has laid out an interpretive model for mid-nineteenth-century American culture linking what she calls the "pornography of pain" with both the mastery and reduction of actual physical suffering and the rise of middle-class privacy.[55] The incessant coverage of punishment and torture in *Détective*, coupled with the magazine's veneer of literary respectability, could in a similar way be understood in the context of a culture of white-collar urban readers for whom privacy was increasing and the actual experience of physical pain was ever more remote.

The coverage of exotic foreign violence tapered off after the magazine's first couple of years, to be replaced with an "anthropologizing" of crime within France itself, particularly Paris. There was nothing new about the interest in criminal underworlds, of course; the distinctive feature of *Détective*'s crime reporting in the 1930s was the focus on separate, highly structured criminal milieus, which contrasted with the turn-of-the-century vision of an amorphous, working-class *armée du crime*, symbolized by the teenage Apaches.[56] Certainly the Apaches had their codes and languages, but these were nothing like the laws of interwar organized crime, the archetypal milieu as prominent in Paris at this time as it had been in Chicago, Corsica, and Marseille.

Le milieu—which really did take off after World War I—was a recurrent feature of the magazine throughout the 1930s.[57] One of the first articles to detail its customs and rules, "As the Accordion Plays," was written by Henri

Danjou, who made much of his own immersion in this glamorous underworld. Thanks to his old friend, a mobster named Bébert, the men of the milieu "got to know and respect me, trusting that if I wrote about their customs I would do so as a loyal companion, without betraying them."[58] With Bébert as his guide, Danjou goes literally underground, into one of the mob's dives, reporting with both a filmmaker's and an anthropologist's eye. The musicians in the jazz band, he writes, "are dressed in red and lit from below which, when the dancing starts and the white lights go out, gives them a demonic appearance."[59] The dive has three spaces: an outer one, into which "civilians" wander; the area near the stage, where the pimps hold court; and a backroom, where important business gets settled. The waiters, known as *louffiats* and clad in white jackets, "know how to speak both the language of the milieu and that of other men."[60]

Much is made, in this and other articles, of honor among thieves and the integrity of *la loi du milieu*. Bébert lays out for his journalist friend some of the fundamentals of the milieu's code of honor: you don't keep hitting an outnumbered man; women think it's a dishonor if their man has to work; men can have two women—a main squeeze and a *doublard*—but if one man steals another's, he must pay in either money or blood; and if you "sing," you're in for it. Another of Danjou's pieces, "Justice in the Milieu," tells of a man named Maurice who borrowed the papers of one Carlos to go to Paris, and once there stole all the savings of Carlos's widowed mother. When Carlos later gunned down Maurice at the Crystal Bar, the authorities called it murder, but the milieu knew it was justice. As one of Danjou's informant friends remarks, "The courtroom judges would not understand. We don't have the same understanding of honor. Will you be able to get it?"[61] Such themes have become so ubiquitous in Western popular culture, from film noir to *The Sopranos*, that it is easy to underestimate how mesmerizing these articles must have been to readers at the time.

The Paris of the 1930s contained many such parallel universes. There were worlds of ritualized debauchery, such as the rue de Lappe near the Bastille, where real gangsters (called *marlous*) and their venal girls (the *pierreuses*) mingled with slumming upper-class types in disguise, usually gawking American tourists "who come and see abroad what they would never accept at home."[62] There were bars all over the heart of Paris, from Montmartre to the Latin Quarter, where men in drag hailed one another and gossiped tidbits like, "Look at Suzy, she's a bundle of nerves tonight, you can tell that big darling isn't used to going out."[63]

Accounts of gay nightlife, abundantly illustrated with photographs of drag queens, became a recurrent feature of the magazine starting in 1932, in part because of two murders of high-profile gay men in Paris's entertainment industry: Oscar Dufrenne, the owner of the large nightclub Le Palace, was stabbed in his office by "a sailor" in 1933; and Louis Leplée, another club owner and a successful impresario who had recently launched Edith Piaf's career, was killed in his own bed by four men in 1936. In the wake of Leplée's murder, a piece by Luc Dornain dwelled with pitying reprobation, and in voyeuristic detail, on the "pathetic" pleasures of middle-aged transvestites. By way of context, Dornain asserted, "There is no milieu more closed, jealous, and self-satisfied than that of homosexuals. There is none which more closely imprisons its followers, and from which it is harder to get away."[64] This assumption that male gay life was highly structured and closed is quite different from reporters' depictions of lesbian nightlife in 1933, which profess surprise that any of the female couples gyrating on the dance floor would be "sincere" in their sexual urges: women involved with other women were assumed to be either doing it for the money or strung out on drugs.[65]

Most alien and frightening, perhaps, was *la zone*, the no-man's-land at some of the old city gates that constituted Paris's last outpost of deep misery and uncharted violence: "*La zone!* . . . That immense belt which encircles Paris with foul-smelling mud, broken down huts, mounds of garbage, *terrains vagues*—horrendous sewer where death and illness hold sway. Tragic breeding ground where hatreds ferment." *La zone*, however, also has "its laws, its men of the milieu, its tough guys. And sometimes at night on the *terrains vagues* which resemble large scabs, fights of honor break out, scores are settled."[66] *La zone* might seem lawless, but its otherness was also rule-bound. Depictions of life in these areas were awful in a conventionally Zolaesque way, a catalog of family breakdown and violence, which included prostitution, alcohol, beatings, and incest.

The "zone" was the lowest rung on Paris's ladder of criminal worlds, as a 1932 article explained. At the top to of the Paris "jungle," you had the criminal aristocracy of Montmartre, who sold vice to a wealthy, international clientele; below them, you had the procurers of the northern city gates, with their flashy ties and shiny shoes; to the west, the gamblers and car thieves of the Quartier des Ternes; then the small-time crooks of the Boulevard de la Chapelle; and finally, the lowest of the low, the desperate criminals of the zone beyond the northern boulevards.[67] *Détective*'s largest group of Parisian readers most likely consisted of middle- and lower-middle-class readers residing on the Left Bank or the eastern sections of the Right Bank. The magazine treated them to a criminal anthropology of those northern sections of the city in which they rarely set foot.

The sensational depiction of urban criminal underworlds, from medieval dens of thieves to the fin de siècle Apaches, was part of a long tradition that *Détective* merely updated with tales of modern mobsters and homosexual decadence. Far more innovative was the sensationalizing of rural crime, a theme that became increasingly common in the magazine's later years. One of the first articles on the subject, an April 1932 overview titled "Villages of Crime," offered a gothic take on life in the French countryside, punctuated with examples of specific crimes. Peasants living close to nature, the article explained, had primitive instincts and nursed long-standing resentments. Their limited horizons made them grasping and self-interested; to these problems one could add the theft and violence committed by tramps and day laborers, which had increased with the recent rise in unemployment.[68] One article recounts the murder of an old farmer, possibly by a young woman who may have been his mistress; the old man's widow (allegedly) hisses at the reporter, "You don't know! You can't know! It's infernal here! This place is the village of hatred!"[69]

Greed and bestial desire feature prominently in these hellish tales of the village. Men burn down their enemies' farms and shoot their families; in the Southwest, a farmer beats both of his mistresses and has them wear metal chastity contraptions, insisting that he's done nothing wrong—how else would you control them? The dissolute Louisette (or was it one of her several lovers?) bludgeons her married paramour to death under what the article's title labels "The Apple Tree of Passion."[70] One rural family prone to murder and betrayal is described under the headline "The House of Atreus"; a village where a serial killer operates is "The Hamlet of Fear," and a rural gorge where bodies are found becomes "The Ravine of Death."[71] Most urban workers spent their summer vacations in these villages of hatred, fear, and passion, but this apparently did not blunt their interest in the sordid goings-on in someone else's farm.

As cultural historians have long demonstrated, narratives about crime have much less to do with the actual incidence of wrongdoing in a given society than about the identities, values, and fears of the groups that produce and consume these texts.[72] The argument offered here follows in that tradition. Prices and advertisements in *Détective* offer clues about the social identity of the magazine's readers; a survey of its contents provides insights into to the mentality of upwardly mobile urban workers in interwar France. Unlike most of its trashier imitators, such as *Police Magazine* or *Police et Reportages*,[73] *Détective* affirmed its cultural respectability by flaunting the names of its better-known collaborators, carrying advertisements for prestigious Gallimard authors, and asserting the moral and anthropological value of its *grands reportages*. At the same time, the magazine allowed readers to visit worlds of crime from which they felt safely removed: the insides of prisons, the antechambers of death, Parisian ganglands, *la zone*, even a countryside that now felt remote. The magazine reassured readers about who they were not (cruel foreigners, urban riff-raff, violent and greedy rurals), while tantalizing them with who they wanted to be: readers of "good literature." This "weekly film at home" fully partook of a new mass culture, while at the same time it spoke to the cultural standards and ambitions of civil servants, bank employees, and office workers. For a decade or so—before more urgent international concerns made the *fait divers* irrelevant and crime in general less entertaining—*Détective* pulled readers in on the strength of its inventive cultural hybridity.

NOTES

1. Robert Darnton, "Journalism: All the News That Fits We Print," in *The Kiss of Lamourette: Reflections in Cultural History* (New York: W. W. Norton, 1990), 60–93; the essay was originally published under the subtitle in *Daedalus* in 1975. For a recent synthetic version of Darnton's thoughts about the construction of news, see "An Early Information Society: News and the Media in Eighteenth-Century Paris," *American Historical Review* 105, no. 1 (February 2000): 1–35.

2. Darnton, "Journalism," 85–86.

3. *Détective*, #116, January 15, 1931.

4. Pierre Assouline, *Gaston Gallimard: Un demi-siècle d'édition française* (Paris: Balland, 1984), 212.

5. Jürgen Habermas, *The Structural Transformation of the Public Sphere: An Inquiry into a Category of Bourgeois Society*, trans. Thomas Burger and Frederick Lawrence (Cambridge, Mass.: MIT Press, 1989); see especially chapter 6 on twentieth-century developments.

6. See, for instance, Craig Calhoun, ed., *Habermas and the Public Sphere* (Cambridge, Mass.: MIT Press, 1992).

7. Assouline, *Gaston Gallimard*, 33–96.

8. Ibid., 208–9.

9. Ibid., 189.

10. *Détective*, #52, October 24, 1929.

11. Editorials in *Détective*, #122, February 26, 1931.

12. Catherine Maisonneuve, "*Détective*: Le grand hebdomadaire des faits divers de 1928 à 1940," mémoire de maîtrise, Université de Paris, 1974, 11; editorial in *Détective*, #413, September 24, 1936.

13. Sigrid Hueber, "Les magazines de faits divers dans les années trente," mémoire de maîtrise, Université de Versailles, 2004, 63–64.

14. Claude Bellenger, *Histoire générale de la presse française* (Paris: Presses Universitaires de France, 1972), 3:510–99.

15. *Détective*, #105, October 30, 1930. André Gide kept an extensive collection of *faits divers* clippings, elements of which he worked into his novels. See David Walker, *Outrage and Insight: Modern French Writers and the "Fait Divers"* (Oxford: Berg, 1995), 53–54.

16. Geneviève Bollème, *La Bibliothèque bleue: Littérature populaire en France du XVIIIe au XIXe siècle* (Paris: Julliard, 1971).

17. Michel Foucault, *Discipline and Punish: The Birth of the Prison*, trans. Alan Sheridan (New York: Vintage, 1979), chaps. 1 and 2.

18. Louis Chevalier, *Classes laborieuses et classes dangereuses à Paris pendant la première moitié du XIXe siècle* (Paris: Hachette, 1984); Dominique Kalifa, *L'encre et le sang: Récits de crimes et société à la Belle Époque* (Paris: Fayard, 1995).

19. Georges Auclair, *Le Mana quotidien: Structures et fonctions de la chronique des faits divers* (Paris: Anthropos, 1970); Walker, *Outrage and Insight*, chaps. 3–5.

20. Walker, *Outrage and Insight*, chap. 4. The most famous examples are Lafcadio in Gide's *Les caves du Vatican* and the eponymous heroine of Mauriac's *Thérèse Desqueyroux*.

21. Sophie Darblade-Mamouni, *L'affaire Papin* (Paris: Éditions de Vecchi, 2000); Rachel Edwards and Keith Reader, *The Papin Sisters* (Oxford: Oxford University Press, 2001).

22. Walker, *Outrage and Insight*, 94.

23. Gérard Durozoi, *Histoire du mouvement surréaliste* (Paris: Éditions Hazan, 1997), 193–239.

24. Marcel Montarron, *Tout ce joli monde* (Paris: La Table ronde, 1965), 13.

25. Ibid., 11.

26. Ibid., 39.

27. For salaries, see Gérard Jacquemet, "Aspects de la condition des milieux populaires dans un quartier de Paris entre les deux guerres mondiales," in *Villes et campagnes (XVe–XXe siècles)*, ed. Françoise Bayard (Lyon: Presses Universitaires de Lyon, 1977), 354.

28. *Détective*, issues of July 10 though August 31, 1930. Of the 102 addresses identified in Paris, the distribution is as follows: 1st, 4; 2nd, 3; 3rd, 3; 4th, 3; 5th, 8; 6th, 3; 7th, 2; 8th, 2; 9th, 4; 10th, 4; 11th, 6; 12th, 6; 13th, 5; 14th, 6; 15th, 6; 16th, 4; 17th, 10; 18th, 5; 19th, 11; 20th, 7.

29. Delphine Gardey, *La Dactylographe et l'expéditionnaire: Histoire des employés de bureau, 1890–1930* (Paris: Éditions Belin, 2001), 44–46, 101–2. For a slightly earlier period, see Lenard Berlanstein, *The Working People of Paris, 1871–1914* (Baltimore: Johns Hopkins University Press, 1984), 148. On the mobility of women, see Antoine Prost, "Les Peuples du 18ème arrondissement en 1936," in *Paris, le peuple: XVIIIe–XXe siècles*, ed. Jean-Louis Robert and Danielle Tartakowsky (Paris: Publications de la Sorbonne, 1999), 59–76.

30. *Détective*, #67, February 6, 1930.

31. Ibid., #97, September 4, 1930.

32. Simone de Beauvoir, *La Force de l'âge* (Paris: Gallimard, 2003), 150–54.

33. Ibid., 150.

34. *La Révolution surréaliste*, #12, December 15, 1929, 45–47.

35. Walker, *Outrage and Insight*, chap. 5. Breton and his colleagues put together a volume of poems and artworks celebrating the Nozière crime: *Violette Nozières* (Brussels: Nicolas Flamel, 1933).

36. See Luc Boltanski, "Taxonomies sociales et luttes de classes: La mobilisation de la 'classe moyenne' et l'invention des 'cadres,'" *Actes de la recherche en sciences sociales* 29 (September 1979): 75–105; and, more generally, Luc Boltanski, *Les Cadres: La formation d'un groupe social* (Paris: Éditions de Minuit, 1982). For contemporary commentary, see, for instance, Jean Lhomme, *Le Problème des classes: Doctrines et faits* (Paris: Librairie Sirey, 1938); and Georges Izard, *Les classes moyennes* (Paris: Rieder, 1938).

37. Maurice Halbwachs's *Les Classes sociales* (Paris: Centre de documentation universitaire, 1937); and *Esquisse d'une psychologie des classes sociales* (Paris: Marcel Rivière, 1964). The latter was originally published in 1938.

38. *Détective*, #1, November 1, 1928.

39. Ibid.

40. On the alienation of voters from parliamentary politics, see Eugen Weber, *The Hollow Years: France in the 1930s* (New York: W. W. Norton, 1994), chap. 5.

41. Maisonneuve, "*Détective*," 15–53.

42. Kalifa, *L'Encre et le sang*, chap. 3. See also Assouline, *Gaston Gallimard*, on Albert Londres, and Christian Delporte on the history of journalists, *Les Journalistes en France, 1880–1950* (Paris: Éditions du Seuil, 1998).

43. Hueber, "Les magazines de faits divers," 63–83.

44. *Détective*, #13, January 24, 1929.

45. Ibid., #16, February 14, 1929.

46. Ibid., #30, May 23, 1929; #17, February 21, 1929.

47. Ibid., #90, July 17, 1930.

48. Ibid., #96, August 28, 1930.

49. Ibid., #90, July 17, 1930.

50. On *le grilling*, see, for instance, ibid., #213, November 24, 1932.

51. Ibid., #258, October 5, 1933.

52. Ibid.

53. See, for instance, a piece on pogroms, ibid., #186, May 19, 1932; an editorial protesting Germany's request for the extradition of a Jew, #236, May 4, 1933; and an article on the Gestapo's activities in Paris, #336, April 4, 1935.

54. Ibid., #258, October 5, 1933.

55. Karen Halttunen, "Humanitarianism and the Pornography of Pain," *American Historical Review* 100, no. 2 (April 1995): 303–34.

56. Kalifa, *L'encre et le sang*, 146.

57. Jérôme Pierrat, *Une histoire du milieu* (Paris: Denoel, 2003); Marcel Montarron, *Histoire du milieu de Casque d'Or à nos jours* (Paris: Éditions Plon, 1969).

58. *Détective*, #47, September 19, 1929.

59. Ibid.

60. Ibid.

61. Ibid., #67, June 2, 1930. For other discussions of mob law, see #198, August 11, 1932; and #205, September 29, 1932.

62. Ibid., #129, April 10, 1931.

63. Ibid., #176, March 10, 1932.

64. Ibid., #390, April 16, 1936.

65. Ibid., #252, August 24, 1933.

66. Ibid., #216, December 15, 1932.

67. Ibid., #218, December 29, 1932.

68. Ibid., #180, April 7, 1932.

69. Ibid., #212, November 17, 1932.

70. Ibid., #239, May 25, 1933; #241, June 8, 1933; #300, July 26, 1934.

71. Ibid., #326, January 24, 1936; #347, June 20, 1935; #362, October 3, 1935.

72. Salient works of cultural history that adopt this perspective are Chevalier, *Classes laborieuses et classes dangereuses*; Judith Walkowitz, *City of Dreadful Delight: Narratives of Sexual Danger in Late-Victorian London* (Chicago: University of Chicago Press, 1992); and Karen Halttunen, *Murder Most Foul: The Killer and the American Gothic Imagination* (Cambridge: Harvard University Press, 1998.)

73. Hueber, "Les magazines de faits divers."

PART 2

PRINT, PAPER, MARKETS, AND STATES

✑ THREE

WHO WERE THE BOOKSELLERS AND PRINTERS OF
EIGHTEENTH-CENTURY FRANCE?

Thierry Rigogne

At any given point during the eighteenth century, there were more than two hundred master printers and more than six hundred booksellers in France.[1] They formed the crucial link connecting authors with readers: printers gave form to texts and, with the help of binders, turned them into books, which booksellers placed in the hands of readers. We know surprisingly little about the men and the women who made books and sold them throughout France during the age of Enlightenment. Were they humanists or merchants? Did they disseminate the Enlightenment or uphold tradition? Did they produce and sell legal or pirated books, underground or legitimate literature? Did Parisians stifle provincials? Did foreign presses compete with the French ones? The usual questions are *mal posées* as they posit false dichotomies. No neat categories can account for the vibrant world of eighteenth-century print. In fact, each printer and each bookseller engaged in all sorts of activities, most legal, a few illicit, and many of them in the gray areas in between. Some of their concerns were basely mercantile, others more elevated, and they saw no incompatibility between culture and profits. The same men and women could sell clandestine atheistic pamphlets while their presses churned out prayer books for the local bishop. Competing and trading with booksellers and printers in other towns, they formed vast networks that linked provincial cities with one another, with Paris, with villages and small towns, and with the rest of Europe.

Robert Darnton has given us many unforgettable individual portraits, dragging into the spotlight a number of anonymous "foot soldiers of the Enlightenment." Out of the arid business letters of the Société typographique de

Neuchâtel, he brought back to life such colorful characters as the semiliterate peddler Noël Gille "dit la Pistole," whose phonetic spelling turned his orders for forbidden books into poetic puzzles, or the indefatigable Nicolas Gerlache, the former journeyman tanner turned bookbinder turned book peddler and smuggler who would do anything to keep his Metz bookstore and reading cabinet afloat. Darnton also guided us through the world of Montpellier booksellers and led us on many incursions deep into the world of book people.[2] For all the warm humanity that infuses his portraits, we must ask ourselves how representative such men and women were. Robert Darnton himself situates them on the margins of the book trade. But how exceptional were they, and what was the norm in the industry?

Our knowledge of the activities of eighteenth-century printers and booksellers is so thin that we are only starting to map out how many there were and where they plied their trades. Teams of French scholars are currently at work producing a series of much-needed prosopographical studies on eighteenth-century *gens du livre* (book people) in northern France, Paris, Lyon, and Rouen.[3] Their efforts thus far highlight the difficulties faced by scholars who research the activities of individual printers and booksellers: namely, that archivists hardly preserved any business records from the period. The administrative apparatus in charge of policing the book trade, on the other hand, produced a vast central file. Among hundreds of boxes lie a few extraordinary sets of records that have remained unexplored, or rather underused, for decades.[4] Two comprehensive administrative surveys, in particular, document the situation of printing and bookselling in each French city that housed a printing shop or a bookstore.[5] These inquiries offer snapshots of the book trade and printing industries at two critical junctures: in 1700, as the budding central administration set out to reshape the kingdom's print trades, and in 1764, when the first overhaul had been completed, the Enlightenment had bloomed, and consumption had taken off. Drawing on these surveys, this essay sketches a profile of French booksellers and printers as they evolved through the eighteenth century. With market forces, intellectual trends, and government action transforming the print trades, individual printers and booksellers adjusted to changing conditions. In the process, they redefined their trades, but they also shook up the entire system that governed the production and diffusion of culture in France.

In the eighteenth century, the central royal administration consolidated the French printing industry. Created in 1699 as a branch of the *chancellerie*, the Direction of the Book Trade restricted the number of cities allowed to house printing presses, and it severely cut the number of printers in each of them. True to Colbertian principles, it sought to concentrate printing into fewer, better-equipped, and more prosperous workshops that would also be easier to police. Royal authorities set printer quotas for Paris in 1669 and 1686, which they extended piecemeal to major provincial centers. Following the 1700 survey, Chancellor Louis Phélypeaux de Pontchartrain generalized printer quotas in all provincial towns in 1704. In 1739, Chancellor Henri-François d'Aguesseau issued tougher new targets, which Chancellor Guillaume de Lamoignon de Blancmesnil fine-tuned in a last batch of decrees in 1759.[6] In addition to setting quotas, royal authorities took over printer licensing and beefed up the regulatory apparatus.[7]

As always in Old Regime France, implementation lagged far behind royal decree due to exceptions, evasion, delaying tactics, lobbying, and a lack of enforcement powers. Yet, by the second half of the eighteenth century, survey results showed that the number of printing shops had dropped sharply in the provinces, from 372 in 1701 to 247 in 1764.[8] Fewer printers plied their trade in fewer towns.

The remaining printers grew larger as they swallowed up the business of unlucky competitors who had been forced to close shop by the administration, buying out their presses and valuable types. For instance, Metz's three printers possessed eight presses overall in 1701, but the two who remained in 1764 owned a combined nine.[9] Across the entire kingdom, a sharp one-third drop in the number of provincial workshops left the total number of presses remarkably unchanged between 1701 and 1764.[10] Each surviving shop owned more presses.

Presses, however, give only the crudest indication of economic activity. The intendant of Metz reported that only four of Joseph Antoine's six presses were set up in 1764.[11] Indeed, idle presses routinely gathered cobwebs in the back of workshops or remained unassembled.[12] In the absence of production statistics, workforce sizes constitute the best available index of activity. Printers had to keep precious capital tied up in extra presses and even more expensive sets of types to meet surges in activity, seasonal or otherwise, but they could adjust labor costs by hiring and firing journeymen to meet changes in demand. Typically, a core of journeymen ran the presses throughout the year, while printers added workers to complete specific jobs by dipping into the pool of itinerant journeymen who traveled around France.[13] The three workshops in Metz employed seven workers overall in 1701, but the two remaining in 1764 kept a total of sixteen.[14] Over the first two-thirds of the eighteenth century, the workforce employed in all French printing shops nearly doubled, on aggregate.[15] By all measures, the royal administration had consolidated the printing industry into fewer, larger, better-equipped, and busier printing shops.

The survivors of the great printer shakeout thrived. Because the newly appointed Director of the Book Trade Antoine de Sartine asked intendants and their local *subdélégués* to assess the *facultés* (loosely, the wealth) of printers and booksellers in each city, his 1764 survey offers a unique glimpse at the prosperity of provincial printers. Overall, respondents qualified printers with terms that grouped them into five broad categories: the wealthy, the well-off, the middling or modest, the struggling, and the poor (see table 1).[16]

Printing was a prosperous industry in 1764.[17] Half the provincial printers were described as well-off, with a sizeable group of wealthy men and women above them. Conversely, hardly any printers lived in poverty. A small portion struggled to stay afloat—many of them relying on ancillary activities to supplement the meager income they derived from their presses—while nearly one-third were of middling means, characterized as "modest," "mediocre," or "limited" by respondents. Printer-booksellers fared much better than the dwindling population of those who did only printing.

The path to fortune was the same regardless of whether a printer sold books. Profits depended on the size of the local market, one's market share, and the intensity of the competition among printers. Local market size was driven less by population than by the presence of institutions. At the onset of the age of

Table 1 Assessment of printers' fortunes in the 1764 survey

	Printer-booksellers	Printers without bookstores	Total printers
Wealthy	25 (12%)	1 (4%)	26 (11%)
Well-off	107 (51%)	10 (42%)	117 (50%)
Middling	66 (31.5%)	10 (42%)	76 (33%)
Struggling	10 (5%)	0 (0%)	10 (4%)
Poor	1 (0.5%)	3 (12%)	4 (2%)
Total	209 (100%)	24 (100%)	233 (100%)
No information*	18	2	20

*Answers that lumped printers or booksellers into both the well-off and middling categories without giving specific numbers for each were assigned to each category, proportionally to the national average for printers and booksellers, respectively. These affected Lyon (eleven printer-booksellers and twenty-four booksellers), Toulouse (ten and thirteen), Lille (six and five), and Nantes (seven booksellers). Localities with no information at all include Bordeaux and Dijon, along with small towns (Bourg-Saint-Andéol, Chalon-sur-Saône, Saint-Omer, Senlis, Stenay, and Trévoux for printers).

bureaucracy, administrations of all types, old and new, extended their reach, grew larger, and became more efficient, in particular by relying on print to standardize and circulate forms, memoranda, decisions, or announcements. Successful printers secured contracts with large institutions such as intendances, *parlements*, bishoprics, universities, and any of the urban institutions that ordered a dizzying variety of printing jobs. In many cities, printers split the market along institutional lines and kept prices high by not competing with one another for major clients. Where such formal or informal cartels did not exist, profits suffered.

The ideal situation for printers could be obtained in a city like Montpellier, where only two printers served a complete set of all major regional administrations (with the exception of the *parlement* of Languedoc, located in Toulouse). Job printing kept "both printers busy all year-round," noted the intendant in 1764, "and it is a very lucrative activity." Augustin-François Rochard was "reputed to own more than 100,000 livres," a hefty sum for a printer "of mediocre abilities in his craft." "A very uneducated woman and unable to run the shop by herself," according to the same intendant, the widow of Jean Martel "ha[d] not had the time to get rich yet" because her husband had died recently, "but she [could] not but make very considerable profits each year" following her late husband, who had bequeathed 150,000 livres to his second son. For the sake of comparison, Toulouse barristers owned average fortunes of between 35,000 and 40,000 livres, putting them in the well-off part of the population.[18] Rochard printed for the intendance, the tax farms, the municipality, and the bishop, while Martel supplied the prestigious university, the military authorities, and the provincial estates. Without competition, the intendant deplored, the two printers charged "on a much more expensive footing than the other printers in the province."[19] Some took their business to Avignon or Toulouse, but most clients had no choice but fatten Rochard and the widow Martel.

Most wealthy printers resided in France's main cities, which housed the largest institutions. A few others were big fish swimming in smaller ponds. In Quimper, a Breton town with a population of about six thousand in 1764, the town's single printer-bookseller, the sixty-seven year-old Simon-Marie Perrier, was "reputed to own forty thousand ecus [240,000 livres]," according to the *subdélégué*.[20] The most mundane jobs were often the most lucrative. With only eleven thousand inhabitants and bereft of major institutions save a bishopric, Angoulême housed two printers in 1764, who were "hardly busy" and not particularly enterprising, in the *subdélégué*'s opinion. Yet, with a single journeyman on only two presses, the forty-eight year-old Abraham-François Robin had amassed "more than 100,000 livres in assets, all in bills or in cash," "supplying ledger books and stamped paper" for the tax administration.[21]

Living comfortably, and sometimes handsomely, off job printing, provincial printers rarely ventured into the highly competitive waters of book publishing. Not only did publishing require heavy outlays of cash for much-delayed, uncertain returns, but provincials also knew the deck was stacked in favor of a dozen large Parisian publishers who had virtually monopolized all the royal privileges for new works since the second half of the seventeenth century.[22] By 1764, hardly any provincial printers published new books under privilege, which has often been mistaken as evidence of a provincial decline.[23] Not only do the labor figures and the data on wealth show a robust printing industry, but provincials could also cash in on a series of publishing endeavors that circumvented the Parisians, ranging from widespread pirating and niche publishing, especially on the lower end of the market, to feeding a lively market for regional- and local-interest publications.

Almost anything that sold in France was quickly pirated by presses across the kingdom's borders or in the foreign enclaves of Avignon and Lorraine (until the latter was incorporated into France in 1766). French publications were also pirated in major provincial cities such as Lyon, Rouen, and Toulouse, as well as in smaller centers such as Châlons-sur-Marne and Clermont-Ferrand.[24] Presses in Troyes, Rouen, Limoges, Orléans, Poitiers, and Lyon churned out cheap popular literature such as *Bibliothèque bleue* chapbooks, almanacs, and books of piety or devotion in the thousands. In 1764, the *Almanach de Milan* alone brought the Troyes printer-bookseller Jean Garnier an annual income of more than 150,000 livres.[25] Local- and regional-interest publications ranged from college textbooks and other schoolbooks to compendia of legal decisions by the *parlements* and other courts of justice, works of local history, and the ever-growing productions of urban cultural institutions, from universities to learned academies. Their core readership was primarily local, often regional, and only rarely national. On the other hand, if print runs were often limited, sales were usually assured and many institutions subsidized publications.

The most successful printers amassed so much wealth that they no longer needed the profits from their businesses to maintain their comfortable lifestyles. The intendant of Caen estimated in 1758 that the city's quota of four printers could be best met by closing the shop of the eighty-one-year-old Pierre-François Doublet because he was "very rich and in a condition to do without his printing shop."[26] In 1737, Doublet was running three presses mostly for the tax farms, but he was already wealthy enough to have married his only daughter to a judge in the Caen *bailliage-présidial* court of justice.[27] Throughout France, wealthy printers and their offspring were able to move up in local society, and in 1764, all printers, no matter what their fortune, were considered to be "honest" and "living honestly" with excellent reputations, in the words of royal officials.[28] Many occupied notable positions in their communities, such as alderman and mayor in Alençon, *grand juge* in the consular jurisdiction in Angoulême, hospital administrator in Quimper, and captain of the bourgeois militia in Brest.[29] Even without official titles, most printers lived like Dax's Roger Leclercq, "an honest man among the town's other bourgeois and under general public approval."[30] Printers fit squarely within the bourgeoisie at the heart of the French provincial town and city.

The ability of a printer to invest outside his or her business, such as in dowries, land, real estate, or *rentes* (annuity-bearing loans), separated the wealthy and the well-off from the middling, whose only income stemmed from work. Carcassonne's Jean-Baptiste Coignet was "not wealthy, but he live[d] off his work," a condition that was the lot of most artisans and shopkeepers. A middling printer such as Laval's Louis-François Ambroise "may have, according to public estimation, twelve to fifteen hundred livres of income," as relayed in the 1764 survey, slightly more than Marguerite Paulet, the widow of François de Lolme Bergeron in Mende, who "might earn one thousand to twelve hundred livres, including the regular income from her bookselling and printing business."[31] To provide an order of magnitude, in Normandy around the same time, a semiskilled worker, such as a carpenter or a roofer, earned about seventeen sous a day (or 0.85 livres in decimal terms).[32] Employing a single journeyman on two presses each, Ambroise and Bergeron ran very small workshops in small towns. They fit the evaluation the Strasbourg intendant gave of his city's printers in 1764: "Regarding their wealth, although it is generally mediocre, they nevertheless meet all their obligations." The Toulouse printers' and booksellers' guild put a more positive spin on the condition of its members, describing them as earning "enough to live honorably and whenever they have savings, they increase their assets little by little."[33] Those in narrower markets or facing tough competition had little choice but to work hard and patiently string together small profits year after year.

As one would expect of established urban masters, printers tended to be old. The average provincial typographer was just shy of fifty years old in 1764. There was, of course, great variation around the median age of forty-nine, from the twenty-three year-old Barthélemy Cristo from Bourges, the youngest and one of the most reckless, to the eighty-two-year-old Jacques Aulney du Ron-cerey, the dean of typographers, established in Lisieux in 1708. Provincial printers generally set up shop late in life, at the age of thirty-two on average, but on the other hand, they had years of accumulated experience, having been masters for an average of seventeen years in 1764.[34]

The printers of 1701 were five years younger on average—forty-five as opposed to fifty—having started their career earlier (at twenty-seven instead of thirty-two).[35] A delayed establishment reflected how printers adjusted to royal policies. With its quotas, shop closures, and takeovers of printer licens-ing, the central administration transformed the ways printers set up shop. It forced families to revise their strategies. The sons of master printers, who had previously entered the profession freely, particularly in major centers such as Rouen or Caen, were no longer guaranteed to succeed their fathers, all the less so as the administration increasingly filled printer vacancies by organiz-ing competitions in which it pushed its own candidates.[36] Masters held on for as long as they could to positions that were becoming harder to obtain albeit increasingly profitable. Their successors had to wait longer, while other avenues toward establishing themselves, such as moving to another town or marrying a master's daughter or widow, became glutted.

In a world in which artisans who defined themselves by their trade passed businesses from father to son, families built their strategies around male chil-dren. Printers who descended from typographic dynasties flouted their lineage. Artisan dynasties were all the more precious as they were rare and tenuous. Over several generations, a family had to avoid accidents of demography (early deaths of parents or children, infertility, or the inability to beget males), business mishaps (such as bankruptcies or closures by the royal administra-tion), and myriad other possible disruptions, such as a son uninterested in taking over the business or keen on upward social mobility toward more exalted stations. In forty-six small towns unaffected by printer suppressions, the lines of succession between 1701 and 1781 show that, over the span of eight decades, only nine printers out of fifty-three were able to pass their shop to an heir bearing their name.[37] Likewise, in the nine largest provincial print centers (Lyon, Rouen, Toulouse, Bordeaux, Lille, Limoges, Nantes, Rennes, and Stras-bourg), which were hit hard by quotas and shop suppressions, exactly one hundred families owned printing shops in 1701, but in 1764 the names of only thirty-one of these still hung above the doors of workshops.[38] Powerful forces thwarted the printers' efforts at creating dynasties. In big cities, the guilds regrouped after shop closures and did everything possible to ensure that all printer positions would stay in the hands of a small number of typographic families. If sixty-nine printing families had fallen by the wayside between 1701 and 1764 or had merged into others through marriage, the thirty-one families that had endured now held as much as 57 percent of the remaining shops. To look at it from a slightly different angle, the sons of local master printers ran two-thirds of all workshops within the nine largest centers in 1764. A few other printers came from local bookseller families or from typographic dynasties in nearby cities, which left outsiders barely any chance to crack the tight world of big-city printers—usually by marrying daughters or widows.[39] Some guilds managed to control printer recruitment more effectively than others did. Bordeaux and Rennes kept all positions for printers' sons, while Rouen and Limoges admitted a few newcomers connected to the printing community, but no real outsiders. Lyon, Toulouse, Nantes, and Lille remained less closed, though connections remained vital. Finally, Strasbourg, which did not have a guild, stood out in 1764 with not even one of its five printers having roots in local printing families.[40] In other words, despite regulatory pressures, the printing industry did not coalesce into a dynastic oligarchy in the eighteenth century. If the guilds shut out many big cities to outsiders, the situation remained more fluid than one might have expected, particularly in small towns, but also in some major centers.

As printers without bookstores went into rapid decline, printer-booksellers came to dominate the printing industry.[41] Meanwhile, in the second half of the eighteenth century, retail booksellers—that is, dealers who did not print books—emerged as a driving force in the book trade. Constituting 71 percent of all bookstores in 1781, up from 56 percent in 1701, retailers created a web of stores that spanned the entire kingdom and brought books into more and smaller towns.[42] After only a modest rise during the first six decades of the eighteenth century, provincial retail bookstores proliferated in the late 1760s and in the 1770s (from 369 in 1764 to 506 in 1781).[43] Stores opened at a rapid pace to meet soaring book demand. A powerful combination of factors sparked a reading boom in the second half of the century. Demographic expansion and urbanization gave a boost to cities and small towns, milieus more conducive to print in general. Economic prosperity bolstered consumption—in fact, some historians speak of a "consumer revolution." Rising literacy created more readers, while the taste for reading spread throughout the population, and better roads and faster mail services made it easier to ship books to a reading public increasingly conceiving itself as national.

Whereas the administration shut down printing shops and thereby reduced the number of bookstores run by printer-booksellers, it never monitored the number of retail booksellers and rarely weighed in on their affairs. No royal decree was required to open a retail bookstore, as opposed to a printing shop. In the kingdom's twenty-eight guild cities, mastership constituted the only requirement for retail booksellers, while in all other localities a mere police authorization sufficed. As a result, new bookstores opened throughout France, in cities already well supplied and in small towns that had never housed any.

The profile of retail booksellers is harder to delineate than that of printers because the rare surveys undertaken on booksellers lack biographical information. Moreover, it was often impossible to distinguish bona fide booksellers, recognized by the authorities, from a wide variety of interlopers.[44] If mercers and peddlers, for instance, were authorized to sell almanacs and short brochures, they hardly ever stuck to just those items. Meanwhile, binders, schoolteachers, used-clothes dealers, and notaries, among many others, sold books illicitly. A 1776 memorandum by the printers' and booksellers' guilds of Lyon, Rouen, Toulouse, Marseille, and Nîmes estimated there were "about three thousand booksellers or sellers of books in the kingdom," implying a ratio of more than two interlopers for each legitimate bookseller.[45] Focusing solely on booksellers recognized as such by local authorities, the 1700 survey showed no difference in profile between retail booksellers and printer-booksellers in terms of age, date of establishment, or experience.[46] The trades had not yet diverged.

We lack proper data to track how the profile of retail booksellers evolved over the century.[47] We do know, however, that in the late 1760s and 1770s, several new types of booksellers swelled the retail trade. First, many printer-booksellers whose workshops the Direction of the Book Trade had shut down continued as retailers only. Jean-Baptiste Voisin, whose printing shop "had subsisted for over a hundred years" but was suppressed in 1759, was "reduc[ed]," in the words of the Limoges intendant, "to [becoming] a bookseller and a binder to raise and feed [his] six children."[48] In Bar-sur-Aube, Germain-Menimin Vitalis became a bookseller only when his father's death triggered the suppression of the family printing shop.[49] Both Voisin and Vitalis started out as booksellers with not only an established store and stocks of books, but also precious trade experience. Bringing a little stock and a different type of experience were interlopers already selling books who settled down as legitimate booksellers. The peddler Garsein "used to tour the province with a stock of books," reported his *subdélégué* in 1764, but "having made himself known, he established himself in Dax."[50] Many took advantage of the exceptional sale of bookseller licenses (brevets) in 1767, an expedient through which the crown raised cash to repay debts accumulated during the Seven Years' War (1756–63) by selling masterships in all trades.[51] Outsiders who had struggled on the fringes of the book trade instantly gained legitimacy, particularly in guild cities where they had encountered dogged corporate opposition. In Bordeaux, for instance, six men, including a Protestant paper seller, became official master booksellers under the guild's jaundiced eye.[52] Finally, market opportunities attracted enterprising individuals not always best qualified to seize them. Many quickly went under, but new booksellers constantly emerged to take their place.

The influx was encouraged by Parisian and provincial publishers or wholesalers seeking more outlets for their publications. Hoping to develop strong commercial ties, they extended credit to help newcomers build their stocks, set up networks of "correspondents," and pushed commission sales.[53] In 1764, the Agen retailer Jean Boé turned to Jean Chappuis for all his supplies, which the Bordeaux printer-bookseller "sen[t] him under condition of sale."[54] As regulations barred printers and booksellers from owning more than a single store, the larger booksellers created what were in effect satellite branches. Some were mere business partnerships, while others were run by relatives. The Castres printer-bookseller Pierre-Guillaume-Dominique Robert, the son of a Toulouse printer-bookseller, declared that he bought all his books in his birthplace, where no fewer than four family members kept stores in 1764.[55]

Established booksellers constantly bemoaned the intrusion of newcomers, painting them as illicit carriers of dangerous books. Printer-booksellers were the most vocal in conflicts that pitted established booksellers, who upheld a printing-dominated worldview structured by privileges, protected markets, and institutional clients, against newcomers who embraced their position as retailers following market demand. Book retailing and printing followed diverging paths as the century progressed. Although Sartine toyed with the idea of bookseller quotas in 1768, a form of laissez-faire left the book trade open to the free play of market forces throughout most of the century.[56]

Bookselling was attractive because book demand was booming while access to the profession was easy and required little capital. But this also meant stiffer competition for thinner profits than in printing. Retail booksellers were thus much less prosperous than printer-booksellers overall (see table 2). Nearly half of them were described as owning only a middling fortune in 1764, and as many as one in five was struggling. If one-quarter of retailers were well-off, wealthy store owners were more rare than poor ones.

Table 2   Assessment of booksellers' fortunes in the 1764 survey

	Printer-booksellers	Retail booksellers	Total booksellers
Wealthy	25 (12%)	4 (1.5%)	29 (6%)
Well-off	107 (51%)	79 (26.5%)	186 (37%)
Middling	66 (31.5%)	144 (48%)	210 (41%)
Struggling	10 (5%)	63 (21%)	73 (14%)
Poor	1 (0.5%)	9 (3%)	10 (2%)
Total	209 (100%)	299 (100%)	508 (100%)
No information	18	37	55

Wealthy retailers kept large stores in major cities, such as Jean Leblond in Orléans or Pierre Machuel in Rouen.[57] They could be publishers or wholesalers as well, but not necessarily. The Montpellier retailer Pierre Rigaud had amassed a fortune estimated in 1764 to be anywhere from 50,000 to 150,000 livres. Although he paraded as a Catholic, "he is a Protestant," revealed the intendant, who described him as "conduct[ing] his trade with great intelligence" and "reputed [as] a very honest man even though he is accused of having many books of his religion and other forbidden ones."[58] Rigaud succeeded by selling everyone in the local community any book they requested, with little regard for legalities.

Well-off retailers either faced little competition in smaller cities or dominated part of the market in larger ones. Booksellers in small towns rarely made a fortune because local readership was too narrow. Middling and struggling retailers often had to complement their income. Binding was by far the most frequent and logical extension to bookselling. Many retailers also sold paper and other writing supplies, such as quills, ink, sealing wax, or portfolios. But others strayed further from the world of print, by teaching school in Boulogne, selling groceries in La Flèche, or retailing hardware in Épernay.[59] The tortuous career of François Riboulet illustrated the porous borders of the book trade. Riboulet had "started as a printer's journeyman, got married, and worked for twelve to fifteen years as a tutor and boarding students. Eight or ten months ago," continued the *subdélégué* for La Flèche in 1764, "he bought part of the stocks of Louis Hovius," a recently deceased bookseller. He "nevertheless plans to board students at his place, being unable to make a living out of his condition as a bookseller and a binder. His fortune is as mediocre and as limited as it gets," concluded the official.[60] Riboulet had to combine binding with boarding to finally get a toe back in the book trade.

Personifying the struggles of men and women on the edges of the world of print, Riboulet operated in the most vulnerable part of the business lifecycle. Simply put, younger, more freshly established booksellers struggled more than their elders did. Having to put down large sums of money to purchase their initial stocks of books, they could expect a number of lean years before paying off their debts. Throughout their first years, even those lucky enough to inherit a store remained at the mercy of business hazards and accidents, such as the fire that consumed the house, printing shop, and bookstore of Pierre-François Tonnet in Dôle in 1763 or the flood that ruined the books of Tulle's Pierre Chirac in 1756.[61] Over time, however, even meager profits would stack up to form a cushion. Moreover, an established bookseller could more easily find credit to weather a storm or to rebound than could an unknown newcomer. The business lifecycle explains that while the number of bookstores expanded in the 1760s and 1770s, a sign that the trade was booming, more retailers went bankrupt or struggled, reflecting that the proportion of ever-riskier start-ups increased.[62] Making matters worse, the 1767 licenses and the reading boom drew individuals without professional baggage or finances into the trade. Paradoxically, a high rate of failures reflected not only the inherent instability of the book trade, but also the openness and dynamism of the sector.

Often lacking the institutional contacts printer-booksellers had nurtured over the years, new retailers had to offer different types of books to different customers. They focused on the growing demand from individual readers, a market that they, in turn, bolstered. When the outsider Louis Lavigne set up shop in Sens in 1757, with no experience or fortune other than "his industry," he "pushed his trade further than any bookseller had done it in ages," praised the *subdélégué* in 1764. Whereas the printer-bookseller Pierre-Hardouin Tarbé printed mostly for the bishop, selling "church books for the diocese, classics, and a few publications in history, science, and literature" from nearby Paris, Lavigne sold "all sorts of books of all kinds." "He brings in and sells without discrimination all the books he is requested," admitted the royal official before relaying that Lavigne was "even accused of lending them for young men to read without discretion."[63] Supplying whatever his clients wanted, Lavigne also worked to expand the local readership—with great success, it seemed.

Central to the rise of independent retailers such as Lavigne were wholesalers. Publishers sold a large share of their output through book swaps with other publishers, as a way to limit cash outlays. Without any production of their own to swap, retail booksellers needed wholesalers to procure a wide assortment of books. The printer-bookseller and publisher Jean-Marie Bruyset, for instance, had built one of France's largest wholesale businesses (including forbidden and pirated works) using Lyon's crossroad position on the Rhône and on major highways connecting northern France with southern France as well as Germany, Switzerland, Italy, and Spain.[64] In the absence of a strong provincial publishing industry beyond specialized niches and local- and regional-interest publications, retailers and wholesalers turned to foreign presses and encouraged pirating as alternatives to pricey Parisian editions. They also pushed forbidden literature. If certain causes motivated some retailers to circulate dissident ideas about religion, politics, economics, or philosophy, everyone understood that demand was high for forbidden books, and profit margins even higher. Better able to identify such markets, retail booksellers were also freer to seize them.

In the end, much remains unknown about the hundreds of printers and booksellers who disseminated print throughout France. But administrative surveys shed light on how these men and women transformed the production and diffusion of the printed word by adjusting to government policies and by capitalizing on a soaring demand for all forms of print. Under heavy surveillance from the central administration, the printer-booksellers who survived the industry's consolidation thrived on job printing. These prosperous bourgeois worked around restrictions placed by royal policies. Far from being the victims of the large Parisian publishers, provincial printers took their place within broad networks that included Parisian, provincial, and foreign presses, competing at times, but mostly complementing one another and often cooperating. Each individual printer occupied a set of different positions on market continuums that ranged from works under privilege to pirated editions, from authorized titles to forbidden books, from local to regional and national readerships, from institutional to individual audiences. Each individual made choices reflecting his or her own temperament and personal convictions. These decisions were also based on each printer's own competitive position and on specific market conditions, such as the profile of local readers, the competitive rivalry between printers, the ever-variable extent of local policing, and their proximity to other centers of print production, both domestic and foreign.[65] Retailers faced the same choices, although they benefited from broader opportunities, especially in the second half of the century, due to booming demand, an absence of administrative interference, and extraordinarily lax policing in most of the kingdom. A remarkably dynamic book trade attracted an influx of newcomers. If retailers had to struggle harder than printer-booksellers did to get rich, their efforts also put more books in circulation in more cities, towns, and villages.

How did the Enlightenment figure in this picture? Some, like Lyon's printer-bookseller, publisher, and wholesaler Jean-Marie Bruyset, believed in the cause of the philosophes. But for each "enlightened" Bruyset, there was a Barthélemy Cristo equally committed to the opposite cause. In 1764, Cristo's dedication to the embattled Jesuits pushed him to secretly print an incendiary pamphlet by moonlight, or rather by candlelight, which caused a fire that destroyed his entire workshop.[66] And Bruyset himself was above all a hard-nosed business-man, not to mention a renowned pirate.[67] Rather than seeking enlightened publishers in the mold of the Renaissance humanist printer, one should look no further than the dozens of wholesalers and the hundreds of retailers all across France who felt the pulse of markets and ordered whatever their read-ers wanted.[68] Less ideological "foot soldiers" than practical businesspeople, booksellers as diverse as Lavigne in Sens, Garsein in Dax, Rigaud in Mont-pellier, or Bruyset in Lyon nevertheless made the Enlightenment possible. They did so not by pushing certain ideas, but by selling all that made it into print. In this way, they fulfilled the Enlightenment's most exalted mission: to pro-mote the broadest possible diffusion of all ideas.

NOTES

1. See Thierry Rigogne, *Between State and Market: Printing and Bookselling in Eighteenth-Century France* (Oxford: Voltaire Foundation, 2007), 110–17, 163–71.

2. See Robert Darnton's *The Kiss of Lamourette: Reflections in Cultural History* (New York: W. W. Norton, 1990), 113–24, 148–51; *Édition et sédition: L'univers de la littérature clandestine au XVIIIe siècle* (Paris: Gallimard, 1991), 57–86; *Gens de lettres, gens du livre* (Paris: Éditions Odile Jacob, 1992), 231–34; and *The Forbidden Best-Sellers of Pre-Revolutionary France* (New York: W. W. Norton, 1995), 39–51.

3. See Frédéric Barbier, Sabine Juratic, and Michel Vangheluwe, eds., *Lumières du Nord: Imprimeurs, libraires et "gens du livre" dans le Nord au XVIIIe siècle, 1701–1789* (Geneva: Droz, 1996); and Frédéric Barbier, Sabine Juratic, and Annick Mellerio, eds., *Dictionnaire des imprimeurs, libraires et gens du livre à Paris, 1701–1789* (Geneva: Droz, 2007), vol. 1 (A–C).

4. See Ernest Coyecque, *Inventaire de la collection Anisson sur l'histoire de l'imprimerie et la librairie principalement à Paris (manuscrits français 22061–22193)*, 2 vols. (Paris: E. Leroux, 1900; New York: Burt Franklin, 1964).

5. Bibliothèque nationale de France (hereafter cited as BnF), Manuscrits français (hereafter cited as MS fr.) 22124–29. Nouvelles acquisitions françaises 399–400, Estat de la librairie de France sous M. de Pontchartrain, (hereafter cited as 1700 survey); MS fr. 22184–85, Estats de la librairie et imprimerie du royaume en 1764 (hereafter cited as 1764 survey).

6. See Arrêts du Conseil (June 21, 1701, and March 31, 1739) in Claude Marin Saugrain, *Code de la librairie et imprimerie de Paris* (Paris: Aux dépens de la communauté, 1744; Westmead, Farn-borough, Hants., U.K.: Gregg International Publishers, 1971), 201–6; and BnF, MS fr. 22177, fols. 269–329, and MS fr. 22126, fols. 188–89, Arrêts du Conseil (May 12, 1759, and August 15, 1760).

7. See Rigogne, *Between State and Market*, 98–110.

8. These figures are calculated on a "stable" subset covering most of the kingdom outside

Paris (excluded in the 1764 survey), but excluding border changes and anomalies in surveying. For details, see ibid., 240–41.

9. 1700 and 1764 surveys.

10. In 1764, there were 687 presses in 240 printing shops, as opposed to 690 presses in 365 shops in 1701 (information on presses missing for several shops). See 1700 and 1764 surveys.

11. 1764 survey.

12. As many as one in three or four, sometimes one in two, based on surveys.

13. See Robert Darnton, *The Business of Enlightenment: A Publishing History of the "Encyclopédie," 1775–1800* (Cambridge: Harvard University Press, 1979), 219–45; Claude Lannette-Claverie, "Les tours de France des imprimeurs et libraires à la fin du XVIIe siècle," *Revue française d'histoire du livre* 6 (1973): 207–33; and Jacques Rychner, "Le travail de l'atelier," in *Le livre triomphant (1660–1830)*, ed. Roger Chartier and Henri-Jean Martin, vol. 2 of *Histoire de l'édition française* (Paris: Promodis, 1984), 42–61, 57–58.

14. 1700 and 1764 surveys.

15. In 1701, there were 533 journeymen and apprentices in the provinces, and 918 in 1764 (72 percent increase); there were 393 workers in Paris in 1702, and 850 on average between 1769 and 1771 (a 116 percent increase). See 1700 and 1764 surveys. 1702 inspection report by the Paris guild of booksellers and printers, quoted in Sabine Juratic, "Entre tradition et innovation: Les ateliers typographiques parisiens au XVIIIe siècle," *Revue française d'histoire du livre* 106–9 (2000): 133–53, 149; and BnF, MS fr. 22081, fols. 338–54, inspection reports in Parisian printing shops (May 1769, 1770, and 1771).

16. Based on the responses to the 1764 survey and its 1765 follow-up inquiry. "Wealthy" individuals were qualified as "riches," "très riches," "facultés considérables," "fortune considérable," or reported to have more than 50,000 livres. "Well-off" individuals were qualified as "fortune honnête," "aisé," "à l'aise," "assez riche," "facultés suffisantes," or having 10,000–50,000 livres. "Middling" is characterized as "facultés médiocres," "bornées," "modiques," "très minces," living off the revenues of a small shop and store, or having 1,000–10,000 livres. "Struggling" is qualified as "revenus insuffisants," "peine à trouver de quoi vivre," "facultés très médiocres," living off a very small shop and store, and having no other assets. "Poor" is characterized as "pauvre" or "très pauvre."

17. For similar conclusions based on Lyon and Bordeaux printers, see Roger Chartier, "Livre et espace: Circuits commerciaux et géographie culturelle de la librairie lyonnaise au XVIIIe siècle" *Revue française d'histoire du livre* 1, nos. 1–2 (1971): 77–108; and Jane McLeod, "Social Status and the Politics of Printers in Eighteenth-Century Bordeaux," *Social History/Histoire sociale* 23, no. 46 (1990): 301–23.

18. Lenard Berlanstein, *The Barristers of Toulouse in the Eighteenth Century, 1740–1793* (Baltimore: Johns Hopkins University Press, 1975), 47–51.

19. 1764 survey. The late Martel had left very little to his first son because he disapproved of his dissolute lifestyle.

20. Ibid.

21. Ibid.; Paul de Fleury, *Recherches sur les origines et le développement de l'imprimerie à Angoulême* (Angoulême: Imprimerie G. Chasseignac, 1901), 41–42. See also BnF, MS fr. 22073, fols. 329–90, *Mémoire à consulter, pour les libraires et imprimeurs de Lyon, Rouen, Toulouse, Marseille et Nîmes, concernant les privilèges de librairie et continuations d'iceux* (Lyon: Imprimerie Alexandre-Antelme Belion, 1776), 72n34.

22. See Henri-Jean Martin, *Livre, pouvoirs et société à Paris au XVIIe siècle, 1598–1701*, 2 vols. (Geneva: Droz, 1969).

23. See Jean Quéniart, "L'anémie provinciale," in Chartier and Martin, *Le livre triomphant (1660–1830)*, 282–93.

24. 1764 survey.

25. Ibid.

26. Caen, Archives départementales (AD) du Calvados, C 2886, doc. 8, 1758 survey for Caen.

27. AD Calvados, C 2886, doc. 5, 1737 survey for Caen.

28. 1764 survey.

29. BnF, MS fr. 21832, État général des imprimeurs du royaume (1777); MS fr. 22127, fol. 411, letter from Robin to d'Hémery, April 12, 1765; 1764 survey; Georges Lepreux, *Gallia typographica* (Paris: Honoré Champion, 1909–14), 4:187–89.

30. 1764 survey.

31. Ibid.

32. See Mohamed el Kordi, *Bayeux aux XVIIe et XVIIIe siècles: Contribution à l'histoire urbaine de la France* (Paris: Mouton, 1970), 256; and Jean-Claude Perrot, *Genèse d'une ville moderne: Caen au XVIIIe siècle* (Paris: Mouton, 1975), 1039–41.

33. 1764 survey.

34. Ibid. Based on the date at which they obtained their own license by royal decree. In many cases, sons of printers had already been running the shop alongside their parents for some time, either informally or through legal partnerships.

35. They had both been practicing for eighteen years. See 1700 survey.

36. See Jean-Dominique Mellot, *L'édition rouennaise et ses marchés (vers 1600–vers 1730): Dynamisme provincial et centralisme parisien* (Paris: École des chartes, 1998); and Jane McLeod, "A Social Study of Printers and Booksellers in Bordeaux from 1745 to 1810" (Ph.D. diss., University of York, 1987), 21–51.

37. Malassis (Alençon), Viallanes (Aurillac), Battut (Boulogne), Weins (Dunkerque), Martel (Montpellier), Besse (Narbonne), Dalvy (Périgueux), Mallard (Toulon), and Henry (Valenciennes). Six families transmitted shops either through daughters (Condom, Dunkerque, and Le Havre), widow remarriages (Mâcon and Valence), or cousins (Villefranche-de-Rouergue). 1781 data from [Antoine Perrin], *Almanach de la librairie* (Paris: Moutard, 1781; Aubel: P.-M. Gason, 1984). I was unable to track the complete succession line in fourteen cities where printers bore different names in 1701 and 1781.

38. 1700 and 1764 surveys. Based on last names.

39. Sons of master printers in 1764: forty-six out of sixty-eight. Five sons of booksellers: Jean-Marie Bruyset (Lyon), Caranove (Toulouse), Delaroche (Lyon), and Ferrand (Rouen). Two printers from other towns: Henry (Lille) from Valenciennes and Vatar (Nantes) from Rennes. Five sons-in-law of local printers: Christmann (Strasbourg), Dalesme (Limoges), Péterinck (Lille), Pijeon (Toulouse), and Vatar (Nantes); and one journeyman married to a widow: Seyer (Rouen). One local printer's nephew: Buisson (Lyon). No information on the parents of Louis Cutty (Lyon), Jonas Lorenz (Strasbourg), and Geoffroy Regnault (Lyon), all counted as outsiders.

40. Printers in 1764 who were the sons of master printers: Bordeaux, 10 out of 10; Rennes, 5/5; Rouen, 8/10; Limoges, 4/5; Lyon, 7/12; Nantes, 3/5; Toulouse, 6/10; Lille, 3/6; Strasbourg, 0/5. The father of Strasbourg's Christmann had married a printer's daughter, but he never ran the shop himself.

41. In 1701, 278 out of 372 printers were printer-booksellers, 185 out of 247 in 1764, and 207 out of 237 in 1781, on a consistent geographic basis. See 1700 and 1764 surveys; and Perrin, *Almanach de la librairie.*

42. In 1701, there were 356 retail stores out of 634 bookstores, and 506 out of 713 in 1781. See ibid.

43. 1764 survey; Perrin, *Almanach de la librairie.*

44. Only the 1700 survey collected biographical information on booksellers.

45. BnF, MS fr. 22073, fols. 329–90, *Mémoire pour les libraires de Lyon, Rouen, Toulouse, Marseille et Nimes,* 78.

46. Retailers were on average forty-four years of age in 1701, as opposed to slightly over forty-four and a half for printer-booksellers; had established themselves at twenty-seven (identical); and had seventeen years of experience, as opposed to nearly eighteen. Based on data on 259 provincial retail booksellers. See 1700 survey.

47. The 1764 survey gave biographical information on nineteen retailers only, without any indication on how representative they might be.

48. 1764 survey.

49. Ibid.

50. Ibid.

51. Edit concernant les arts et métiers (May 1767) in *Recueil général des anciennes lois françaises,*

depuis l'an 420 jusqu'à la Révolution de 1789, ed. Athanase-Jean-Léger Jourdan, Decrusy, and François-André Isambert (Paris: Belin-Leprieur, Verdière, 1822–33), 22:468; BnF, MS fr. 22066, fols. 143–44, Arrêt du Conseil (October 30, 1767). See Rigogne, *Between State and Market,* 159–63. Printing was a rare exception to the sale of brevets.

52. See Bordeaux, AD Gironde, C 3371, 1768 and 1775 surveys for Bordeaux. In 1781, all but one remained, and one had even become a printer and the guild's syndic.

53. 1764 survey.

54. Ibid.

55. Ibid.

56. See Caen, AD Calvados, C 2886, doc. 10, 1768 survey for Caen; and letter from Vice Chancellor Maupeou to intendants introducing the 1768 survey, May 2, 1768, quoted in Madeleine Ventre, *L'imprimerie et la librairie en Languedoc au dernier siècle de l'Ancien Régime, 1700–1789* (Paris: Mouton, 1958), 45.

57. 1764 survey. Leblond was also a printmaker and print seller.

58. Ibid.

59. Ibid.

60. Ibid.

61. Ibid.; BnF, MS fr. 22126, fols. 420–21, letter from Tonnet to d'Hémery, April 5, 1765; MS fr. 22127, fol. 410, letter from Chirac to d'Hémery, April 25, 1765.

62. See BnF, MS fr. 22073, fols. 329–90, *Mémoire pour les libraires de Lyon, Rouen, Toulouse, Marseille et Nîmes,* 77–78.

63. 1764 survey.

64. Ibid. See also BnF, MS fr. 22128, fol. 291–302, letter from Bourgelat, inspector of the book trade in Lyon, to Sartine, December 24, 1763.

65. On policing and geography, see Rigogne, *Between State and Market,* 36–97, 201–18.

66. 1764 survey; BnF, MS fr. 22125, fol. 68, letter from Guvrit to d'Hémery, February 29, 1764.

67. See Dominique Varry, "Une famille de libraires lyonnais turbulents: Les Bruyset," *La lettre clandestine* 11 (2003), 105–27.

68. See, for instance, Elizabeth L. Eisenstein, "The Libraire-Philosophe: Four Sketches for a Group Portrait," in *Le livre et l'historien: Etudes offertes en l'honneur du Professeur Henri-Jean Martin,* ed. Frédéric Barbier et al. (Geneva: Droz, 1997), 539–50.

FOUR

MAKING THE FAIR TRADER:
PAPERMAKING, THE EXCISE, AND THE ENGLISH STATE, 1700–1815

Leonard N. Rosenband

The "fair trader," proclaimed generations of English officials, needed protection.[1] He was worth cultivating because he paid his full share of the excise duty, the tax on the goods crafted and grown in England's shops and fields. But his numbers never satisfied the state. Despite the swelling ranks of excise officers and the newfound precision offered royal gaugers by instruments such as the hydrometer, illicit producers continued to outwit science.[2] Hidden cellars, casks with false bottoms, counterfeit revenue stamps, and the blind eye of the exciseman, bought with a guinea or two, all drained the Treasury. His trade was "so liable to fraud," lamented the leading papermaker James Whatman II in 1764, "that at least half the paper that is made [in England] pays no Duty at all."[3]

This essay considers the "dishonest traders" in the papermaking industry in England between 1700 and 1815, the manufacturers who bedeviled both Whatman and the English state during the high tide of the fiscal-military regime. Britain's war-making prowess had expanded greatly across the eighteenth century. So, too, had the state's capacity to ferret out and collect the revenues necessary to harden its sinews of power. The number of excisemen mushroomed and their marching orders grew increasingly thorough. Producers in many trades, paper manufacturers included, sought relief in sharp practices. The papermakers slipped untaxed quires into their reams, hid fine sheets in bundles marked second class, and evaded the duty altogether by reusing stamped ream wrappers. As the solicitor general explained to the Court of Exchequer in 1801, "The profits [are] through the multiplication of these instances; we do not often detect them."[4] The attorney general confessed that the honest manufacturer was often compelled to mimic the fraudulent producer: "As this practise was begun one followed another and they were obliged to do so almost in self defence."[5] Moreover, the Commissioners of Excise acknowledged the complicity of grocers, printers, and stationers in the papermakers' evasions. The dishonest traders in paper cast long shadows beyond their own art.

Robert Darnton taught us to consider the legal boundaries that framed past worlds, but even more, to look beyond them in search of everyday creativity and unexpected connections. One of these surprises is the corporate flavor of English papermaking in the age of Adam Smith. There were rivalries and regional tensions in the trade, but it lobbied Parliament as a single body for favor and protection, and often had its way. Honest traders and rogue papermakers alike mastered their art in an atmosphere charged with cabals, conspiracy, and dreams of monopoly. They blunted competition by drawing up mutual price lists for their reams. They briefly closed their mills to humble the rag merchants, whose cast-off linen dominated every papermaker's budget. They also shuttered their shops in vain efforts to drive down the wages of their skilled hands. These intrigues violated both the statute and the common law concerning the restraint of trade, but they went unpunished. When the dishonest trader secured his paper in a loose wrapper or sent it under a counterfeit excise stamp, he met a far different fate. He paid dearly, since his moonlight business threatened the underpinnings of the fiscal-military state. He had entered the contested terrain of his trade, where the master papermakers' semi-clandestine regulation of their craft and its commerce collided with the state's appetite for revenue, its elaborate system of supervision, and its regiments of excisemen.

Parliaments and prime ministers ceaselessly tried to turn the "free" trade of tax-evading papermakers into "fair" trade. The state provided excise officers with intimate details of paper production and commerce, sent these men into workshops and warehouses, and set national standards for the weights and measures of stationery and pasteboard. Historians such as John Orth, John Rule, Peter Linebaugh, and, of course, E. P. Thompson have focused on the numerous attempts by England's governors to undo worker governance of their trades and workbenches.[6] Scholars have paid less attention to the English state's efforts when the regulatory grasp was enjoyed by entrepreneurs.[7] Adam Smith, however, spent many pages on the regulatory reach of the manufacturers. As long as trade and production flowed freely, he concluded, prices inexorably gravitated to their natural level. He celebrated the end of market imperfections imposed by any interest, such as the papermakers. No doubt, he despised the entrepreneurs' attempts to control the costs of labor and raw materials as well as the price of paper. Yet Smith, who was a vigilant Scottish customs commissioner, also mused that the smuggler was often a person who "would have been, in every respect, an excellent citizen, had not the laws of his country made that a crime which nature never meant to be so."[8] Smith, then, was a complicated source for those trying to establish fair trade.

England's papermaking roots were so shallow that its labor relations were exempt from the Statute of Artificers of 1563. John Briscoe secured a royal patent in 1685 "for making English paper . . . as white as French or Dutch paper."[9] But it was not to be: at the turn of the century, Charles Davenant, who was well-informed about the state of the industry, admitted, "We are not come up to the French perfection" in the production of paper.[10] Just before Christmas in 1697, the Commissioners for Trade and Plantations chimed in. Like Davenant, these officials concentrated on the scarcity of rags as a "great hindrance to the progress" of the craft. They also proposed "for the Incouragement" of the art "that all paper imported ought to pay a higher Duty than Paper made at home."[11] Thus the balance between customs and excise duties was prescribed by Parliament in 1711. A foreign ream known in the trade as fine demy bore an impost of 4s. (and more if it originated in Normandy); the excise burden on its domestic equivalent was 1s. 6d.[12] England's paper manufacturers offered a candid defense of this favorable tariff-excise ratio: "that so useful a Manufactory may not be lost to the Nation, and Thousands of People lie starving for want of Employ."[13]

By the middle of the century, English papermaking was maturing. In 1747, an article in the *London Tradesman* concluded, "We are but lately come into the Method of making a tolerable Paper, we were formerly supplied with that Commodity from France, Holland, and Genoa, and are still obliged to these Countries for our best Papers."[14] The talents of Huguenot exiles, the importation of a Dutch device that quickened the shredding of fresh rags, and competitions sponsored by the Royal Society of Arts hastened this progress. Soaring demand, too, played its part: in 1781, the Royal Society announced that the consumption of paper was "every day encreasing."[15] An exultant Matthias Koops proclaimed in 1800 that "by perseverance, convenience in the construction of these manufactures, superior engines [the Dutch device], presses and machines, and improved moulds, [England's] industrious [paper] manufacturers" possessed an "actual pre-eminence" in the trade.[16] But earlier, in the threatening circumstances of 1796, Koops's tune had different lyrics. Should the French secure the "free navigation" of the Rhine and Scheldt, he warned, England's paper producers faced wholesale peril, since "paper manufactories have been long established in France, superior to the English."[17] On balance, Koops probably had it right: England's papermaking instruments likely matched or bettered those of their Continental rivals, while the skill and technique of the English craft may have lagged. Tools had failed to offset fully the advantages of touch, and price competition still troubled the British trade.

When Adam Smith mocked the "clamour and sophistry of merchants and manufacturers," he could easily have been referring to the papermakers.[18] Having heard about a bill "for the better preventing Excessive and Immoderate Gaming," the Company of Playing Card Makers marched to Parliament in 1710.[19] Failing in an earlier bid to put an end to excise charges on their goods, the papermakers petitioned the Treasury in 1765 to continue the "Lenity" in the collection of the paper excise.[20] The "paper hangers and manufacturers" were loud, apprehensive opponents of the negotiations to lower Anglo-French trade barriers in 1786.[21] So England's papermakers had learned how to lobby noisily, but they had also mastered the whisper and the clandestine circular.

The papermakers chatted privately about the cost of labor and cast-off linen, the price and content of their reams, and the toll taken by the excise on their profits. Talk sometimes led to active association. With the market for their wares saturated but rag prices stubbornly high, in 1783 "the paper makers met together to see if they could not get something for they were loosing money by their trade."[22] In order to cap the rising cost of discarded linen, the leading papermakers who gathered at London's George and Vulture Tavern during the 1790s agreed to shut their mills for one month.[23] But this plot failed, as did a later boycott, in which blame was cast on "the seccession of [the] Brethren in Hampshire and Berkshire."[24] Self-regulation was a trying business, especially when potential collaborators put their own self-interest first.

The master papermakers had company in their efforts to command the craft's labor markets. Always a capitalist trade, the production of paper encompassed the synchronized skills of wage-earning journeymen and a substantial array of tools and machines, from carefully wired molds to banks of stamping hammers. It was a seasonal industry, lasting as long as the flow of a mountain stream and the hills of stinking rags that surrounded every mill. The workers' sway rested on the threatened or actual withdrawal of their scarce skills "for wages or customs."[25] By the close of the eighteenth century, the journeymen had organized, and their bosses were only a step behind. In 1788, a cabal of paperworkers had taken shape in Manchester, prompting a printed retort from their employers. "From the Year 1789 to the present Period," England's paper manufacturers raged in 1796, "frequent Conspiracies" had empowered the journeymen to press for higher wages.[26] Parliament banned the paperworkers' unions in 1796, but with skill and paper at premium prices, this measure had less value than the sheets on which it was printed. A year later, the "Kent men struck as a body" and, more ominously, from their masters' perspective, apparently garnered material support "countrywide."[27] In 1799, Parliament outlawed combinations among all workers. The journeymen paperworkers responded by forging a national union in 1800. James Swann was hardly an isolated example when he testified in 1807 that "one of [his] Mills has been standing still from the First of May, in consequence of a Combination among the Men."[28] Still, some workers did break ranks. Wage rates varied widely in Kentish papermaking, Whatman reported, and he had gotten by without paying "overwork" money, a venerable custom of the craft.[29] But in 1823, a pamphlet concluded that the paperworkers, among other artisans, conducted their affairs "as though no such [Combination] Act was in existence."[30]

The paper manufacturers were equally practiced in the art of collusion. For instance, the Buckinghamshire producers resorted to a lockout in 1796 and had been quick to adopt the "document"—that is, the blacklist.[31] In 1800, Parliament barred written agreements among the masters in every trade to reduce the wages, raise the output, or alter the hours of their hands. In April 1801, twenty-three employers leagued together in Kent and Surrey with studied disregard for this act. They would "no longer" submit in "unresisting compliance to the wanton, unnecessary and *extortionate demands*" of their workers.[32] The manufacturers founded their national society in 1803, but solidarity and profits proved an imperfect fit, and some producers snared journeymen with enhanced "wages or customs." Still, this coalition represented the owners of two-thirds of England's papermaking vats and many of the industry's most prominent names.[33]

Several aspects of the Papermakers' Act of 1796 foreshadowed the general measure of 1799. It accelerated the prosecution of alleged malefactors and permitted one justice of the peace, rather than the usual two, to preside. It lacked the paternalist counterweight of wage prescription, but it did include a distinctive, seemingly outmoded mandate: the act set the daily output for every papermaking vat. This benchmark had little effect, since the journeymen sweated until they had scraped the pulp from the bottom of the vats. Still, the state had attempted to resolve one source of tension between masters and men and thereby slow their opposed cabals. William Pitt's regime sought deregulated labor markets in which *master* and *man* reached accord.[34] Surely this formula would tip the scales in most trades in the manufacturers' favor. But the state's eagerness to unravel the ties among both producers and workers suggests that it was more than the handmaiden of capital—the state's interests were primarily its own.

A broadly established daily quota might have also provided the state with a deeper revenue stream—if the excise officials could actually snag the funds. Successive regimes tried to ease the collection of the duty on paper by recasting the basis of assessment. In the seventeenth century, this tax rested on the value of the reams in a nearby town; in the eighteenth, the duty turned primarily on the physical description (type) of the paper; and in the nineteenth, the levy hinged mainly on the weight of the reams.[35] Dishonest trade, however, was both the most successful and the most risky conspiracy practiced by England's papermakers. By its very nature, the scale and frequency of this enterprise must remain unknown, but there are revealing traces. The use of fraudulent stamps, the attorney general admitted in 1805, "is carried on to a very great extent," despite the "extremely high" penalties.[36] "In the compass of thirty miles round" the Houghton works of Lincolnshire, the authorities discovered "no less than thirty different cases of paper sent from this Mill with a false stamp upon it." The engineers of this fraud suffered a £3,000 fine. Their customers must have been remarkably unlettered or indifferent to the forgery, since a character in "the word paper [was] actually reversed" in the impression.[37] But illicit activities were often difficult to detect or prosecute. When white paper was stained to serve as a wall covering, it was subject to a second excise duty. Yet the hangings generally escaped this charge, "to the great Detriment of the Revenue, & fair Traders in the Paper paint'g Business."[38] In 1778, when the paper stainers petitioned the Treasury for aid against their untaxed competition, even the rapacious Treasury demurred, since the proposal "would be not only difficult but oppressive in the Collection."[39]

The excise office in Marlborough complained in 1777 that "Great Quantities of printed or painted paper for which no Duty is paid, are used for covering & lining trunks & Bandboxes ... to the Manifest Injury of the Revenue."[40] The dishonest trader profited by pocketing the excise charges. As a result, he could lower the price of his wares, and, with the wink and nod of a printer, stationer, or even an exciseman, win an undeserved share of the market. Thus

William Jones, a Gloucester producer, bribed an excise officer to mark 5,754 pounds of his paper as 2,784, which saved him slightly more than eighteen pounds.[41] Such schemes proliferated as the papermakers' cabals failed to restrain the cost of labor and rags. They became even more attractive as the debt-ridden English state raised the excise burden on paper dramatically in 1781, and again in 1801, and tightened collection.[42] The consequences were evident in Whatman's accounts: before 1781, he chalked up 4 percent of his costs to the excise; by 1785, he was handing over 20 percent.[43]

The Treasury's harvest from the duty on paper expanded enormously during the last decades of the eighteenth century, perhaps at the expense of output itself. To preserve domestic production, Parliament offset the soaring inland duty with sharply rising levies on imported reams. Adam Smith despaired in 1776 that the "mercantile interest," in which he enrolled manufacturers, had captured England's economic policy and distorted it to its own advantage.[44] Now the state sought to capture the mercantile interest in order to glean a greater share of its profits. To do so, it would have to transform dishonest traders in paper into fair traders. That is, the state intended to deregulate the industry and put an end to the traditional covenants and illicit know-how that had long permitted papermakers to evade the excise and govern much of the business in their reams. It was a tall order.

The state's plan rested on a flock of excise officers, surveyors, and collectors. By 1725, about a third of all of England's government officials labored in the excise department.[45] They were not placemen; instead, they were well trained, rigorously supervised, and regularly rotated to forestall collusion.[46] Expected to master the practices of a host of trades, from tanner to tallow chandler and papermaker, they were sometimes at the mercy of the producers. For example, the exciseman John Turner replied to a reprimand with the admission "that he thought the Trader knew the Law better than himself."[47] An excise bureau reminded the inspectors that legitimate variance in "Length and Breadth" marked even the best producers' sheets. And the hydrometer notwithstanding, the officers learned that "a Judgement may be formed of the Quality from the Fineness of the Texture and Thickness of the Sheets."[48]

Surveillance was active. William Durham was trapped by a trail of numbers: he remitted to the excise "little more than half the Amount paid by his Predecessor in the same Mill, although he had erected an additional Vat."[49] In other cases, intuition and experience provided the key: "Something or other had led to suspicion of great frauds in the paper manufacture in that part of the Country." Substantial temptation invariably surrounded the work. The officers responded to these blandishments frequently—so frequently, in fact, that many papermakers fell prey to a fresh inspector who failed to play the game. Thomas Wilmott grew so accustomed to the efficacy of a few guineas that "he hardly thought it possible that the bribe should be refused."[50] What such collusion put at risk was clear to the court: "The whole revenue might be defrauded and the fair trader might be exposed to very considerable loss and the fraudulent trader derive considerable benefit."[51] Small wonder that the court fell heavily on a producer who removed paper from his mill after the excise officer had weighed it but before his supervisor got the same chance: "If these outworks are preserved the Enemy never gets into the Citadel."[52]

In 1816, Parliament barred papermakers from using their mills as stationers' shops. The manufacturers also had to cease selling their sheets "on any premises" within two miles of a paper mill.[53] It was a futile gesture, born of long-standing frustration. The excise knew that stationers, expert handlers of paper, were natural confederates of dishonest producers. When the trades were linked in one pair of hands, the danger increased, as the Court of Exchequer explained in 1798: "Though there are certainly many honourable men carrying on those businesses together yet no doubt there are great opportunities of defrauding the Revenue." In this case, the defendant had amassed a collection of stamped ream wrappers ready for reuse.[54] Though obligated to destroy these covers once they had removed the quires, stationers and printers habitually preserved them and passed them back to the producers. Thus the next packet from the mill arrived duty-free. Mark Woodhead and a fellow intriguer had benefited from this dodge "in not less than 44 instances," the court charged in 1813.[55] A manufacturer's fate was sealed by wrappers "extremely carefully kept in a drawer perfectly entire. . . . They therefore must have come back contrary to law into his possession."[56]

Cutting the cords of complicity preoccupied the excise commissioners. "Very loosely tied" bundles doomed one producer, for they "gave rise to a little suspicion that a trick was intended."[57] The authorities were on the lookout for bulging reams, strings strained to the breaking point, and knots unraveling under the pressure. They realized that "by the making up of more Quires in a Ream or Bundle or more Sheets in a Quire than the Law allows . . . some Capital Frauds have been carried on."[58] They were familiar with the handiwork of men like Samuel Hutton, who stuffed seventy-two sheets into his quires rather than the legal twenty-four, and then scratched the true dimensions of his shipment into the stamp.[59] And they knew that the fair trader, once under-priced, did not have to look far to learn the tricks of maintaining his trade.

The Court of Exchequer carefully assessed penalties for artless dodges. Poor William Durham, guilty of a long string of evasions, was "not entitled to the least Favour, but on the Contrary appears a very proper Subject for an Example."[60] Douglas Hay claimed that English courts ruled through a measured equation of uncompromising majesty tempered by moments of mercy.[61] To be sure, the court did not extend the full measure of pain to every unfair trader in paper. Arthur Lee, the court conceded, had violated a statute but without intent to "defraud the Revenue." Consequently, the court considered it "sufficient to take but one penalty although by his conduct he has incurred many penalties."[62] In exchange for the "mercy" shown to Ralph Lomas, the solicitor general hoped that the West Riding manufacturer would avoid the "bad examples that may have been set him in [his] family." If Lomas stayed on that course, it would be "bad business"—for the Treasury, too, which risked losing receipts.[63] The court routinely factored in a felon's assets before reckoning his liability. Unlucky Robert Turner's advocate questioned whether "the [court's] object be to ruin this man." The attorney general's reply was succinct: "I believe he is quite safe. . . . [He] is a person of very considerable property."[64] Smaller producers, convicted on several counts and subject to failure, sometimes got away with the penalty for a single offense. In the state's calculus, majesty and mercy mattered, but so did the receipts from a working mill—even if its treacherous master required particular attention.

"Little else is requisite," Adam Smith observed, "to carry a state to the highest degree of opulence from the lowest barbarism, but peace, easy taxes, and a tolerable administration of justice; all the rest being brought about by the natural course of things."[65] Accordingly, he would have been dismayed by the rising duty on paper, the enterprising and severe excise officials, and the lack of rest for British guns during much of the eighteenth century. He may have recognized his thoughts in the desire of England's rulers to rid both labor and product markets of illicit "contracts" and arrangements. But he certainly would have understood that the government, in championing this sort of deregulation, was concerned primarily with its own purse. When entrepreneurial self-regulation did not trouble the state's interests, the state did not trouble the entrepreneurs. When this self-regulation clashed with the state's needs, the excise labeled these transactions as dishonest trade and pursued the culprits relentlessly. The British fiscal-military state's hunger for revenue was too great to trust to the natural course of things.

NOTES

1. On the British fiscal-military state and its policies, see John Brewer, *The Sinews of Power: War, Money, and the English State, 1688–1783* (Cambridge: Harvard University Press, 1990); Martin Daunton, *Progress and Poverty: An Economic and Social History of Britain, 1700–1850* (Oxford: Oxford University Press, 1995), 477–559; and Niall Ferguson, *The Cash Nexus: Money and Power in the Modern World, 1700–2000* (New York: Basic Books, 2001).

2. On measurement and the excise, see William Ashworth's splendid *Customs and Excise: Trade, Production, and Consumption in England, 1640–1845* (Oxford: Oxford University Press, 2003), part 5.

3. British Library, Add. MS. 38,203, James Whatman II, "Some Reasons That Make It Necessary to Alter the Present Method of Levying the Excise on British Made Paper."

4. The National Archives (hereafter cited as TNA): Public Record Office (hereafter cited as PRO), CUST 103/49, "The Attorney General Versus John Gray and Others," December 4, 1801, 808.

5. TNA: PRO, CUST 103/15, "The Attorney General Versus James Coles," February 26, 1785, 241.

6. John Orth, *Combination and Conspiracy: A Legal History of Trade Unionism, 1721–1906* (Oxford: Clarendon Press, 1991); John Rule, *The Experience of Labour in Eighteenth-Century English Industry* (New York: St. Martin's Press, 1981); Peter Linebaugh, *The London Hanged: Crime and Civil Society in the Eighteenth Century* (Cambridge: Cambridge University Press, 1992); E. P. Thompson, *The Making of the English Working Class* (New York: Vintage, 1963).

7. One notable exception to this generalization is D. C. Coleman, "Combinations of Capital and of Labour in the English Paper Industry, 1789–1825," *Economica*, n.s., 21 (February 1954): 32–53.

8. Adam Smith's musings on the smuggler's plight are quoted and discussed in Ashworth, *Customs and Excise*, 165.

9. Quoted in D. C. Coleman, *The British Paper Industry, 1495–1860: A Study in Industrial Growth* (Oxford: Clarendon Press, 1958), 69.

10. Quoted in ibid., 53.

11. British Library, Sloane MS 2902, Commissioners for Trade and Plantations, "Paper Manufact^r," December 23, 1697.

12. Harry Dagnall, *The Taxation of Paper in Great Britain, 1643–1861: A History and Documentation* (Queensbury: In collaboration with the British Association of Paper Historians, 1998), 12–13, tables 2 and 3.

13. Quoted in Alfred Shorter, *Paper Making in the British Isles: An Historical and Geographical Study* (New York: Barnes and Noble, 1972), 44.

14. Quoted in Richard Hills, *Papermaking in Britain, 1488–1988: A Short History* (London: Athlone, 1988), 67.

15. Quoted in Coleman, *British Paper Industry*, 171.

16. Matthias Koops, *Historical Account of the Substances Which Have Been Used to Describe Events, and to Convey Ideas, from the Earliest Date, to the Invention of Paper* (London, 1800), 72–73.

17. Matthias Koops, "A Developement of the Views and Designs of the French Nation" (London, 1796), 201.

18. Quoted in Brewer, *Sinews of Power*, 248.

19. Quoted in ibid., 238.

20. TNA: PRO, CUST 48/17, "Petition of the Paper Makers of Great Britain," 1765.

21. John Ehrman, *The British Government and Commercial Negotiations with Europe, 1783–1793* (Cambridge: Cambridge University Press, 1962), 46, esp. n. 10.

22. TNA: PRO, CUST 103/15, "The Attorney General Versus James Coles," February 26, 1785, 218.

23. D. C. Coleman, "Combinations of Capital and of Labour," 39.

24. Quoted in ibid., 41.

25. Quoted in Coleman, *British Paper Industry*, 266.

26. *Journals of the House of Commons* 51 (April 19, 1796): 585.

27. On this incident, see the summary notes by Jean Stirk in John Balston, *The Whatmans and Wove (Vélin) Paper: Its Invention and Development in the West* (West Farleigh, Kent, U.K.: J. N. Balston, 1998), 307.

28. British Parliamentary Papers, *Fourdrinier Committee*, 1807, xiv, 18.

29. Thomas Balston, *James Whatman, Father and Son* (London: Methuen, 1957), 119.

30. Quoted in E. H. Hunt, *British Labour History, 1815–1914* (Atlantic Highlands, N.J.: Humanities Press, 1981), 197–98.

31. Coleman, *British Paper Industry*, 263–64.

32. Quoted in Coleman, "Combinations of Capital and of Labour," 44.

33. Ibid., 45.

34. On this vision, see Leonard N. Rosenband, "Comparing Combination Acts: French and English Papermaking in the Age of Revolution," *Social History* 29, no. 2 (May 2004): 172.

35. Rupert Jarvis, "The Paper-Makers and the Excise in the Eighteenth Century," *The Library*, 5th ser., 14, no. 2 (June 1959): 101.

36. TNA: PRO, CUST 103/57, "The Attorney General Versus Sarah Jones," June 7, 1805, 461–62.

37. TNA: PRO, CUST 103/48, "The Attorney General Versus William Lupton and Robert Turner," July 3, 1801, 546–47. The verdict is on p. 599.

38. TNA: PRO, CUST 43/2, July 17, 1764.

39. TNA: PRO, CUST 48/19, "Report on the Memorial of the Paper Stainers," October 7, 1778.

40. TNA: PRO, CUST 43/81, October 7, 1777.

41. TNA: PRO, CUST 103/64, "The Attorney General Versus William Jones," May 15, 1807, 228, 238.

42. For hikes in the paper excise, see Dagnall, *Taxation of Paper*, esp. 24–43.

43. Balston, *James Whatman*, 71, table G.

44. Adam Smith, *An Inquiry into the Nature and Causes of the Wealth of Nations*, ed. Edwin Cannan (New York: Random House, 1937), book 4.

45. Ashworth, *Customs and Excise*, 119.

46. Ibid., 117–30.

47. TNA: PRO, CUST 40/36, May 19, 1818.

48. TNA: PRO, CUST 43/49a, March 5, 1782.

49. TNA: PRO, CUST 48/68, "Report" on the petition of William Durham, April 25, 1817.

50. TNA: PRO, CUST 103/47, "The Attorney General Versus Thomas Wilmott," February 20, 1801, 173, 175.

51. TNA: PRO, CUST 103/69, "The Attorney General Versus Henry Compton," December 1, 1810, 615.

52. TNA: PRO, CUST 103/47, "The Attorney General Versus Charles Wilmott," February 20, 1801, 169.

53. TNA: PRO, CUST 48/68, "Memorial of George Stretton," April 5, 1817.

54. TNA: PRO, CUST 103/41, "The Attorney General Versus John Hunter," December 5, 1798, 444–45.

55. TNA: PRO, CUST 103/76, "The Attorney General Versus Mark Woodhead and Another," December 3, 1813, 262.

56. TNA: PRO, CUST 103/36, "The Attorney General Versus Thomas Charlock and John Hill," July 1, 1795, 230.

57. TNA: PRO, CUST 103/74, "The Attorney General Versus Ralph Lomas," June 25, 1812, 177.

58. TNA: PRO, CUST 43/49a, March 5, 1782.

59. TNA: PRO, CUST 103/41, "The Attorney General Versus Samuel Hutton," July 5, 1798, 117.

60. TNA: PRO, CUST 48/68, "Report" on the petition of William Durham, April 25, 1817.

61. Douglas Hay, "Property, Authority and the Criminal Law," in *Albion's Fatal Tree: Crime and Society in Eighteenth-Century England*, ed. Douglas Hay, Peter Linebaugh, John G. Rule, E. P. Thompson, and Cal Winslow (New York: Pantheon Books, 1975), 17–63.

62. TNA: PRO, CUST 103/60, "The Attorney General Versus Arthur Lee," May 23, 1806, 511.

63. TNA: PRO, CUST 103/74, "The Attorney General Versus Ralph Lomas," June 25, 1812, 183–84.

64. TNA: PRO, CUST 103/48, "The Attorney General Versus William Lupton and Robert Turner," July 3, 1801, 554.

65. Quoted in Donald Winch, *Adam Smith's Politics: An Essay in Historiographic Revision* (Cambridge: Cambridge University Press, 1978), 4.

✑ FIVE

COMMERCE WITH BOOKS:
READING PRACTICES AND BOOK DIFFUSION AT THE HABSBURG
COURT IN FLORENCE (1765–1790)

Renato Pasta

Robert Darnton's pathbreaking work on the social history of ideas has made scholars aware of the key role that eighteenth-century booksellers had in spreading the ideologies of the Enlightenment. Although he has never provided a theoretical definition of what the Enlightenment was, his refreshingly old-fashioned approach to scholarship concentrates on the relationship between books and the Revolution, and it hinges on archival research in contrast with the fashionable abstractions of postmodernist methodological discourse.[1] The pattern that emerges appears to be more checkered than what book historians and specialists on the eighteenth century used to believe before the 1980s. We are now aware both of the wide diffusion of Enlightenment language before 1789 and of the social and institutional constraints that limited its potential for change after 1770. This essay aims at exploring some aspects of book diffusion and the practice of reading in a specific context: the Habsburg-Lorraine court in Florence during the second half of the eighteenth century. There, French books and Enlightenment ideologies circulated freely, but court life also hosted other, less radical influences, such as natural law, jurisdictionalism, Jansenism, and the language of gradual progress and brotherhood fostered by the international networks of Freemasonry. The essay aims to offer a nuanced view of high culture in one of the centers of intellectual and political life during the age of reform in Italy.

In 1771, Peter Leopold, Habsburg Grand Duke of Tuscany, ordered that the twenty-thousand-volume library of the Medicis be transferred from the royal residence in Pitti Palace to the public library in Florence, the Magliabechiana, an institution donated by Antonio Magliabechi to the city and opened for public use in 1747.[2] The decision to move the Medici collections out of Pitti reflected the wish to increase the stock of printed matter available in the Magliabechiana, thereby promoting the "pursuit of happiness" in town and the moral betterment of the reading public. Practical motivations also lay behind Peter Leopold's move. As his family rapidly expanded, they started to need the rooms used to house the Medici library. The first child of the grand ducal couple, Francis, was born to Maria Louise of Bourbon-Parma and Peter Leopold in 1768. He was to succeed his father as emperor in 1792. The second male child, Ferdinand, born in 1769, became Grand Duke of Tuscany in 1791, following Leopold's accession to the imperial throne in Vienna in 1790. Between their marriage in 1765 and the death of Leopold II, the grand ducal couple bore fifteen children, many of them surviving the death of their parents. Thus, freeing up living space at Pitti became urgent, and the relocation of the Medici library seemed an appropriate solution.[3] Most of the Medicis' book collections are now preserved in the holdings of the Biblioteca Nazionale, Florence. They provide scholars with several heterodox and libertine works that Magliabechi, himself working at the core of a network of erudite and princely correspondents, had eagerly bought around the turn of the eighteenth century. Some volumes belonging to the Medici collection were dispersed among the Florentine and Tuscan libraries in 1771/72 and double exemplars were auctioned off. Some texts reached the new library of the Imperial Cabinet of Physics and Natural History, which had been established in 1766 and opened to the public in 1775.[4] Other volumes were donated to the library of the University of Pisa. At an intellectual and organizational level, therefore, Peter Leopold's choice represented a rational distribution of the existing collections for the benefit of the grand duchy's learned institutions. It reflected the Habsburgs' cultural politics in Italy and compares, albeit on a minor scale, with the reorganization of research institutions in Lombardy that Maria Theresa carried out in the early 1770s, especially after the suppression of the Jesuits in 1773.

The evidence for this essay rests primarily, but not exclusively, on the printed catalog of the private grand ducal library that was assembled in 1771 in order to compensate for the loss of the older Medici volumes. The *Catalogue des livres du Cabinet particulier des LL. AA. RR.*[5] presents a remarkable set of manuscript comments written either at the bequest of the sovereign or directly by the grand duke himself. In this catalog, the ruler cast his judgment on many works concerning education and the practice of government. The *Catalogue* lists 1,571 titles, mostly French texts printed in Paris and the Netherlands. The new collection must have been assembled by a prominent, but as yet unidentified, bookseller in Paris working on behalf of the Habsburg-Lorrainers and in contact with both the Tuscan diplomatic service and the experienced finance minister in Florence, Angelo Tavanti. The *Catalogue* and the accompanying marginalia reveal an outright rejection of antiquarianism and an embrace of "useful" knowledge—a concern that welded together the ideologies of the Enlightenment with a more conservative outlook in matters of ethics and religion. The collection was intended to serve as the working library of the prince. In his role as statesman, Peter Leopold perused a variety of books that were either available on the shelves of his office—the Segreteria intima di Gabinetto at Pitti Palace—or had been acquired on the international book market. Thus the *Catalogue* represents an initial stage in the development of the princely collections, and further information must be culled to understand the ruler's engagement with books. Brissot de Warville's *Bibliothèque philosophique du législateur*, for example, was often consulted in the lead-up to the establishment of a new criminal code, which suppressed torture and the death penalty in November 1786. Brissot's legal collection was an especially influential book in the late Enlightenment, and included Cesare Beccaria's *Dei delitti e delle pene*, translated into French by Étienne Chaillou de Lisy (1773)—a version that was closer to the original text than the translation by André Morellet (1766).[6] Beccaria and Brissot loomed large in the blueprint for a written constitution that Peter Leopold meant to issue in his states. Although this project never materialized, it stands out as an achievement of Enlightenment constitutional thought, and the grand duke continued to work on it until his premature death in 1792. By that time, Leopold's private books in Florence had been included in the new princely collection that Ferdinand III rapidly expanded in the 1790s.

Political economy was also important to the Habsburgs. Many of Peter Leopold's advisers in the late 1760s and 1770s emerged as experts on finance and administration. They maintained contacts with some of the charismatic leaders of Physiocracy,[7] such as Victor Riqueti de Mirabeau, who in 1769 dedicated his book *Les économiques* to the grand duke. Other Physiocratic writers were also contacted when the Tuscans strove to reform taxation at home and considered the possibility of developing a modern land-tax register (*catasto*), which would implement the principle of *impôt unique*.[8] Even though the scheme floundered due to the embittered opposition of the landed elites, the Physiocrats continued to inspire government officials and literati at Florence well after the decline of the Physiocratic *secte*. But Physiocracy did not represent the only economic discourse in Tuscany. Anne-Robert-Jacques Turgot's failed reform projects between 1774 and 1776 proved crucial in evaluating the role of economic and institutional reform at Florence. The relationship worked both ways, as the Tuscans kept the philosophe informed about their activities at home and diffused a most favorable interpretation of Peter Leopold's government abroad. It is hardly surprising, therefore, to find many works in the field of political economy lining the shelves of the grand ducal library. The *Catalogue* testifies to this, listing titles by Melon, Dutot, Forbonnais, Uztariz, Mandeville, and Galiani as available at Pitti. Like so much of the sensitive or clandestine information that circulated in the last decades of the Old Regime, these works and others, shipped in from Paris, did not pass through normal commercial channels. Often, Habsburg diplomats were involved in the trade and the books first reached Tommaso Piccolomini, the minister for foreign affairs; only at a somewhat later stage were they dispatched to Pitti.

Few documents survive to reveal Peter Leopold's acquisitions policy.[9] The Tuscan agent in Paris, Raimondo Niccoli, processed purchase orders on the Parisian book market. In the spring of 1771, for example, he bought and sent to Florence a copy of the abbé Chappe d'Auteroche's *Voyage en Sybérie*, which the Count Franz Xaver Rosenberg-Orsini, a top Habsburg diplomat and mentor to the grand duke, had ordered him to acquire. A most loyal servant to the empress, Rosenberg-Orsini masterminded Leopold's reform strategy up to 1771, and the close relationship he developed with the young Prince is evidenced in the warmth of their correspondence, now preserved in the Kärntner Landesarchiv, Klagenfurt.[10] Similarly, in 1771 Piccolomini asked Niccoli in Paris to purchase three of the most prohibited books circulating in Catholic Europe at that time: Baron d'Holbach's *Système de la Nature*, published under the cloak in November 1769; Voltaire's deist "manifesto" *Le dîner du comte de Boulainvilliers*; and his remarkable *Relation du bannissement des Jésuites de la Chine*.[11] Voltaire emerged as a key author in the readings of the Italian literati. Not surprisingly in the intellectual contexts of the "blue peninsula," which was usually cut off from the materialist aspects of the Enlightenment, Voltaire was first perceived as the playwright who had provided France with its epic poem, *La Henriade*, and then as the great historian of the *Essai sur les moeurs et l'esprit des nations*. Voltaire's *Contes*, on the other hand, elicited mixed feelings as they began to circulate south of the Alps. In any case, Voltaire's propaganda was crucial in the Italian diffusion of Newton's worldview. Newtonianism had established firm roots among the Tuscan literati since the early 1740s, when Voltaire's

La métaphysique de Newton[12] was translated in Florence. Another work proved essential for the diffusion of the Newtonian ideology in Italy, Francesco Algarotti's *Newtonianismo per le dame* (1739), which the Roman Catholic Church quickly prohibited. The text circulated widely in Europe and was also available (in French) on the shelves of the Habsburg grand duke.[13] The evidence provided in the *Catalogue* suggests that Voltaire's reception at the court remained ambivalent. *L'histoire de Pierre le Grand* and the *Abrégé de l'histoire universelle* in the Néaulme edition of 1754, both of which are listed in the *Catalogue*, are praised for their style but criticized for their content, which the grand duke found superficial and shorn of erudition.[14]

"In Italy people study and use their reason," remarked d'Alembert in the *Encyclopédie*.[15] This comment may well apply to the inner circles of Leopold's court in Florence. In fact, the learned circles read too much, according to the lamentations of the Roman Curia. In the late 1750s and 1760s as well as later, the popes issued stern prohibitions on the reading of immoral and heterodox texts, in French and in Italian, which were flooding the peninsula. The oppositional strategy then deployed by the Church was meant to preserve ecclesiastical control over the minds of the "simple folks": namely, women and youth.[16] This strategy proved largely ineffective and its failure had lasting effects. At the end of the century, during the short-lived republican *triennio* (1796–99), many classics of the Enlightenment received a new lease on life, as editions, translations, and quotations in the periodicals of (mainly) French texts—including some materialist or atheistic tracts—reached a growing literate class. Although Italy did not experience an "effondrement de l'appareil de côntrole" during the *siècle des Lumières*, as Daniel Roche suggested for France, the constraints of Counter-Reformation ideology were then forever broken.[17]

Peter Leopold's stock of French and Italian books mirrored a somewhat domesticated version of the Lumières. The sovereign's opposition to Roman clerical influence may well have stemmed from Pietro Giannone's *Civil History of the Kingdom of Naples* and Paolo Sarpi's polemics against the popes.[18] Both texts complement the ruler's esteem for Claude Fleury's pro-Jansenist ecclesiastical history. Leopold's books included some key texts of the Enlightenment, beginning with the first edition of Rousseau's second *Discours* and d'Alembert's *Sur la déstruction des Jésuites en France*. Hume was largely represented by his *History of England* and by the French version of his *Essai sur le commerce*. Algarotti, Mably, Beccaria, Bolingbroke, and Machiavelli were also readily available at the Pitti Palace, as was Locke's *Essai sur l'entendement humain* in the translation by Pierre Coste, which was perused at the court despite its prohibition by the church in the 1730s.[19] The impact of this work in Italian enlightened discourse was paramount, as Muratori's readings of the English philosopher suggest.[20] Readings of Locke in Florence took place in a quite different historical context. After the publication of the *Encyclopédie* at mid-century, which was reedited twice in Tuscany after 1759, the very notion of "public happiness" acquired new, heterodox meanings. The Leghorn version of Diderot and d'Alembert's *Dictionnaire* was paid for and defended against the encroachments of the church by Peter Leopold himself. D'Alembert was widely appreciated south of the Alps because his public reputation as a re-spected mathematician seemed to mitigate the untenable anti-Christian views of the philosophes. Not surprisingly, his five-volume *Opuscules mathématiques* is listed in the library at Pitti.[21] But the grand duke's delight in natural phi-losophy and chemistry also favored the appointment of the leading Italian phys-iologist of the time to the head of the Imperial Cabinet of Physics in 1766. Felice Fontana was born in Rovereto, a town just south of Trent, and, like his brother Gregorio at the University of Pavia, he belonged to the organizational network of the Freemasons.[22] A materialist at heart, even though he never explicitly admitted it, Fontana had also been appointed as a teacher to the young Habsburg-Lorraine archdukes. He took his task seriously, especially after his return from the grand tour that had led him and his young companion, the physicist Giovanni Fabbroni, through most of western Europe and England.[23] In Paris, they both became affiliated with the Masonic lodge Les Neuf Soeurs in 1778, and the personal and professional ties they established at the time proved fruitful both for their careers and for the institutional and cultural connections of the Imperial Cabinet of Physics.

In 1785, Charles Dupaty visited Florence and conversed with Peter Leo-pold at some length. He was considered a "Venerable" of the Parisian lodge Les Neuf Soeurs, and his views on the Tuscan government at that time lie at the core of his *Lettres sur l'Italie en 1785*, an often-quoted work that was read by diplomats, literati, and rulers on the Continent. Dupaty remarked that the archdukes, whom he had met at Pitti, proved conversant in many languages and were voraciously reading Locke's *Essai sur l'entendement humain*. Appar-ently, they had already digested the works of Condillac and Montesquieu. Peter Leopold devoted painstaking attention to the literary education of both his subjects and his children.[24] As his *Notes sur l'éducation publique* bear out, the sovereign saw the *Encyclopédie* as a means to foster the moral and material improvement of society—an end that had to be pursued steadily but gradually, beginning with the education of the noble and bourgeois elites.[25] Similarly, the grand duke emphasized the intellectual meaning of the abbé Coyer's *Plan d'éducation publique* and stressed the value of Locke's *Some Thoughts Concerning Education.* The English philosopher provided the epistemological and ideological background to some of the reforms the Lorrainers strove to achieve in the field of higher education and learning. Both fields acted together within the Tuscan government's plan to reduce clerical influences in local society, fight against superstition and Baroque piety, transform the secular clergy into an agent of state social control, and break away from the lasting heritage of church encroachments on public life.[26] It would be wrong to see in Leopold's schemes for progress a strategy dictated solely by the French Enlightenment. Practical motivations stood firmly behind the government's decisions in matters of social control and economic change. The grand ducal couple's moral behavior reflected Augustinian religiosity more than the libertine strand of the French Enlightenment (as evidenced by their graves in the Kapuzinergruft in Vienna, the austere setting of which bespoke evangelical ethics more than worldly virtue). And Maria Theresa herself maintained an attachment to the Catholic creed, which, despite the libertine inclinations of her husband (himself a dedicated Freemason), she passed on to her children. It is not surprising, therefore, to see that the 1771 *Catalogue* of the ruler's library listed among its entries Jacques-Bénigne Bossuet's *Histoire des variations des églises protestantes* and *Connoissance de Dieu,* while J.-J. Duguet's *Institution d'un Prince,* a text originally intended for the education of the pupils of the House of Savoy, emerges as one of the books that Peter Leopold and his brethren had perused during their youth at the Hofburg.[27] The grand duke recommended these kinds of readings to his offspring to foster their religious understanding. And the small section in the *Catalogue* devoted to religion suggests an interest in both Augustinian piety and Jesuit preaching. But the grand duke himself was never inclined toward mysticism or Baroque devotion, though he took seriously the moral messages of the Gospels.

Reading practices at the court reflected eclectic tastes and preoccupations, running from politics and religion to natural philosophy and literature. Novels, including some British texts of narrative and romance, continued to be ranked below the "serious" works of history, geography, architecture, and science, at least according to the marginalia in the 1771 *Catalogue.* A similar hierarchy is reflected in the diary of Giuseppe Pelli Bencivenni, the *Efemeridi,* which recorded the reading experience of the Florentine nobleman from 1759 to his death in 1808.[28] Pelli read everything, including the libertine and "pornographic" works of the French. Although he relished them, he maintained the view that novels and pamphlets were spiritually inferior to history, religion, antiquarianism, and the Latin and Italian classics. No Latin classics in their original language are to be found in the library of Peter Leopold and Maria Louise. As opposed to what emerged in the German-speaking part of Europe at the end of the century, the spell of Greece was faint in Florence and the classics resurface in the *Catalogue* only in their Italian and French translations. But the heritage of Rome and Greece remained paramount at Pitti, as the numerous ancient history books listed in the *Catalogue* suggest. As to light literature and novels, they were still deemed dangerous for the youth. The sovereign kept his library locked up, and leisure reading was allowed only in the presence of the mother: "All books are locked up, and I have the key, except those that are needed for teaching, books can be read only in the presence of my wife . . . after I have read and approved them."[29] Some exceptions, however, were considered. Thus, if *Tom Jones*, the novels by Richardson, and Marivaux's *La vie de Marianne* were dismissed as "boring and cold," La Fontaine's *Fables* were common reading for the young at Pitti, as they proved a good guide to understanding the ancient myths and tropes. The same is true for masterpieces of pedagogy and education, such as Fénelon's *Télémaque*, which the prince regarded as a key text for the spiritual growth of the young. Similarly, Andrew Ramsay's *Les voyages de Cyrus* and the abbé Terrasson's embryonic bildungsroman *Séthos* were recommended reading. A "very well-written moral novel," *Sethos* was "full of the best [moral] maxims and most useful for the young," a marginal note commented. Fénelon, Terrasson, and Ramsay provided a common set of values for some of the deepest convictions of the Masonic lodges on the Continent, varied and contradictory as those institutions were.[30] Original sin figures seldom in these texts, though it is not entirely absent. Emphasis is placed on the potential for individual salvation through works and on *bienfaisance.* Politeness and friendship are imperatives for commoners and crowned heads alike. Talent and merit are valued for revealing that all are born equal. Peter Leopold liked these kinds of books very much. *Les voyages de Cyrus* was singled out as a "very agreeable novel, written with wit, useful for its morale and for the knowledge of the world."[31] The book prompted one further comment by the ruler, as the allegories embroidered in the narrative represented a soft-spoken introduction to the duties and secrets of rule.

Emphasis on the tenets of good government and "virtue" emerge as a leit-motif in Peter Leopold's recommendations about reading, and here Montesquieu plays an important role. The Amsterdam edition of his *Oeuvres* was singled out as an "excellent, very interesting, and profound book, a text that is most true and wise. It ought to be read by the young, who should meditate on its contents."[32] Montesquieu's *Considérations sur la grandeur et la décadence de l'empire romain* stood at the top of the archduke's history readings, for men and women alike. The Roman Catholic Church had included these works in its index of 1751, but the prohibition was not respected in Florence. Similarly, Burlamaqui's *Principes du droit de la nature et des gens*, a classic in natural law theory, was recommended in the Yverdon print of 1766–68 as a "good, classical work about legal theory, useful for study by the young."[33] And J. F. von Bielfeld's *Lettres familières* deserved Leopold's praise as "beautiful, enjoyable, and instructive, most useful for the young."[34] Dedicated to Voltaire, Bielfeld's work, which circulated among the crowned heads of Europe, praised Freemasonry warmly. "The most solemn brotherhood that ever existed," this organization was singled out as a cosmopolitan pole of learning and education that paved the way to Bielfeld's utopian scheme for the improvement of the human lot. Love and harmony, he wrote, made the "interest of this society" converge with the "interest of human kind as a whole"[35]—a view reflecting a topos of Freemason ideology since the 1730s. The *Lettres* were cast in the language of monarchical power and suggested that under the aegis of an "enlightened" sovereign, Astrea, the goddess of justice, would return to bring peace and plenty on earth. Bielfeld's message was highly political. The Prussian ideology of national growth, agricultural improvement, and *Bildung* stands out clearly in Bielefeld's treaty as well. His *Institutions politiques* was also perused at the Florentine court; thus Peter Leopold's books included both the belated *Speculum principis* by the Jansenist Jean-Joseph Duguet and the Protestant tract by Bielefeld, which suggests the ambivalence of enlightened discourse in Habsburg Italy.

The Habsburg court in Florence was in constant contact with its major counterpart in Vienna, the Hofburg. In the 1770s and 1780s, Florence developed into a node of political and bibliographical communication between Italy and the German-speaking areas of the empire. A former Jesuit and future archbishop of Vienna, Sigmund-Anton von Hohenwart taught the grand ducal children history and acted as a go-between in relationships with the German world, both Catholic and Protestant.[36] He introduced Heinrich Pestalozzi to Peter Leopold and fostered their exchange of ideas about education. Hohenwart also befriended a top-ranking confrère of the Illuminaten Order, the Dane Frederik Münter, who toured Italy in the 1780s.[37] Münter visited Florence, Siena, and Pistoia, where he met Scipione de' Ricci, the Jansenist bishop and

Augustinian reformer of the Tuscan "national" church. By the time of their
encounter, de' Ricci's downfall had already come to pass, but the conversations
between the two reformers demonstrate a common interest in the much hoped
for reunion of the Christian churches; further, both were loyal supporters of
Leopold's attempt to overhaul state/church relations. Anticurialism and opposition to papal politics brought these men together, despite their differences
over culture and religion. Münter met several Freemasons in Florence and soon
recognized the strength of popular opposition to religious change and economic laissez-faire. Much like Herder, who met the grand duke in 1789 and
reported extensively about his visit,[38] Münter cast favorable judgment on the
Habsburg-Lorraine top-down reforms, which he considered to mark a new
beginning for a more moral public life. Herder, for his part, also remarked on
the "spirit of the German government" detectable in the Austrian's rule in
Florence[39]—a fact resented by both the general population and the elite.

The elite circle at the court did often develop contacts with the literary
underworld. In 1787, Francesco Saverio Catani, a playwright *aux gages des
libraires*, asked the Société typograhique de Neuchâtel to send him books that
he would sell in Florence.[40] He wrote to his skeptical Swiss correspondents
that he had ties with Baron Franz-Thomas von Bassus in Poschiavo, a town
in the Swiss Graubünden that functioned as a meeting point for members of
the Bavarian Illuminaten, whose spread south of the Alps he was encouraging. He was keenly interested in what was going on in Tuscany, as suggested
by his correspondence with Carlantonio Pilati, a prominent Freemason from
Trent who was then in Florence. Much like the future revolutionary Filippo
Buonarroti, Catani tried to eke out a living by selling prohibited or obscene
books to an eager audience of Florentines. Probably a Freemason who had
been initiated in either Florence or Pisa, Buonarroti earned little from his
under-the-cloak trade, except for a light penal sentence. Catani and Buonarroti
maintained contacts with many members of the elite. *Semi-letterati* ("halfway
men of letters," as Pelli Bencivenni dubbed them), in the 1780s they deployed
a pamphlet attacking the church and the scattered surviving Jesuits. This
strategy hinged on both the commercial interest in news about the court of
Rome and on the Habsburgs' tolerant attitude toward the press. Their stories
will remind the reader of Robert Darnton's extensive work on the underground
booksellers of the French Enlightenment. Indeed, case studies such as those
of Catani, Buonarroti, Francesco Becattini, and a few other scribblers reveal
social stratification in the ranks of the Florentine "philosophers." With a population of eighty thousand by the end of the *siècle des Lumières*, Florence housed

a *basoche* of clerks and would-be attorneys who copied unorthodox manuscripts and circulated them in the cafés, taverns, barbershops, and markets. These writers are evidence of the spilling over of political messages beyond the circles of the elite into more vernacular venues of debate. The numerous artisans of Tuscany participated in these discussions as well, since the grand duke had suppressed their fraternities. Moreover, charity was declining and everyday life was becoming harsher for the poor. Intellectuals fared better, but the low life of literature remained the lot of most newsmen, translators of French, and compilers, some of them defrocked monks or jobless, university-trained members of the professions. In greater numbers than in Milan or Turin but fewer than in Naples and Venice, these would-be authors suffered the hardships of the literary trade at the time, which was characterized by both an increasing interest in tracts on politics and the economy and the spreading thirst for news typical of the end of the Old Regime.[41]

Social life at Florence expanded before the turn of the century. Next to the maze of literary institutions and academies that the Habsburgs tried to discipline and control, several salons opened their doors to the natural philosophers, artists, men of letters, and diplomats who toured Italy. Eugenia Bellini, the daughter of the brilliant physician Antonio Cocchi, maintained a conversation that charmed many visitors, including some Freemasons of the new generation, such as the jurist Giovanni Carmignani, a skillful commentator on Beccaria, and the lawyer Lorenzo Collini, who would later play a key role as a writer and a spokesman for liberal political ideas in Florence and Italy. The Paduan writer Melchiorre Cesarotti was also one of her guests, and he visited the *conversazione* in Marquess Federigo Manfredini's palace, where other Freemasons gathered. Melchiorre Delfico, a charismatic leader of the Lumières in southern Italy, attended the salon of Teresa Pelli Fabbroni, whose importance was second only to that of Madame d'Albany.[42] Wilhelm and Alexander von Humboldt corresponded with Fabbroni, who also hosted several northern European Freemasons. Many of these figures gained access to Ferdinand III, as they had with his father's court before March 1790.

What does this all mean? Even though institutional Freemasonry disappeared from Florence after 1738,[43] Peter Leopold's court at Pitti and at l'Imperiale, a splendid mansion on the slopes of the hill of Arcetri, often hosted Freemasons. In 1783, Gustav III of Sweden visited Florence and met the sovereign, with whom he discussed politics and the economy. The king admired the reformed Hospital of Santa Maria Nuova. Intellectual ties between Sweden and Tuscany had long before been established through the web of research institutions in both countries.[44] Uppsala University, where Linnaeus's legacy survived, remained a center of "philosophical" exchange with the Imperial Cabinet of Physics in Florence. Gustav III's mentor, Count Carl Frederik von Scheffer, befriended Mirabeau the elder and corresponded with his protégé, Giorgio Santi, a medical doctor who had long lived in Paris and was later appointed head of the Botanical Garden of Pisa.[45] Both Scheffer and the king of Sweden belonged to the Swedish Freemasonry—an institution that also counted the king's brother among its fellows. Florentine contacts with the panoply of German courts and Residenzstätte led to an exchange of political, economic, and bibliographical information that deserves closer investigation, as Wandruszka's biography of Peter Leopold suggests. And Habsburg Italy, including the kingdom of Naples after 1776, thrived with Masonic literati and civil servants. During the 1780s and 1790s, European Freemasonry experienced a change in its relationship to state and society as the "national" identity of its lodges became more pronounced. The importance of rituals gained momentum, and ceremonies became more complex as a means of establishing clearcut boundaries between insiders and outsiders. The conflict between Les Neuf Soeurs and the Grand Orient of France, for instance, expressed these growing tensions.[46] Despite all this, there were some common values that shaped the Freemasons' public behavior before 1789, such as faith in the possibility of human progress, moral as well as material. Similarly, the esoteric rituals of the Freemasons mirrored an underlying conviction in the universal truths of legal and moral equality. Freemasonry was never "democratic," as some historians argue, nor was it "liberal," according to the postrevolutionary meaning of these words.[47] The lodges' internal hierarchies in France, Piedmont, and Austria remained solidly in place and the practice of polite conversation, music making, and leisurely reading never threatened the existing order.[48] At the top level of government and rule, the lodges supported at most a "view from the top" of society, centered on property rights and laissez-faire. Within the language of Physiocracy and natural law theory, property had emerged in the last quarter of the century as a means to the gradual fulfillment of social and economic needs. Peter Leopold agreed with this view, despite his aloofness in matters concerning the Freemasons' rituals and beliefs. His extensive reading of Enlightenment constitutionalism never led him to discard the role of the monarchy or to support *political* liberty (as opposed to *civil* liberty and equality before the law). One of his eulogists, Prince Sigismondo Chigi, made this clear in his (mediocre) verses. The "honor of the Austrian people, Solomon of Italy,"[49] the Habsburg grand duke had established a lasting peace among his subjects, and their happiness and politeness would only increase through dedicated work and the respect of rank. In Chigi's poem on laissez-faire and the maintenance of property rights, the observance of legal obligations and contracts was coupled with a paean in praise of "virtue." His verses sound like an epitaph for the Tuscan age of reform, a time when literacy rose, scholars and "philosophers" propounded on the principles of government, the military had disbanded—and revolution was nowhere in sight.

NOTES

1. For bibliographical references to Robert Darnton's work and for a critical assessment of his views on the eighteenth century, see Haydn T. Mason, ed., *The Darnton Debate: Books and Revolution in the Eighteenth Century* (Oxford: Voltaire Foundation, 1998).

2. Renato Pasta, "La Biblioteca aulica e le letture dei principi Lorenesi," in *Vivere a Pitti: Una reggia dai Medici ai Savoia*, ed. Sergio Bertelli and Renato Pasta (Florence: Olschki, 2003), 351–88; Orsola Gori, "Una Corte dimezzata: La reggia di Pietro Leopoldo," in Bertelli and Pasta, *Vivere a Pitti*, 291–349. On public libraries in Florence, see Emmanuelle Chapron, "'Ad utilità pubblica': Politique des bibliothèques et pratiques du livre à Florence au XVIIIe siècle" (Genéve: Droz, 2009).

3. General histories of Tuscany in the eighteenth century include Furio Diaz, Luigi Mascilli Migliorini, and Carlo Mangio, *Il Granducato di Toscana: Dalla Reggenza agli anni rivoluzionari* (Turin: UTET, 1998); and Eric Cochrane, *Florence in the Forgotten Centuries, 1527–1800* (Chicago: University of Chicago Press, 1973). See also Maria Augusta Timpanaro, *Per una storia di Andrea Bonducci (Firenze, 1715–1766)* (Rome: Istituto Storico Italiano per l'Età Moderna e Contemporanea, 1996); Maria Augusta Timpanaro, *Tommaso Crudeli (Poppi, 1702–1745): Contributo per uno studio sulla Inquisizione a Firenze nella prima metà del XVIII secolo*, 2 vols. (Florence: Olschki, 2003); and Jean-Claude Waquet, *Le Grand-Duché de Toscane sous les derniers Médicis: Essai sur le système des finances et la stabilité des institutions dans les anciens états italiens* (Rome: École française de Rome, 1990).

4. See Simone Contardi's *La Casa di Salomone a Firenze: L'Imperiale e Reale Museo di Fisica e Storia Naturale (1775–1780)* (Florence: Olschki, 2002); and "The Origins of a Scientific Institution: Felice Fontana and the Birth of the Real Museo di Fisica e Storia Naturale di Firenze," *Nuncius: Journal of the History of Science* 21, no. 2 (2006): 251–63.

5. Florence, de l'Imprimerie Granducale, 1771. The Biblioteca Nazionale, Florence, preserves one copy of the catalog, call number Palat. 1.5.1.6. Another copy, which belonged to Maria Louise of Bourbon-Spain, is extant in the collections of the Newberry Library, Chicago, call number Z491.C277. I am grateful to Dr. Paul Gehl of the Newberry Library for providing a photocopy of this text, which includes a few pages missing from the exemplar in Florence.

6. Jean Pierre Brissot de Warville, *Bibliothèque philosophique du législateur*, 10 vols. (Berlin: Société typographique de Neuchâtel, 1782–85), in Biblioteca Nazionale, Florence, call number Palat. 20.8.2.12. Peter Leopold's library included several other works by Brissot. Some information about Chaillou de Lisy of Bourges available in Cesare Beccaria, *Carteggio, 1769–1795*, ed. Carlo Capra, Renato Pasta, and Francesca Pino, vol. 5 of *Edizione nazionale delle Opere di Cesare Beccaria*, ed. Luigi Firpo and Gianni Francioni (Milan: Mediobanca, 1996), 418–21.

7. The intellectual movement for economic and political reform that François Quesnay promoted since the late 1750s. See Catherine Larrère, *L'invention de l'économie au XVIIIe siècle* (Paris: Presses Universitaires de France, 1992).

8. See Mario Mirri's "Per una ricerca sui rapporti fra 'economisti' e riformatori toscani: l'Abate Niccoli a Parigi," *Annali dell'Istituto Gian Giacomo Feltrinelli* 2 (1959): 55–120; and "La Fisiocrazia: Un tema da riprendere," in *Studi di storia medievale e moderna per Ernesto Sestan* (Florence: Olschki,

1980), 2:703–60. See also *Catalogue*, 255, Victor Riqueti de Mirabeau, *L'Ami des hommes, ou traité de la population*, 6 vols. (Hamburg: Hérold, 1764). At the same location, several texts discussing the issue of taxation and of *impôt unique* can be found: *Catalogue*, 129, Le Mercier de la Rivière, *L'ordre naturel et essentiel des sociétés politiques* (London: Nourse, 1767); *Catalogue*, 293, Victor Riqueti de Mirabeau and François Quesnay, *Philosophie rurale ou économie générale et politique de l'agriculture* (Amsterdam: Les Libraires associés, 1763).

9. See, however, Chapron, "Des bibliothèques "a pubblica utilità."

10. Orsola Gori, "Famiglia e governo nelle lettere di Pietro Leopoldo a Rosenberg," in *La passione della storia. Studi in onore di Giuliano Procacci*, ed. Francesco Benvenuti, Sergio Bertolissi, Roberto Gualtieri, and Silvio Pons (Rome: Carocci, 2006), 162–81. On Rosenberg, see Adam Wandruszka, *Leopold II*, 2 vols. (Vienna: Verlag Herold, 1963–65).

11. Florence, Archivio di Stato, Segreteria degli Esteri, Appendice 2. Niccoli also mailed to Florence one copy of Ferdinando Galiani's anti-Physiocratic work *Dialogue sur les commerce de bleds* (Paris: Merlin, 1769). Niccoli to Rosenberg, Paris, January 15, 1770 (Florence, Archivio di Stato).

12. Paolo Casini, *Newton e la coscienza europea* (Bologna: Il Mulino, 1983), 79–99; Laurence Macé, "Voltaire en Italie (1734–1815): Lecture et censure au siècle des lumières," 2 vols. (Ph.D. diss., Paris: Université Paris-Sorbonne, 2007).

13. *Catalogue*, 299, Francesco Algarotti, *Le Newtonianisme pour les dames, ou entretiens sur la lumière, les couleurs et l'attraction*, 2 vols. (Paris: Montalant, 1739).

14. *Catalogue*, 161, 181.

15. Quoted in Paolo Casini, "'On étudie et on raisonne en Italie': Geometria, scienza e Lumi in Italia," in *Studi settecenteschi*, vol. 16, of *L'enciclopedismo in Italia nel XVIII secolo*, ed. Guido Abbattista (Naples: Bibliopolis, 1996), 85–96.

16. Patrizia Delpiano, *Il governo della lettura: Chiesa e libri nell'Italia del Settecento* (Bologna: Il Mulino, 2007).

17. Daniel Roche, "Le livre: Un objet de consommation entre l'économie et la lecture," in *Histoires du livre: Nouvelles orientations*, ed. Hans Erich Boedeker (Paris: Maison des Sciences de l'homme/IMEC, 1995), 230.

18. *Catalogue*, 138, Pietro Giannone, *Histoire de Naples: Traduit de l'italien, avec des nouvelles notes, réflexions et médailles fournies par l'auteur*, 4 vols. (The Hague: P. Gosse, 1742). The book was judged an "excellent history, well written and with fire, the author of which has been cruelly prosecuted because of his writings against the Roman Court" (*Catalogue*, 138). See also *Catalogue*, 205, for further remarks concerning Giannone, and pp. 165–66, Paolo Sarpi, *Histoire du démêlé de Paul V avec la République de Venise* (Avignon, 1759).

19. See, respectively, *Catalogue*, 5, 76, Jean-Jacques Rousseau, *Discours sur l'origine de l'inégalité parmi les hommes* (Amsterdam: M. M. Rey, 1755); *Catalogue* 185, 75, Jean Le Rond d'Alembert, *Sur la destruction des Jésuites en France* (Paris, 1767); d'Alembert, *Mélanges de littérature, d'historie et de philosophie*, 5 vols. (Amsterdam: Châtelain et fils, 1767); *Catalogue*, 170, David Hume, *Histoire de la maison de Stuart sur le trône d'Angleterre* (selections in French from his *History of England*) (London, 1766); *Catalogue*, 271, Hume, *Essai sur le commerce, le luxe, l'argent, l'intérêt de l'argent, les impôts, le crédit public et la balance du commerce* (Paris: Saillant, 1767); *Catalogue*, 107, John Locke, *Essai philosophique sur l'entendement humain* (Amsterdam: Schneeder, 1761); *Catalogue*, 82, Gabriel Bonnot de Mably, *Les entretiens de Phocion sur le rapport de la morale avec la politique* (Amsterdam, 1763) (also available in Italian); *Catalogue*, 10, Henry Saint-John, Lord Viscount Bolingbroke, *Lettres sur l'esprit de patriotisme* (London, 1750); *Catalogue*, 214, Bolingbroke, *Testament politique écrit par lui-même* (London, 1754); *Catalogue*, 18, Nicolò Machiavelli, *Opere complete*, 8 vols. (Paris: M. Prault, 1768) (the grand duke also subscribed to the Florentine edition of Machiavelli's works, 6 vols., G. Cambiagi, 1782, *Catalogue*, 175–76).

20. Ludovico Antonio Muratori was also listed in the *Catalogue*, 45, with the splendid, ten-volume edition of his *Rerum italicarum scriptores* (Arezzo: Bellotti, 1767–73).

21. *Catalogue*, 291, *Opuscules mathématiques, ou Mémoires sur différens sujets de géométrie, de méchanique, d'optique, d'astronomie* (Paris: David, 1761).

22. Renato G. Mazzolini, "Felice Fontana," in *Dizionario biografico degli italiani* (Rome: Istituto dell'Enciclopedia Italiana, 2004), 48:663–69; Ugo Baldini, "Gregorio Fontana," in *Dizionario biografico degli italiani*, 48:681–89.

23. Renato Pasta, *Scienza, politica e rivoluzione: L'opera di Giovanni Fabbroni (1752–1822) intellettuale e funzionario al servizio dei Lorena* (Florence: Olschki, 1989).

24. Charles Dupaty, *Lettres sur l'Italie en 1785*, 5 vols. (Paris: P. G. Simon and H. Nyon, 1789); Wandruzska, *Leopold II*, 2:151.

25. In Pietro Leopoldo di Toscana, *Scritti inediti sull'educazione*, ed. L. Bellatalla (Lucca: Pacini Fazzi, 1990), 27–37.

26. Bibliography about the ecclesiastical reforms and the suppression of convents, monasteries, and some religious congregations in Tuscany is plentiful. See Antonio Zobi, *Storia civile della Toscana dal MDCCXXXVII al MDCCCXLVIII*, 5 vols. (Florence: Molini, 1850–52), esp. vol. 2; Carlo Fantappiè, *Riforme ecclesiastiche e resistenze sociali: La sperimentazione istituzionali nella diocesi di Prato alla fine del'antico regime* (Bologna: Il Mulino, 1986); Bruna Bocchini and Marcello Verga, eds., *Lettere di Scipione de' Ricci a Pietro Leopoldo*, 3 vols. (Florence: Olschki, 1990); and Gabriele Turi, *Viva Maria: La reazione alle riforme leopoldine (1790–1799)* (Florence: Olschki, 1969).

27. *Catalogue*, 388, where also Bossuet's *Politique tirée des propres paroles de l'écriture sainte* (Paris: Cot, 1709) is recorded: "Excellent book, primarily for the education of the young and for its principles about ethics, virtue, and religion." On Jean-Joseph Duguet, see Mario Rosa, *Settecento religioso: Politica della ragione e religione del cuore* (Venice: Marsilio, 1999), 75–110. *Catalogue*, 410, indexes two editions of Blaise Pascal's *Les Provinciales* (Cologne: N. Schoute, 1669; P. de la Vallée, 1739). The catalogue lists 186 titles in the field of religion, including *Advent-Predigen in der hochlöblischen Stift-Kirchen by Sanct Dorothee* (Vienna: Kurzböck, 1763) (*Catalogue*, 396); *Oeuvres spirituelles de Mgr. Fénelon, Précepteur des Enfants de France*, 4 vols. (1767) (*Catalogue*, 403); and Claude Fleury, *Les moeurs des Israelites et des Chrétiens* (Paris: Hérissant, 1763) (*Catalogue*, 407).

28. Biblioteca Nazionale, Florence, Sala Manoscritti, call number NA, 1050, Giuseppe Pelli, *Efemeridi*, 78 vols. The first set of volumes (1759–73) is available online at http://www.bncf.firenze.sbn.it/progetti/index.html.

29. Quoted in Alessandra Contini, "'La naissance n'est qu'effet du hasard': L'educazione delle principesse e dei principi alla corte Leopoldina," in Bertelli and Pasta, *Vivere a Pitti*, 425.

30. Gian Mario Cazzaniga, "Massoneria e letteratura: Dalla 'République des lettres' alla letteratura nazionale," in *Le muse in Loggia*, ed. Gian Mario Cazzaniga et al. (Milan: Unicopli, 2002), 11–32; Contini, "La naissance n'est qu'un effet du hazard." For the comment on *Séthos*, see *Catalogue*, 33; for Ramsay's text, *Catalogue*, 123.

31. *Catalogue*, 164.

32. *Catalogue*, 268; see also *Catalogue*, 128, Montesquieu, *Oeuvres*, 3 vols. (London: Nourse, 1767).

33. *Catalogue*, 120. *L'essai sur les passions et les caractères*, 2 vols. (The Hague, 1748), on the other hand, was considered bad for youths: "The style of this book is not agreeable; there are some good reflections, but all in all they are very superficial: the chapters concerning women and marriage are quite bad; above all at the end of chapter 2 we find very bad maxims of behavior, which are most dangerous for the young" (*Catalogue*, 89).

34. *Catalogue*, 268, J. J. Burlamaqui, *Principes du droit de la nature et des gens* (Yverdon: [De Felice], 1766–1768) 8 vols.; 80, J. B. Bielfeld, *Lettres familières et autres de Monsieur le Baron de Bielfeld* (The Hague: P. Gosse Jr. and D. Pinet, 1763).

35. Bielfeld, *Lettres familières*, 11–12.

36. Antonio Trampus, "Secolarizzazione e Restaurazione: Sigismund von Hohenwart tra Venezia e Vienna," in *Säkularisationsprozesse im Alten Reich und in Italien: Voraussetzungen, Vergleiche, Folgen*, ed. Claudio Donati and Helmut Flachenecker (Bologna/Berlin: Il Mulino/Duncker und Humblot, 2005), 269–90.

37. Wandruszka, *Leopold II*, vol. 2.

38. Herder's report to Duke Carl August von Sachsen-Weimar, written in October 1789, was first published in 1866 and is reprinted in Wandruzska, *Leopold II*, 2:193–202.

39. Johann Gottfried Herder, *Italienische Reise, 1788–1789*, ed. A. Meier and H. Hollmer (Munich: C. H. Beck, 1989), 482.

40. Renato Pasta, *Editoria e cultura nel Settecento* (Florence: Olschki, 1997), 225–83. STN's contacts at Florence include Buonarroti, Catani, the booksellers Jean Bouchard, Giuseppe Pagani, Luigi Carlieri, Filippo Stecchi, and R. Del Vivo, as well as Senator Lorenzo degli Albizzi.

41. For a comparative analysis of the literary job market, see Anna Maria Rao, "Le mouvement des Lumières à Naples dans le contexte européen: Les structures du travail intellectuel," in *Jenseits der Diskurse: Aufklärungspraxis und Institutionenwelt in europäisch komparativer Perspektive*, ed. Hans-Erich Bödeker and Martin Gierl (Göttingen: Vandenhoeck & Ruprecht, 2007), 465–89.

42. Liana Elda Funaro, "'All'Armata e in Corte': Profilo di Federigo Manfredini," *Rassegna storica toscana* 2, no. 40 (1994): 239–76; Giovanni Rosini, *Elogio di Teresa Pelli Fabbroni* (Pisa: [Molini e Landi], 1813); information on Bellini's circle found in Timpanaro, *Per una storia di Andrea Bonducci*.

43. The bibliography concerning the history of Freemasonry has expanded in recent years. See Gian Mario Cazzaniga, ed., *Storia d'Italia: Annali 21: La massoneria* (Turin: Einaudi, 2006); Fulvio Conti, ed., *La massoneria a Firenze* (Bologna: Il Mulino, 2007); and Fulvio Conti, ed., *La massoneria a Livorno* (Bologna: Il Mulino, 2006).

44. Ferdinando Abbri, *Un dialogo dimenticato: Mondo nordico e cultura Toscana nel Settecento* (Milan: Angeli, 2007).

45. Pasta, *Scienza, politica e rivoluzione*; Vieri Becagli, "Il 'Salomon du Midi' e 'L'Ami des hommes': Le riforme leopoldine in alcune lettere del marchese di Mirabeau al conte di Scheffer," *Ricerche storiche* 7, no. 1 (1977): 137–98; Becagli, "Georg-Ludwig Schmidt d'Auenstein e i suoi 'Principes de législation universelle': Oltre la fisiocrazia?," *Studi settecenteschi* 24 (2005): 215–52.

46. Florence, Archivio di Stato, Archivio Pelli Fabbroni, 470, Giorgio Santi to Giovanni Fabbroni, Paris, December 30, 1778.

47. See Margaret C. Jacob's *The Radical Enlightenment: Pantheists, Freemasons, and Republicans* (London: Allen and Unwin, 1981); and *Living the Enlightenment: Freemasonry and Politics in Eighteenth-Century Europe* (Oxford: Oxford University Press, 1991). On Jacob's interpretation of Freemasonry as an agent of the "Radical Enlightenment" and democracy on the Continent, see Giuseppe Giarrizzo, *Massoneria e illuminismo* (Venice: Marsilio, 1994), 430, 434; Paolo Casini, "Biografia, scienza e illuminismo," *Intersezioni* 15, no. 1 (1995): 23–40, esp. 26–27; Renato Pasta, 'Nugae academicae': Divagazioni su Beccaria, le riforme e l'illuminismo," in *Cesare Beccaria: La pratica dei "lumi,"* ed. Gianni Francioni and Vincenzo Ferrone (Florence: Olschki, 2000), 139.

48. Gerardo Tocchini, *I fratelli d'Orfeo: Gluck e il teatro musicale massonico tra Vienna e Parigi* (Florence: Olschki, 1998).

49. Sigismondo Chigi, *Dell'economia naturale, e politica, all'Altezza Reale di Pietro Leopoldo Arciduca d'Austria, e di Boemia, Granduca di Toscana* (Paris: G. F. Valade, 1781), vv. 97–98.

PART 3

POLICE AND OPINION

SIX

INVASION OF LORIENT:
RUMOR, PUBLIC OPINION, AND FOREIGN POLITICS IN 1740S PARIS

Tabetha Ewing

Louis XV, attended by queen and mistress, was in good humor at the château de Choisy, despite news from Brittany of the British invasion of Lorient. He settled at table, according to Madame de Luynes, to enjoy a good meal when a sudden headache sent him to bed. Doctors assured all present that Louis's indisposition was nothing like the illness he had contracted at Metz two years earlier in the presence of another mistress, when infection invaded his body, and the Austrians his territories.[1] Whereas loyal subjects in 1744 blamed the adulteress, in 1746 Parisians cited the crisis in Brittany as cause. The king was sick with mortification, they said, "occasioned by the bad news His Majesty received from Brittany."[2] Broadly speaking, Parisian talk and opinions on war and diplomacy were royalist and, once Louis XV went to war, king-centered. Unsurprisingly, in the earliest accounts of the invasion, its chain of metaphorical associations reestablished the nexus between the state, the king's body, and the social body. And yet the specific dynamics of the event's circulation in contemporary news media, and in open discussion, suggest a shift in agency from traditional political authority to a speaking public. This public was recognized by, and perhaps came into being through, police surveillance of such places of sociability as cafés, bars, royal gardens, theaters, and gambling "academies." Police spies' dated manuscript reports of mostly anonymous conversations are archived as "gazetins de police" or "discours de Paris." In public talk following the Lorient crisis, a Parisian police agent identified a form of speech he called "public opinion." Public opinion, here, was an agentive, if unofficial, voice of patriotism.

The British expedition under General Sinclair descended on Brittany at Quiberon near the port town Lorient in early October 1746.[3] The town was a strategic target. Founded only in the late seventeenth century, it had a population that came from all over Brittany, mostly to work for the Compagnie des Indes. It housed the Compagnie's shipbuilding concern, arsenal, treasury, and precious merchandise from Asia and the Pacific. Its trade fair attracted buyers from all over France. It was a company town reputed to maintain contentious relations with local nobles and workers.[4] In October 1746, Lorient's defenses were inadequate. The great provincial lords were in Paris or on the front in Flanders when the British arrived in a fleet of fifty vessels, including nine ships of line, six frigates, and two *galiotes à bombes* carrying 4,500 men in all. British forces marched through several villages en route to Lorient, setting one on fire before ordering the town's surrender. The commander in charge of the Breton *milice* was ready to sign a capitulation when the inexperienced militiamen, instead of sounding a parley, signaled a general alarm. Sinclair might have responded with an attack, but Admiral Lestock signaled that the winds had changed. With the fleet at risk of dispersal, Sinclair ordered a retreat. When the Breton officials arrived with the town keys, the British were not there to accept them.[5] Confusion reigned from Versailles to Paris about what exactly took place during that week in October. Once the details were known— the hasty capitulation and the hasty retreat—both sides were *chansonnées*, or lampooned in song. As far as anyone could tell, as one song put it, the situation was saved by mutual fear.

The French minister of the navy, Jean Frédéric Phélypeaux, comte de Maurepas, wrote soon after the descent that its positive outcome was due to misjudgment rather than the efforts of French forces. "It is not so much that [the British] were repulsed, or even that we were disposed to vigorously defend [the port]"; rather, "British overestimation of Lorient's firepower and fear of rising winds led them to abandon the enterprise so precipitously."[6] Horace Walpole would later quip that due to high winds, the adventure gained the British only a few cows, geese, and turkeys but provided humorists with much richer fodder.[7] Indeed, it did not take long for satirists to launch their attack. Several songs of uncertain provenance circulated in Paris. Their verses drew explicitly on manuscript accounts of the invasion that emphasized the undue mutual fear between the opponents. This one is sung to the air "Si t'avais connu M. de Catmat":

Frenchmen and Englishmen, join in prayer
To thank God for his miraculous aid
Men of great heart
Spread terrible carnage
In making you timorous
He saved you both.[8]

Historians concur that nothing consequential happened. "A bold maneuver would have delivered all of the Compagnie des Indes's riches, merchandise, and hardware to the English," assessed the historian duc de Broglie.[9] The failed invasion has been relegated to a short page in the history books on the War of Austrian Succession, rightly submerged beneath the impending French victory at Rocoux (a grim, bloody battle that engaged two hundred thousand men) and the Austrian-British invasion of Provence later that year.[10] In the history of modern French public culture, however, it merits a prominent place.

Concern about the veracity of the news coming from Lorient and its impact on public opinion was expressed by many, including those at the highest administrative levels. The duc de Luynes, based on Maurepas's assessment, lamented, "The multitude of troops of all ranks assembled on this particular occasion at Lorient generates a continual variation and an enormous uncertainty in the news that we received."[11] Rumors about the invasion—mediated by manuscript and printed gazettes, provincial letters, and hearsay—affected the French public, undermining confidence in the Compagnie des Indes's stocks, royal ministers, and official information. Parisians anticipated further that the Compagnie would use the crisis as a pretext to withhold dividends.[12] Public confidence in royal ministers also declined due to rumors that the controller-general of finances and the minister of the navy had neglected the town's defenses. France's official *Gazette* announced both the invasion and the retreat in its October 22 issue, weeks after the events had occurred. It celebrated local defense maneuvers, which many Parisians, including the minister of the navy, would have found laughable. The *Gazette d'Amsterdam* reported the news more rapidly, just days after Parisians began hearing about it, but its interpretation of events kept changing: Lorient was taken, it had not been taken; damages were minimal, damages were significant. In other words, the gazettes reflected the confused state of communications. Uncertainty at Versailles, coupled with the usual official reticence around military setbacks, contributed to the reflexive quality of public opinion in Paris.[13]

According to one police observer, the Breton winds perhaps had blown

change over the Parisian landscape of everyday speech, at least with respect
to the way certain circles discussed politics. Officials followed talk about this
event closely, and around October 25, discussion in Parisian cafés and salons
was particularly rich. As alluded to above, in transcribing one conversation, a
police spy made use of the term "public opinion" (*l'opinion publique*), perhaps
for the first time ever in a police report. "There are people," the police spy
began, "who hazard their opinions on the means we should employ to keep
the English from our shores."[14] He was surprised that they were not satisfied
with the usual public complaints about the indolent, ineffective decision makers at Versailles.[15] He would have expected to hear ministers (or generals) being
blamed for military reversals, echoing the mutual slander of courtiers, which
had noticeably begun to infiltrate Parisian public places since 1742. He would
also have expected to hear blame cast on the "treacherous" Protestants living
on the west coast of Brittany. The dialogue, in fact, resembled many Parisian
café conversations about military strategy recorded in the police archives. So
why, then, was this experienced contemporary listener surprised by it? Perhaps because of the vigor of the discussion:

> Some of them wanted to march sufficient force to keep [the British] from
> establishing a [military camp]. . . . They were in small number. It is easy
> to see why the greater number did not rally around this sentiment. Oth-
> ers think that the surest means would be to have M. de Saxe's victorious
> army enter Holland, which would be easy for him to invade. . . . Two
> advantages would result from this expedition. The first would be to oblige
> England to recall all of its forces to deploy in Holland, thereby fulfilling
> its commitments to the Republic. The other advantage would be to divert
> Austrian troops from Italy or, even, Provence.[16]

Some people in the café argued that a detachment from the king's army in
the Netherlands should come to the province's rescue. Others thought that
the army should use its strength to create a diversion that would force Britain
to withdraw its forces. These were difficult decisions, indeed. Once the in-
vaders were established, they would be hard to dislodge. But dividing the main
army ran other risks. The majority of speakers agreed that the solution was to
invade the United Provinces. The debate was rapid-fire as possibilities were
proposed and eliminated. Even reading these passages more than 250 years
later, an audible quality comes through. Something about the debate—perhaps the particularities and timing of the topic, the range of people involved

in the discussion, or its overall tone—jarred the listening police spy. He heard something new in this conversation that is not obvious to the historian.

Based on an extensive reading of the *gazetins de police* from this period, the violent focus on the Dutch did mark a topical shift in talk away from direct action against France's declared enemies, Austria and Britain. This shift may have reflected the stunning performances of smaller powers, Prussia and Piedmont-Sardinia, whose impact on the war had been decisive. Alternatively, it may have been about the Dutch people and the United Provinces as a state. In his memoirs, the marquis d'Argenson noted the rise in Paris of a broad-based hostility against the Dutch in 1747, cultivated, he said, by his opponents at court.[17] Late 1746 may have been the starting point for this hostility. In either case, public opinion decided at the end of this conversation that the entire war would end as disastrously as the bloody battle of Asti if the Dutch were not invaded and cowed.[18] According to one anonymous café interlocutor, "Public opinion is to say that we will not be able to end this war happily if we do not crush one of our enemies or their allies" and "that one way or another we put Holland out of combat."[19] They argued that the Dutch would become as dangerous as the crafty Charles-Emmanuel of Piedmont-Sardinia (who had tricked French forces into battle) if they were not reduced to "une ruine totale."[20] The speakers recognized the seriousness of their decision, or "resolution," as a commitment to the destruction of their neighbor and trading partner: "The resolution is harsh, in truth, but in [these] pressing circumstances . . . we cannot search for other, more politic [resolutions]. Daring projects, determined execution. These are the remedies for all urgent ills." Excessive care and slow reactions would only make things worse.[21] Respondents objected to this sentiment because, they said, Dutch allies would surely fly to their rescue. The hard-liners replied that aid would come too late: "Holland will be invaded before help arrives."[22] Though far from official policy, this café conversation seems to have represented far more than empty words to its speakers.

The calls for violence present in this conversation were missing in other accounts, which described the event as unspeakable ("on n'ose point [en] parler") or of too little importance to discuss. Compared to the verses and bons mots expressed in other conversations about the invasion, talk here was bold. It went beyond satire, grumbling, and blaming by advocating violent action. Oddly, few accounts of Lorient's alleged invasion mentioned suffering, terror, and trauma. If foreign invasion was thought to pose a radical challenge to royal sovereignty and dynastic continuity, marking the potential death of one state and birth of a new one, then this silence is remarkable.[23] Nor were such concerns absent from reports on other battles. The Austrian invasion of Genoa, for example, contrasts with that of Lorient. In contemporary accounts, the horrors visited on the Genovese territories by Maria Theresa's armies were unconscionably excessive: "They violated divine and human law: churches disturbed and pillaged, sacred vessels stolen and profaned, they slit the throats of old men, disemboweled women, chopped up children, roasted, and ate them with exquisite barbarism."[24] These narrative excesses, which served to explain the impending liberation movement and social revolution in Genoa, were missing in accounts on Lorient. Yet, the café conversation following Lorient was vigorous, calling for action that was swift, brilliant, and to the quick, where perhaps "the quick" (*vif*) conjured up the now-lost sense of living flesh.

The most descriptive accounts of the invasion circulated in the manuscript newsletter "Lettres de province," sent from Brittany to Madame de Doublet's famous salon in Paris.[25] (Such newsletters often served as copy for printed gazettes.) The author's name was excised, but indications in the letter show that he was a local Breton notable. He began his story of the invasion with the moment he spotted the incoming British fleet. He described having rallied local troops, hastening his wife and child away from danger, and attempting to influence military decision making. The writer's heroics were set against the cowardly antics of his local peers, including the comic military misfiring that would be repeated in later accounts of the event. He expressed ire against the unpatriotic commanders, the colonel-marquis de l'Hôpital and the colonel-marquis d'Heudicourt, who led the war council that decided to hand the town over to the enemy. L'Hôpital, the Breton wrote, was a "poltroon," an utter coward: he deliberated too slowly, attempted a hasty surrender, and failed to pursue the fleeing enemy. According to this account, the Breton correspondent and other brave gentlemen of the province trembled with rage. Dropping to his knees, he attempted to recall one of the commanders, General Voluire, to his duty and sensitize him to the dishonor this surrender would bring about. Lorient, he insisted, was important to the king and useful for the state. Despite these entreaties, L'Hôpital rode out with a hostage to surrender to the British. Yet, upon his arrival, he found only indications of the Britons' hasty retreat. Had he arrived eight minutes earlier, the correspondent wrote, Sinclair would have received this "disastrous resolution," placing Lorient in British hands.

The Breton correspondent's letters defined the event in terms of colorful acts of espionage and individual feats of daring and cowardice. The large, local Protestant population may have increased the sense of exposure to Britain. The peasantry in this account showed neither loyalty nor disloyalty to the crown, but rather seemed to react only in response to basic needs. Pitchfork-bearing peasant women, for example, killed a British soldier who had attempted to take a cow from them. Sinclair hanged a Breton who had served unsuccessfully as a British spy. A Compagnie employee and his wife were in the pay of the British. Strikingly, all these concerns point to uneasy social divisions and fear of treachery in this part of Brittany, in which internal threats loomed more ominously than the encroaching foreign enemy did. Examples of praiseworthy conduct stressed the reverse: courageous displays of loyalty to the region and the king. The provincial letter writer commended a Compagnie engineer and munitions officer for these qualities. They figured as a part of the imagined resolution, which in this account was bold leadership and a vigorous defense accomplished by civic-minded subjects loyal to the *patrie.*

Parisian talk and the Breton letters evoke two different forms of civic engagement. "Public opinion" in Paris *called* for decisive action but *was* nothing more than public-minded discussion. The provincial letter writer took action at ground zero. He was a participant in and an observer of the unfolding military event, yet he took the time to send a lengthy exposé to a Parisian salon. He insisted that his account was "no novelistic fabrication," but rather "the most exact truth without exaggeration." Yet, in his open condemnation of the resident military command, this eyewitness eschewed any pretense of objectivity, seeking rather to influence as much as inform. Other letters from Brittany that arrived in Paris emphasized different aspects of events, finding L'Hôpital less blamable (or were less willing to criticize him).[26] Public judgment followed that of the Breton correspondent, despite the king granting L'Hôpital honors as the bearer of the good news. L'Hôpital, in Parisian conversations and verses, was a coward. Parisians, the *gazetins* recorded, could hardly believe that the same man who hid his face from the enemy dared show it at court, "insofar as he alone is to blame for the English descent."[27] The word of the day in Paris and Brittany, to take one example, became "poltron" or "poltronnerie," in reference to the general and his troops.[28]

Some of the city's salons were forums for dialogues on matters of state.[29] Their *habitués* evaluated provincial letters for general use—copying them for their correspondents, excerpting them in *nouvelles à la main*, and cribbing from them to craft verses. The translation of events from provincial letters to other public genres (like song) was a familiar itinerary in this period. But the café debate that took place after the Lorient invasion had an unfamiliar quality to the police agent who transcribed it. The indication of newness points to the important role police agents played in this culture of transcription. As proto-ethnographers, they gave literary form to disembodied Parisian voices, assembling quotations, laughs, and gestures into coherent debates and summary opinions. They compared opinions from different locations and formulated debate on the page by juxtaposing disconnected fragments. As observers, they reflected on past conversations and tried to anticipate future ones. In dialogue with their superiors and the subjects under surveillance (who sometimes knew they were present), they learned over time to hone in on what they were supposed to hear and tune out the noise. They collated and aggregated opinions in nonmathematical ways, distilling them into anecdotes or simple statements, such as "All of Paris was devastated yesterday."[30] As police transcriptions of Parisian talk, these *gazetins* were intended for official readers; however, enterprising *gazetiers* distributed them clandestinely to subscribers and sometimes to a larger public. Occasionally, the city's lieutenant general of police authorized the clandestine distribution of *gazetins* to influence popular opinion. If provincial letters informed and biased Parisian opinions, police agents played a key role in framing "public opinion" as a genre of talk in their reports.

To return to the café conversation that took place after Lorient, the police agent's surprise came from its form, he noted, not its content. Yet according to other surveillance reports, such publicly aired advice and expressions of opinion concerning current events were not so exceptional. The most continuous collection of *gazetins* from 1725 to 1747 indicates that every major military or diplomatic event elicited the public commentary of self-proclaimed experts. What gave this observer pause, perhaps, was the palpable assertiveness of the armchair statesmen's resolve, which was difficult to convey in a police report. In the performative language of official bodies or institutions, *to resolve* was a key word in decision-making processes and carried specific, formal effects. The conversation in the café mimed that official performance and, thus, may mark the coming into being of political, public speech as a genre and café interlocutors as its interpretive community. The space could have been a café or salon or any place where people talked about talk. While this community could not make its decisions, or "resolutions," become official policy, it could decide who was allowed to be a part of its speaking community, what was said, and what such talk meant.

In the end, the British descent on Lorient incited the airing of decisive, public-minded solutions. Criticizing the incompetence and self-interest of officials, public interlocutors engaged in a spirited dialogue over national interests, which were not conceived of as different from those of the king. As police observers described it, public opinion was dynamic. It represented nothing more than dialogue, relied on no special knowledge, and often fed on rumor alone. It rested not on traditional authority but on the common sense of ordinary people. It drew examples from recent events, the details of which were known only through hearsay. It spoke *as* no one in particular and *to* no one in particular. Nevertheless, in its reflexivity, it implied its own authority; and in its performativity, it implied its own effectiveness. In producing opinions, subjects did not refer to the authority of an all-seeing Louis XV, whose knowledge of the national whole was, theoretically, an effect of the king's two bodies.[31] Instead, they referenced rumors, unsubstantiated reports, and ephemera, whose hallmark was their uncontrolled circulation.

As independent and autogenerative as Parisian opinion may have been, it could be inflected by print. Indeed, print played an important role in shaping public opinion. It helped define which views were worthy of discussion. In collecting contradictory accounts, printed sources such as the *Gazette d'Amsterdam* reified uncertainty, reminding readers of their own lack of access to solid information. Official, printed accounts served pragmatically to neutralize exaggerated or erroneous accounts. They also assigned names and dates to events, which, as Will Slauter has shown, had the useful function of settling wagers among those who speculated on news.[32] But it was in the period before the publication of official accounts—a period when Parisians freely circulated news, elaborated on it, debated it, and modified it—that public opinion initially took shape. If this period of uncertainty was frustrating, it was also productive.

The study of public opinion in the eighteenth century has been guided by three different approaches.[33] The first, exemplified by Keith M. Baker, treats public opinion as a *concept* imbued with certain traits, including coherence, authority, and stability, that distinguish it from an ensemble of individual, or "particular," opinions.[34] In this view, public opinion provided ordinary people with a legitimate platform from which to speak. The second, pioneered by Jürgen Habermas and elaborated on more recently by Roger Chartier, treats public opinion sociologically, as a vital component of an emerging civil society that existed independently of the state. This latter approach stresses institutions of publicity, or the "public sphere," through which individuals made reasoned, critical judgments about public policy.[35]

Robert Darnton has pioneered a third approach, the social history of public opinion. Much of his work has examined the myriad opinions held by ordinary and elite subjects.[36] Darnton's scholarship, which has largely focused on the circulation and reception of printed libels and sedition, captures the early modern sensibility of subjects whose aspirations and disappointments were nurtured within a king-centered world.[37] The research for this essay comes out of a larger project on mid-century public opinion, which attempts to build on Darnton's work while focusing specifically on manuscript and oral communications around war and foreign affairs. These topics saturate police surveillance reports, diaries, chronicles, and printed and manuscript gazettes. To be sure, religious controversies, crown/*parlement* disputes, and financial crises played an important role in print and in the growing recognition of public opinion as a legitimate political voice. Yet focusing on these topics almost inevitably leads historians to notions of a public in opposition to the monarchy.

By focusing on war and diplomacy, this essay highlights seemingly paradoxical qualities of early modern speaking subjects and their opinions. They were royalist *and* patriotic, loyal *and* critical.[38] Moreover, these opinions seem to have been less the expressions of rational individuals, as Habermas and his followers would have it, than the result of collective, consensus-seeking deliberations on the common good or the good of the kingdom, practices characteristic of early modern electoral bodies. In forming opinions in this way, the café public often affirmed the legitimacy of existing public offices even if it excoriated a current officeholder.[39] Scholars of eighteenth-century French public opinion have tended to emphasize how the development of public opinion led to a spirit of criticism and gave rise to forces opposed not just to current officials, but also to the regime as a whole. In following the evolution of talk about war and diplomacy, we find public opinion taking an alternative path. On this topic, Parisians were vicarious participants in politics; and, in miming official procedures in their speaking practices, they—together with the police agents who recorded their views and the printed gazettes that diffused and amplified them—developed a "public opinion" in tandem with, and not against, the crown.

NOTES

1. Maurepas's lament, according to Charles Philippe d'Albert, duc de Luynes, "Extrait de la lettre de Mme de Luynes du 5 octobre 1746, à Choisy, à onze heures du soir," in *Mémoires du duc de Luynes sur la cour de Louis XV (1735–1758)*, ed. L. Dussieux and E. Soulié (Paris: Firmin Didot frères, fils et cie, 1860–65), 7:433–34.

2. "Gazetins de police," October 1, 1746, in Feydeau de Marville, *Lettres de M. de Marville, lieutenant général de police, au ministre Maurepas (1742–1747)*, ed. A. de Boislisle (Paris: Champion, 1905), 3:46.

3. For a detailed history of the War of Austrian Succession, see Reed Browning, *The War of Austrian Succession* (Stroud, U.K.: Alan Sutton Publishing Ltd., 1994).

4. See Yann Lukas, *Lorient: Histoire d'une ville* (Quimper: Éditions Palatines, 1997).

5. M. J. Hébert, *Lorient* (Paris: Challamel, n.d.), 28–29; E. Mancel, *Chronique lorientaise: Origine de la ville Lorient, son histoire et son avenir* (Lorient: Librairie de Charles Gousset, 1861), 101–11.

6. Jean-Frédéric Phélypeaux, comte de Maurepas, to Archbishop of Bourges, October 17, 1746, in Marville, *Lettres de M. de Marville,* 3:51–52.

7. Horace Walpole, 4th Earl of Orford, quoted in Albert de Broglie, *Maurice de Saxe et le marquis d'Argenson* (Paris: Calman Lévy, 1891), 1:430.

8. "Français et vous anglais, réunissez vos vœux / Pour remercier Dieu d'un secours merveilleux; / Les cœurs trop généreux / Font un carnage affreux; / En vous rendant peureux / Il vous sauve tous deux." "Chansons Clairambault," Bibliothèque nationale de France, Manuscrits français 12715, fol. 171; see also "Une descente des anglais," in Jean-Fréderic Phélypeaux Maurepas, *Recueil Clairambault-Maurepas: Chansonnier historique du XVIIIe siècle,* ed. Émile Raunié (Paris: Quantin, 1882), 7:79–80.

9. Broglie, *Maurice de Saxe,* 1:429.

10. Browning, *War of Austrian Succession,* 281–86, 288–90.

11. Luynes, *Mémoires du duc de Luynes,* 7:448.

12. Edmond-Jean François Barbier, *Chronique de la Régence et du règne de Louis XV (1718–1763), ou Journal de Barbier* (Paris: Charpentier, 1866), 4:186–87.

13. "Gazetins de police," October 25, 1746, in Papiers Marville, Bibliothèque historique de la ville de Paris (hereafter cited as BHVP), MS 721 (rés. 23), fol. 149.

14. "De L'Orient, le 10 Octobre 1746," *La Gazette de France,* #43, October 25, 1746; "De Paris le 7 Octobre," *La Gazette d'Amsterdam,* #82, October 14, 1746; "Du Port Lorient le 4 Octobre," "De Paris le 10 Octobre," #83, October 18, 1746; "De Paris le 14 Octobre," #84, October 21, 1746; "De Paris le 17 Octobre," #85, October 25, 1746; "De Paris le 21 Octobre," #86, October 28, 1746; "De Paris le 25 Octobre," #87, 1 November 1746; "De Paris le 23 Octobre," #88, November 4, 1746.

15. "Gazetins de police," October 25, 1746, fol. 149.

16. Ibid., fols. 149v–150.

17. René Voyer d'Argenson, *Journal et mémoires du marquis d'Argenson* (Paris: P. Jannet, 1858), 3:79.

18. Charles-Emmanuel, king of Piedmont-Sardinia, used a diplomatic technicality and promises of peace to lure French armies into a trap. A Piedmont army attacked the French garrison at Asti on March 5, 1746, forcing a surrender that led to five thousand French captives. Browning, *War of Austrian Succession,* 262.

19. October 25, 1746, BHVP, MS 721 (rés. 23), fol. 150v.

20. Ibid.

21. *Gazetins,* Bibliothèque universitaire de Poitiers, Papiers d'Argenson, carton P52.

22. The latter exchange was edited out of the version of this report in the d'Argenson papers. October 25, 1746, BHVP, MS 721 (rés. 23), fol. 150v.

23. These remarks paraphrase Michel Foucault's comments on what Étienne Pasquier called the "other succession," which links explicitly to the international Protestant-Catholic struggles. See *"Society Must Be Defended:" Lectures at the College de France, 1975–1976,* trans. David Macey (New York: Picador, 2003), 118–19.

24. Anonymous, *Journal de ce qui s'est passé à GENES et dans son Territoire depuis l'irruption que l'armée autrichienne et piémontaise a faite dans les vallées de Polcevera et de Bisagn jusqu'à sa retraite* (n.p., 1747), viii.

25. François Moureau, *Répertoire des nouvelles à la main: Dictionnaire de la presse manuscrite clandestine, XVIe–XVIIIE siècle* (Oxford: Voltaire Foundation, 1999), entry 1738.3.10.

26. Charles Bougouin fils, *Descente des Anglais en Bretagne et siège de Lorient en 1746* (Nantes: Imprimerie Vincent Forest et Émile Grimaud), 12.

27. Papiers d'Argenson, carton P52. This song, quoted in the beginning of this essay, devotes several verses to L'Hôpital's ineptitude.

28. A Breton woman had strong words for her compatriots once the dust settled: "Les commandants des troupes réglées et gardes côtes sont des sots, les Bretons des poltrons, et tout ce qui appartient à la compagnie des Jean f[outre]" (The commanders of the regular troops and the coast guard are idiots, the Bretons are weaklings, and all who belong to the Compagnie are unreliable jackasses). November 27, 1746, Papiers d'Argenson, carton P52.

29. The salons of Marie-Thérèse Rodet Geoffrin and Marie de Vichy-Chamrond, marquise du Deffand, are two examples, but there are many others. See Dena Goodman, *The Republic of Letters: A Cultural History of the Enlightenment* (Ithaca: Cornell University Press, 1994), 41, 75–76, 139; Antoine Lilti, *Le monde des salons: Sociabilité et mondanité à Paris au XVIIIe siècle* (Paris: Fayard, 2005); and Tabetha Leigh Ewing, "Rumor and Foreign Politics in Louis XV's Paris During the War of Austrian Succession" (Ph.D. diss., Princeton University, 2005).

30. "Gazettes à la main," July 10, 1744, BHVP, MS 625, fol. 21.

31. See especially chapter 5 of Ernst H. Kantorowicz, *The King's Two Bodies: A Study in Mediaeval Political Theology* (1957; repr., Princeton: Princeton University Press, 1997). While some scholarly disagreement exists about the persistence into the eighteenth century of the medieval, dualistic theory of the body, there seems little doubt that contemporaries actively reimagined the relationship between the king's natural body and the body politic. See, for example, Alain Boureau, *Le simple corps du Roi: L'impossible sacralité des souverains français, XVe–XVIIIe siècle* (Paris: Éditions de Paris, 2000); and Sara E. Melzer and Kathryn Norberg, eds., *From the Royal to the Republic Body: Incorporating the Political in Seventeenth- and Eighteenth-Century France* (Berkeley: University of California Press, 1998).

32. Will Slauter, "Forward-Looking Statements: News and Speculation in the Age of the American Revolution," *Journal of Modern History* 81, no. 4 (December 2009): 759–92.

33. Roger Chartier and Keith Michael Baker, "Dialogue sur l'espace public," *Politix* 26, no. 2 (1994): 15.

34. See Robert Darnton's *The Forbidden Best-Sellers of Pre-Revolutionary France* (New York: W. W. Norton, 1995); *The Great Cat Massacre, and Other Episodes in French Cultural History* (New York: Vintage, 1985); "Public Opinion and the Communication Networks in Eighteenth-Century Paris," in *Opinion*, ed. Peter-Eckhard Knabe (Berlin: A. Spitz, 2002), 149–230; and "Mlle Bonafon et 'La Vie Privée de Louis XV,'" *Dix-huitième siècle* 35 (2003): 369–91. See also Arlette Farge, *Subversive Words: Public Opinion in Eighteenth-Century France*, trans. Rosemary Morris (University Park: Penn State University Press, 1994); Farge, *Les fatigues de la guerre* (Paris: Le Promeneur, 1996); and other works on Paris: Dale Van Kley, *The Damiens Affair and the Unraveling of the Ancien Régime, 1750–1770* (Princeton: Princeton University Press, 1984); and Lisa Jane Graham, *If the King Only Knew: Seditious Speech in the Reign of Louis XV* (Charlottesville: University of Virginia Press, 2000).

35. Keith Michael Baker, *Inventing the French Revolution: Essays on French Political Culture in the Eighteenth Century* (Cambridge: Cambridge University Press, 1990), esp. chap. 8.

36. Jürgen Habermas, *The Structural Transformation of the Public Sphere: An Inquiry into a Category of Bourgeois Society*, trans. Thomas Burger (Cambridge: Polity Press, 1989); Roger Chartier, *The Cultural Origins of the French Revolution*, trans. Lydia G. Cochrane (Durham: Duke University Press, 1991).

37. James Van Horn Melton re-theorizes the "enlightened public sphere," arguing for the importance of early modern institutions. See *The Rise of the Public in Enlightenment Europe* (Cambridge: Cambridge University Press, 2001).

38. On national sentiment and royal patriotism, particularly in the second half of the eighteenth century, see David A. Bell, *The Cult of the Nation in France: Inventing Nationalism, 1680–1800* (Cambridge: Harvard University Press, 2001). On the importance of foreign affairs to emerging notions of citizenship in the British context, see Linda Colley, *Britons: Forging the Nation, 1707–1837* (New Haven: Yale University Press, 1992).

39. On the literary public sphere, see, for example, Chartier, *The Cultural Origins of the French Revolution*. On the distinctions between early modern and modern procedures for collective decision making, see Pierre Bourdieu, *Language and Symbolic Power*, trans. Gino Raymond and Matthew Adamson (Cambridge: Harvard University Press, 1999).

SEVEN

BOOK SEIZURES AND THE POLITICS OF REPRESSION IN PARIS, 1787–1789

Thomas M. Luckett

In addition to the routine investigation of civil disputes and common crimes in their immediate neighborhoods, Parisian *commissaires de police* in the eighteenth century sometimes came to specialize in repressing a particular category of crime throughout the whole city. While one *commissaire* regularly raided the capital's taverns searching for AWOL soldiers, another arrested prostitutes in the streets, and still another arrested men for homosexual solicitation. In the late 1780s, the *commissaire* Pierre Chénon, known as "Chénon père," was in charge of seizing illegal books. He had been a *commissaire* since 1743, and his office, or commissariat, stood in the heart of Paris on the rue Baillet near the church of St-Germain-l'Auxerrois. The lieutenant general of police, Louis-Thiroux de Crosne, frequently ordered Chénon to search bookstores and ambulant vendors for specific titles, and for any other works that "appeared suspect." When he was unavailable, de Crosne typically turned to Chénon's son, Marie-Joseph Chénon, whose commissariat stood just a few blocks away in the rue Saint-Honoré, near the corner of the rue d'Orléans. "Chénon fils," who had become a *commissaire* in 1773, was probably best known in Paris as the policeman who had arrested Cagliostro in the diamond necklace affair of 1785.[1] As with the many other tasks assigned to police *commissaires*, book seizures generated detailed reports.[2]

As a royal appointee, the lieutenant general of police was directly responsible to the royal council, and his priorities had to reflect those of the current administration. Besides maintaining public order in the capital, he was expected to support ministerial policy by policing public expression and suppressing criticism of Versailles. Yet the ministry itself kept changing, and with it the body's policies. De Crosne became lieutenant general in 1785, replacing the controversial Jean-Charles-Pierre Lenoir, and he would step down four years later after the fall of the Bastille. His tenure thus spanned three very different administrations: those of Charles-Alexandre de Calonne, Etienne-Charles de Loménie de Brienne, and the second ministry of Jacques Necker. In very different ways, each of the three tried and ultimately failed to solve the complex set of problems that were sapping the regime: economic depression, fiscal insolvency, magisterial intransigence, a rising tide of both urban and rural revolt, and an increasingly radicalized intelligentsia. Moreover, honoring long-standing tradition, each head of government tried to shore up his own popularity by scapegoating his predecessors.

The list of books that the Paris police seized or attempted to seize on the eve of the Revolution thus reveals the contradictory goals and shifting strategies of a politically unstable government. Through research into the Chénon papers, I hope here to contribute to a larger historical literature—especially including studies by Robert Darnton and the late Robert L. Dawson—that has sought to reconstruct the bibliography of works that the police actively repressed in France in the waning years of the Old Regime.[3] At the same time, I hope to show that attention to the precise chronology of book seizures can inform our understanding of the political history of the pre-Revolution. As we shall see, the Chénons' raids on Parisian bookstores represented not only a failed but also a counterproductive attempt to dampen political opposition to the monarchy, and it may actually have contributed to the forces driving France toward revolt.

Typically, Chénon père, accompanied by a police inspector, would arrive unexpectedly and move swiftly through several bookshops, briefly questioning their owners about particular titles. They all knew the routine. When he seized a work, Chénon usually wanted to know where it came from and how many copies had been sold, and the shopkeepers patiently supplied answers that may or may not have been true. Straining credulity, they often added that they were unaware that the book in question was illegal. The imprisonment of booksellers, whether shopkeepers or colporteurs, was not generally necessary—though admittedly much less indulgence was shown for the hapless smugglers, usually impoverished, caught carrying shipments of books through the customs gates that led into the city. Rarely did the police succeed in seizing copies of the same book on two separate days, which suggests that titles were in fact removed from sale after the first seizure. We should thus not dismiss their efforts as ineffectual.

Between January 1787 and June 1789, the Chénons and their colleagues in Paris seized or attempted to seize more than 130 publications, or an average of more than four per month, but the pace of seizures varied greatly from month to month and appears to have been most intense at moments of political crisis. Many of the authors of these works are obscure, but others had significant political or literary careers, including the marquis de Condorcet, Nicolas Bergasse, Jacques Pierre Brissot, the comte de Rivarol, Jean-Louis Carra, Simon-Nicolas-Henri Linguet, Olympe de Gouges, Jean-Paul Marat, and even the young Antoine-Louis-Léon de Saint-Just. The most frequently seized author in this period was the comte de Mirabeau, with five separate titles: *Dénonciation de l'agiotage*, *Lettre remise à Frédéric-Guillaume II*, *Le Rideau levé*, *Histoire secrette de la cour de Berlin*, and *Lettre du comte de Mirabeau à ses commettans*. The types of books seized varied considerably and included all the great prohibited genres of the day: attacks on the royal government or on the *parlements*, anti-clerical and anti-Christian works, pornographic books and illustrations, and personal libels.

The bibliography of books seized by the *commissaires* allows us to dispel at least two prominent myths that have developed in the secondary literature. First, modern accounts of the French pre-Revolution often imply mistakenly that censorship of the press throughout France all but ended after Brienne's council decree of July 5, 1788, in which the king asked "all informed persons . . . to send information or memoirs relating to the coming convocation" of the Estates-General. Jacques Godechot, for instance, comments that "this was a roundabout way of granting the freedom of the press."[4] Yet, in Paris at least, the frequency of book seizures—having fallen off considerably since the ministry's confrontation with the *parlement* in the autumn of 1787—actually rose again after October 1788. They reached new heights in the spring of 1789 even as the Estates-General began to meet, then ceased abruptly for six months following Chénon père's final book seizure on June 20, 1789. Moreover, many of the works seized under the second Necker ministry specifically concerned the form of the coming Estates-General, proving that the July decree afforded no new immunity at all.

It has also become commonplace among historians of Paris to consider that the Palais-Royal, as a private domain of the liberal duc d'Orléans, lay outside the jurisdiction of the Paris police and was thus immune to book seizures. For instance, Godechot writes that the Palais-Royal was "a privileged place where the police could not penetrate."[5] This turns out to be untrue. Indeed, more than half of all raids targeted the dozen or so booksellers of the Palais-Royal. A royal council decree of September 4, 1787, suspended the immunities of the Palais-Royal and other privileged places, authorizing the Paris guard to enter these premises, but even before this date the Chénons frequently conducted raids there.[6] Bookstores in the rue Saint-Honoré and the rue Saint-Jacques were also frequently raided by the police. Further, Chénon routinely searched the colporteurs who worked the gardens and cafés of the Palais-Royal's great inner courtyard, some of whom actually claimed to be illiterate and thus ignorant of what they were selling.

Perhaps the greatest interest in studying book seizures in Paris during the pre-Revolution is what they can tell us about the cultural politics of the royal council as it confronted the final crises of the Old Regime. In summary, Calonne's attempts to manipulate the press at the time of the Assembly of Notables were clumsy and ultimately counterproductive. Brienne's recourse to book seizures and the imprisonment of booksellers during his great struggle with the magistracy in the fall of 1787 and the summer of 1788 were far more ironfisted but may have contributed to his unpopularity. Most surprising, though, are the policies of Necker. Having begun in the autumn of 1788 by largely eliminating censorship, he soon moved back to a policy of book seizure that rivaled that of Brienne in its severity. Paradoxically, however, by suppressing the works of his critics, the liberal Necker helped to stifle conservative expression, while giving freer reign to radical reformers. Necker's book-seizing policies may thus have helped to hasten the outbreak of the Revolution.

The convening of Calonne's much anticipated Assembly of Notables on February 22, 1787, did not result in a large number of raids on Parisian bookshops. Rather, the political crisis of the winter and spring of 1787, leading, finally, to Calonne's dismissal in April, was marked at first by relatively lax press censorship in Paris, and then, as the tide began to turn against the finance minister and his policies, by a belated and ultimately counterproductive attempt to manipulate public opinion through pro-government propaganda. When police suppressed political pamphlets during these months, they tended to suppress the wrong ones, striking out harshly against the conservative and utterly predictable rhetoric of the *parlements* but letting slip a far more damaging work by Mirabeau.

On February 10, the Chénons searched the bookstores of the Palais-Royal and seized sixteen copies of *Instruction sur les assemblées nationales*, published by the Paris bookseller Jean-François Royez, and more than three hundred copies of *Essai historique et politique sur les assemblées nationales*, published by Vincent Petit. By their legal and historical logic, both of these anonymous pamphlets fell squarely within a tradition of parliamentary opposition to royal authority that can be traced back to the work of François Hotman in the sixteenth century. France, it was argued, was a constitutional monarchy whose fundamental laws required the monarch to submit all new laws and taxes to the nation for approval. Under King Clovis, the nation was represented by an annual gathering of knights on the Champs de Mars in Paris, and this institution had subsequently evolved into the various representative assemblies of modern France: the Estates-General, *parlements*, and assemblies of notables. When these bodies defied the royal will and refused to register the king's laws, they were fulfilling their legitimate role as defenders of the nation's liberties. Five days later, the baron de Breteuil (who as minister of the royal household had cabinet-level jurisdiction over the administration of Paris) issued a council decree condemning both works, along with a work on provincial assemblies printed by the Imprimerie Polytype, and temporarily closed the shops of all three publishers. Despite the insipidity of the three pamphlets, Breteuil asserted that they "contain things reprehensible, whether concerning the objects that they claim should be communicated to the Assembly of Notables or in publishing the names of the persons who will compose this assembly."[7]

Chénon père seized or attempted to seize several other anti-ministerial works over the following weeks. One was an anonymous protest against the new customs wall that the administration was building around Paris. Although the *Mémoires secrets*, an underground newspaper, suggested that it was the work of the comte de Mirabeau, historians usually attribute it to one Jacques-Antoine Dulaure.[8] Another pamphlet, *Remerciement et supplique du peuple au roi*, congratulated the king for having called the Assembly of Notables but demanded that he now economize and pay down his debts. The *Mémoires secrets* pointed out that its style seemed to be that of the marquis de Mirabeau, the famous Physiocrat and estranged father of the comte de Mirabeau. On February 22, Chénon père found seventy-six copies of this tract at three bookstores in the Palais-Royal, including that of the bookseller Lefebvre, who admitted that he had received a hundred copies from the marquis himself.[9] The most damning and widely read anti-ministerial pamphlet of the season, *Dénonciation de l'agiotage au Roi et à l'Assemblée des notables*, came from the pen of the comte de Mirabeau, the marquis's son, who boldly put his name on the title page.

On March 15, Pierre Gastel, an illiterate boy of fifteen, was arrested for trying to smuggle a package into Paris that turned out to contain copies of the comte de Mirabeau's tract. Acting on Gastel's testimony, Chénon père immediately searched the shop of Marie-Françoise Vaufleury in the Palais-Royal and found eighteen more copies, the remainder of the 250 she had originally received from her supplier. The following day, Calonne ordered de Crosne to "take the greatest care to prevent the distribution of this work." The authors of the *Mémoires secrets* had first gotten wind of Mirabeau's new diatribe on March 12, but they noted that it was "rare and expensive," and were themselves apparently unable to obtain a copy until March 18. The 232 copies sold by Mme. Vaufleury may thus represent its total circulation, but if the *Dénonciation de l'agiotage* failed to reach a wider public, it is known to have influenced the members of the Assembly of Notables, where it did much to undermine Calonne's credibility. By purporting to expose the prevalence of stock market manipulation and governmental financial corruption, Mirabeau's pamphlet substantiated the notables' growing conviction that Calonne was to blame for the deficit. On March 20, Mirabeau fled to Belgium to avoid arrest, but the damage was done.[10]

Calonne's difficulties controlling the press in early 1787 are probably best illustrated, however, by his curious decision to have the police seize his own, pro-ministerial pamphlet. This requires some explanation. In March, as his relations with the Assembly of Notables degenerated, he attempted to fight them with propaganda of his own. Toward the end of that month appeared a short pamphlet called *Lettre d'un Anglois à Paris*, with a title page falsely claiming it had been printed in London. Readers had little doubt that, in the words of the *Mémoires secrets*, "this tract shows every sign of having been composed by order of the minister of finances." Ostensibly the translation of a letter written on March 18 by an Englishman traveling in France, it has in fact been attributed to one Joseph-Nicolas Barbier-Vémars, a journalist who wrote for the *Journal général de France*. The *Lettre d'un Anglois* begins by praising Calonne for daring to reform the fiscal system of the monarchy, and for attempting to establish elective provincial assemblies without distinction of order, but it quickly turns into a radical denunciation of tax privileges, particularly those of the clergy. Continued opposition to his program in the assembly could only be the result of a clerical cabal. To defeat his critics among the notables, the author concludes, Calonne must take his program over their heads and appeal to the people themselves: "But why shouldn't the projects of the minister be public? Why shouldn't transparency [*publicité*] shield him from the barbs of his enemies? . . . The French administration, even in doing good, has not yet resolved to publish what it does, and so win the acclaim and support of the people."[11]

In fact, Calonne was already following his pamphleteer's advice. He published a major speech that he had delivered to the notables on March 12, both as a separate pamphlet and as an article in the *Journal de Paris*. Then, on March 31, he openly published and distributed a brief apology for his program of reform, denouncing his critics as selfish and unpatriotic. Written by the lawyer Pierre-Jean-Baptiste Gerbier, this six-page diatribe appeared both as the preamble to Calonne's publication of the memoirs he had presented to the Assembly of Notables, and also as a separate extract with which he flooded Paris, sending copies even to the curates so they could read it from the pulpit. "Privileges will be sacrificed!," he claimed. "Yes: justice demands it, necessity requires it. Should we rather impose further burdens on the unprivileged, on the people?" The members of the Assembly of Notables were understandably enraged. In a series of blistering speeches, they denounced his contempt for their authority. Calonne tried to backpedal, claiming disingenuously that the speech and the preamble had been printed without his consent, but he was rapidly losing the confidence of the court. On April 5, acting on orders of de Crosne, and thus presumably at the request of Calonne himself, Chénon père visited the shops of eight booksellers at the Palais-Royal in search of the *Lettre d'un Anglois* yet failed to find a single copy. It was too little too late. On April 8, the king dismissed Calonne.[12]

Compared with the relative laxity, and even ineptitude, of Calonne's policy of book seizures, that of Loménie de Brienne was far more severe, and can be seen as driven by the great political crises he experienced in the autumn of 1787 and, again, in the summer of 1788. Already in August 1787, as the ministry came increasingly into conflict with the *parlements* over forced registration of its new land and stamp taxes, the police became more repressive. In addition to seizing books, they now took the unusual step of arresting booksellers. On August 6, Chénon père seized a half-dozen copies of two pamphlets related to the Kornmann affair (discussed below) from the shop of Mme. Vaufleury in the Palais-Royal and sent her briefly to La Force Prison in the Marais. This same woman had been caught selling Mirabeau's *Dénonciation de l'agiotage* in March. When the Commissaire Guyot questioned her in prison two days later, she reported that the police inspector Henry had searched her shop four or five times over the past few months, looking especially for works by the comte de Mirabeau.[13]

The crackdown continued for another two months. An ordinance of the chief bailiff of the Palais-Royal on September 3, and an act of the royal council the following day, required the booksellers' guild to assist in the seizure of illegal books. On the afternoon of September 11, acting on orders from de Crosne, the inspector Jean-François Royer de Surbois went to the Palais-Royal and arrested two women colporteurs for selling six different anti-ministerial pamphlets. They had between them more than fifty copies of a recent remonstrance of the *parlement* of Brittany—titled *Second arrêté du Parlement de Bretagne du 22 août 1787*—and admitted to having sold nineteen others. Both women appear to have been released the same day. On November 16, Chénon père arrested the widow Marie-Louise Guillaume at her shop in the rue Saint-Honoré for stocking no fewer than nine different titles that supported the *parlements* in their ongoing conflict with the Brienne administration. When asked why she sold such things, she answered "that all the news merchants do so."[14]

Shortly after September 13, de Crosne also closed and sealed the Imprimerie Polytype of the printers Hoffmann and son in the rue Favart. Hailing from Alsace, the Hoffmanns had arrived in Paris in 1785 and patented what they claimed was a new printing technology without movable type, but the true secret of their success was in selling libels. According to the *Mémoires secrets*, they were "suspected of contributing much to printing the flood of clandestine pamphlets on administrative matters and the events of the day with which we have been inundated." The Polytype raid was the single largest book seizure of the pre-Revolution. For reasons that are unclear, Commissaire Chénon père did not actually search the Polytype until October 8. When he did, he drew up a list of no fewer than twelve illegal titles in stock. Based on the account book, he also compiled a second list of twenty-two illegal works that the Hoffmanns had printed between June 21 and September 13, 1787.[15] Despite some duplication between the two lists, the total came to thirty-two works. Thirteen of the thirty-two titles (40 percent) concerned the aforementioned Kornmann affair, a sensationalized sex scandal involving the financier and playwright Pierre Caron de Beaumarchais that had gripped the public since late summer. Though it was not overtly political, Sarah Maza has argued that the Kornmann affair generated trial briefs that amounted to thinly veiled critiques of the royal family. The Hoffmanns printed many of the pro-Kornmann (hence antimonarchical) pamphlets.[16] Most of the other titles likewise criticized royal and ministerial despotism. Two works seized, for instance, concerned the notorious case of Masers de Latude, who had spent thirty-nine years in the Bastille and other state prisons for a youthful practical joke he had once played on Mme. de Pompadour. The Hoffmanns' stock included several copies of the comte de

Mirabeau's *Lettre remise à Frédéric-Guillaume II, roi régnant de Prusse*, in which he called for sweeping political reforms and greater governmental transparency, and their account book showed that they had delivered 1,500 copies to Mirabeau himself.[17] Indeed, considering the sorts of works that the Polytype printed and distributed, it is remarkable that de Crosne had not closed it much earlier.

Just as the conflict over the registration of the land and stamp tax edicts produced a crackdown on the press in the autumn of 1787, so, too, after a relatively quiet winter, did the May edicts—by which Brienne and the guard of the seals, François-Chrétien de Lamoignon, attempted to strip the *parlements* of their power to block royal legislation. In the future, a new "plenary court" would have sole authority to register taxes and laws common to the whole kingdom, and unlike the *parlements*, its magistrates would be appointed by and directly responsible to the king. On June 5, 1788, Chénon père searched all the shops of the Palais-Royal but failed to find a single copy of either the *Histoire du siège du Palais* or the *Mémoire remis à M. le comte de Thiare*. The first described in detail the heroic efforts of the *parlement* of Paris to resist the arrest of two of its most radical members on the night of May 4–5. The second was a formal statement from an assembly of nobles at Rennes protesting the creation of the plenary court and denouncing the king's ministers as criminals. In July 1788, in addition to raids on bookstores, arrests also began to multiply. On July 12, Chénon père searched in vain for the *Apologie de la Cour plénière* at a shop in the rue Monceau-Saint-Gervais and arrested its owner, Jean-Louis Lacloye. He claimed to have sold only twelve copies but was suspected of having sold the entire print run. Allegedly a serious study by the abbé Vélin, a respected antiquarian, the *Apologie* was, in fact, a satirical piece in which the author claimed to prove that the ancient plenary court was a "court of rejoicing," not a court of justice. Before the Christian conversion, festivities at the plenary court had culminated in human sacrifice, a custom that the author proposed to revive by executing the king's ministers.[18]

Lacloye was sent to La Force prison, as were two colporteurs arrested a week later in the gardens of the Palais-Royal for hocking a pro-government pamphlet, *Mon coup-d'œil*. Their offense seems to have been the sarcastic cry with which they advertised it to the public: "News from the government." At the end of July, Chénon père arrested the widow Pailly on suspicion of having sold a pamphlet titled *Les mânes de Madame la présidente Le Mairat*, which attacked Lamoignon. On August 9, he also arrested one Laurent Duguin, a lawyer's clerk at the Palais de Justice, and seized manuscripts of several illegal works from his room in the rue aux Fèves.[19] It is difficult to guess how long such strong measures in the capital would have lasted if the king had not finally dismissed Brienne on August 25 and recalled Necker.

In sharp contrast with Brienne, Necker began his second ministry by instituting a remarkable level of press freedom. Brienne's dismissal, and that of Lamoignon on September 14, provoked ecstatic *réjouissances* in the center of Paris that rapidly degenerated into rioting and street battles with the police throughout the city. Yet despite this challenge to its authority, the new administration attempted, at least during its first two months in power, to implement a policy of transparency. Necker seems to have gambled that public opinion, left to itself, would push conservative magistrates toward the sort of liberal reforms he envisioned for the monarchy. In Paris, book seizures immediately ended, and on September 13, twelve Breton nobles, imprisoned at the Bastille since July for having denounced the king's ministers as criminals, were released. The decision to create the plenary court was revoked on the September 23, and by the beginning of October, even most of those arrested in the course of the riots were freed. On October 10, Necker hosted an open house at the Hôtel du Contôle-Général during which he received Parisians of all classes to hear and discuss their grievances.[20]

It was becoming increasingly evident, however, that conservative forces were undermining his attempts to mold the coming Estates-General to his own purposes. On September 25, the *parlement* of Paris rendered its notorious decision that the Estates-General must take precisely the same form as at its previous meeting in 1614. Attempting to circumvent the *parlement*, Necker reconvened the Assembly of Notables, only to find them every bit as intransigent as they had been for Calonne. To gain something approaching proportional representation for the Third Estate, Necker would need every political tool at his disposal. On November 5, the *commissaires* began once again to raid bookstores. As seizures multiplied over the following months, the most common theme in the works confiscated was overt criticism of either Necker himself or the king.

This trend is illustrated by Necker's conflict with the comte de Mirabeau in May 1789. By a royal council decree of May 7, Necker suppressed Mirabeau's new periodical, titled simply *États-Généraux*, the first two issues of which had appeared the previous week. In Paris, the assembly of electors for the Third Estate voted to condemn the decree. Mirabeau himself immediately responded by continuing publication under a new title, *Lettre du comte de Mirabeau à ses commettans*. He devoted his first issue, dated May 10, to a scathing attack on censorship in general, and on Necker in particular: "Twenty-five million voices demand the freedom of the press. . . . Yet it is now that we face a ministerial veto; it is now, after baiting us with an illusory and treacherous tolerance, that a so-called 'popular' ministry outrageously dares to seal up our thoughts." Mirabeau's biographers typically end the story here, as a victory for Mirabeau. In fact, Chénon fils seized the *Lettre du comte de Mirabeau* from a Parisian bookseller on May 21.[21]

Other titles seized from bookstores during these months include the *Réponse de M. de Calonne à l'écrit de M. Necker* on December 19, the *Principes positifs de M. Neker [sic] extraits de tous ses ouvrages* and the *Lettre de Monsieur le comte de Lauragais à Monsieur Necker* on March 2, the *Correctif à l'opinion publique sur M. Necker* on April 7, and the *Nouvel apperçu sur le discours de M. Necker* on both May 25 and June 6. Together such aristocratic pamphlets presented Necker as an unprincipled despot who was prepared to overthrow France's ancient constitution. At the end of April, in a private letter to General Dumouriez, one exasperated Parisian ridiculed the hypocritical policies of the ministry: "I have not yet been able to find the work you requested, my dear Dumouriez. Could it be one of those suppressed since the press became free? All those that contradict the system of the dominant man are so treated, for the greater good and the propagation of public enlightenment."[22]

Unlike the comte de Mirabeau, most of Necker's critics were on the Right, and his suppression of their works, on balance, aided the Left. The censorship policies of the ministry had thus joined the forces pushing France toward revolution. Remarkably, one book that appears nowhere in the police reports, and was presumably never seized, is the abbé Sieyès's *What Is the Third Estate?* It would appear that Necker favored the dissemination of the single most influential revolutionary tract of 1789 because it took care not to attack him specifically, was not explicitly antiroyalist, and might undermine his enemies in the privileged orders.[23]

In 1787, at the time of the First Assembly of Notables, a satirical pamphlet had laughingly suggested that the king appoint the comte de Mirabeau to the office of prime minister.[24] Two years later, events at Versailles catapulted him to the height of national power. On June 20, 1789, as Mirabeau and his colleagues in the National Assembly took the celebrated Oath of the Tennis Court, swearing not to disband until the king recognized their sovereignty, Chénon père was conducting his last book seizure. He searched unsuccessfully a number of bookstores and binderies for copies of two pamphlets that he had already seized over the previous three days. In the shop of the binder Thieblemont, Chénon instead found 112 copies of a two-volume work that his son had tried and failed to seize ten days earlier. Titled *Organt*, it was a mock-epic poem ridiculing the king and queen by a little-known young writer named Antoine-Louis de Saint-Just. The future "angel of death" thus had the distinction of being the last author seized in Paris before the National Assembly ended such raids.[25]

When Chénon père had confiscated copies of Mirabeau's *Lettre remise à Frédéric-Guillaume II* from the Imprimerie Polytype in the autumn of 1787, he may have noticed that the author called for complete freedom of the press, including libel. "The most complete freedom of the press should be among your first achievements," he advised the new king of Prussia, "not only because the restriction of this liberty prevents the exercise of a natural right, but because any obstacle to the progress of enlightenment is an evil, a great evil." In December 1788, Mirabeau published a separate pamphlet inspired by his reading of John Milton's *Areopagitica*, titled *Sur la liberté de la presse*, in which he wrote, "It is at the very moment that the king invites the French to enlighten him on the fairest and wisest manner to convoke the nation. . . . It is at this moment that, with the most scandalous thoughtlessness, one persecutes in the name of the monarch the freedom of the press more severely, with a more active, devious inquisition than the most unlimited ministerial despotism has ever dared."[26]

When Mirabeau and the constituents came to power, raids on bookstores at last ended, at least for a time. Chénon père and Chénon fils might easily have been ordered into the bookstores of the Palais-Royal to seize royalist diatribes—such as those of Mirabeau's own brother, the vicomte de Mirabeau—but they were not.[27] Instead, after June 20, the seizure of books simply ceased to be part of the *commissaires'* professional duties. Such unprecedented freedom of expression, however, was not to last. By the end of the year, the new *commissaires* attached themselves to individual Parisian districts, without enabling legislation from the National Assembly, and began to search local bookstores for subversive and counterrevolutionary publications. They seem to have begun to do so around the Louvre in mid-December 1789, and then gradually in districts across Paris over the following year or so, but the great *commissaires* of the Paris Châtelet were no longer involved. Typically four or five district police officers would enter a bookstore at once, accompanied by a soldier of the Paris guard, search the entire building, and draw up a report in which they identified themselves only by their signatures. One system of press censorship had been eliminated, and a new, more brutal one had been inaugurated.[28]

NOTES

1. *Almanach Royal, Année MDCCLXXXVII* (Paris: Houry, 1787), 405–6; Ashlee B. Hill, "Commissioner Marie-Joseph Chénon: Censorship, Authority, and Reputation in Pre-revolutionary France" (master's thesis, Portland State University, 2007). On a riot that targeted the office of Chénon fils in August 1787, see Thomas M. Luckett, "Hunting for Spies and Whores: A Parisian Riot on the Eve of the French Revolution," *Past and Present* 156 (August 1997): 116–43. There is no exact English translation for "commissaire de police" as the term was used under the Old Regime, though "police superintendent" may come close.

2. The original papers of the Parisian *commissaires de police* through 1791 are included in the Y series of the Archives nationales (hereafter cited as AN). For 1787–91, the minutes of Chénon père are Y 11430–35; those of Chénon fils are Y 11516–18. When Chénon père and Chénon fils were both unavailable, de Crosne might order any of the city's other forty-eight *commissaires de police* to conduct book seizures, and those reports have also been examined for this study.

3. See Robert Darnton's *The Corpus of Clandestine Literature in France, 1769–1789* (New York: W. W. Norton, 1995); and *The Forbidden Best-Sellers of Pre-Revolutionary France* (New York: W. W. Norton, 1995); and Robert L. Dawson, *Confiscations at Customs: Banned Books and the French Booktrade During the Last Years of the Ancien Régime* (Oxford: Voltaire Foundation, 2006).

4. Jacques Godechot, *La prise de la Bastille, 14 juillet 1789* (Paris: Gallimard, 1965), 179–80, 184–85; Jean Egret, *The French Prerevolution, 1787–1788*, trans. Wesley D. Camp (Chicago: University of Chicago Press, 1977), 190.

5. Godechot, *La prise de la Bastille*, 99; see also Carla Hesse, *Publishing and Cultural Politics in Revolutionary Paris, 1789–1810* (Berkeley: University of California Press, 1991), 19; and Darrin M. McMahon, "The Birthplace of the Revolution: Public Space and Political Community in the Palais-Royal of Louis-Philippe-Joseph d'Orléans, 1781–1789," *French History* 10, no. 1 (March 1996): 19.

6. Hippolyte Monin, *L'état de Paris en 1789: Études et documents sur l'ancien régime à Paris* (Paris: Jouaust, 1889), 472; Siméon-Prosper Hardy, "Mes loisirs, ou Journal d'événemens tels qu'ils parviennent à ma connaissance" (September 1, 1787), 7:206–7, Bibliothèque nationale: MS Fr. 6680–87. Besides those of February–April 1787 discussed below, for an example of a raid at the Palais-Royal prior to September 1787, see "PV^{al} de perquisition chez la V^c Morin, le S. Lagrange, le S. Lejay, le S. Guillot, le S. Lespinasse, le S. Chénu, le S. Chénu, et la D^c Guillaume," March 8, 1785 (Com. Chénon fils), AN: Y 11514A.

7. "PV^{al} de perquisition et saisie de livres chez le Sr Royer et chez le Sr Petit," February 10, 1787 (Com. Chénon père), AN: Y 11430; "PV^{aux} de perquisition chez les S^r et D^c Hardouin, Morin, Denet et Dubois," February 10 1787 (Com. Chénon fils), AN: Y 11516; *Arrêt du Conseil d'État du Roi, qui prohibe et confisque les exemplaires de trois ouvrages concernant l'Assemblée des notables, et interdit les sieurs Hoffmann, imprimeur, Royer [sic] et Petit, libraires, qui les ont publiés* (Paris: Imprimerie royale, 1787); *Instruction sur les assemblées nationales, tant générales que particulières, depuis le commencement de la monarchie, jusqu'à nos jours avec le détail de cérémonial, observé dans celle d'aujourd'hui* (Paris: Royez, 1787); *Essai historique et politique sur les assemblées nationales du royaume de France depuis la fondation de la monarchie jusqu'à nos jours* (Paris: Petit, 1787); *Objets proposés à l'Assemblée des notables par de zélés citoyens: Premier objet, administrations provinciales* (Paris: Imprimerie Polytype, 1787). A decree of March 10, 1787, allowed Royez, Petit, and the Hoffmanns (of the Imprimerie Polytype) to reopen their businesses. Louis Petit de Bachaumont et al., *Mémoires secrets pour servir à l'histoire de la république des lettres en France, depuis MDCCLXII jusqu'à nos jours* (London: Adamson, 1777–89), 34:219–20, 339–40 (February 25, March 30, 1787).

8. "Perquisition chez les Srs Bailly, Roger et Tellier, libraires," February 18, 1787 (Com. Chénon père), AN: Y 11430; Jacques-Antoine Dulaure, *Réclamation d'un citoyen, contre la nouvelle enceinte de Paris, élevée par les fermiers-généraux* (1787); Bachaumont, *Mémoires secrets*, 34:218–19 (February 25, 1787); Friedrich Melchior Grimm et al., *Correspondance littéraire, philosophique et critique* (Paris: Garnier, 1877), 15:45 (April 1787); Joseph-Marie Quérard, *Les supercheries littéraires dévoilées* (Paris: Maisonneuve et Larose, 1964), vol. 1, col. 735.

9. "Perquisition," February 22, 1787 (Com. Chénon père), AN: Y 11430; *Remerciement et supplique du peuple au roi, à l'occasion de l'Assemblée des notables* (Brussels, 1787); Bachaumont, *Mémoires secrets*, 34:220–21 (February 27, 1787).

10. Honoré-Gabriel de Riquetti, comte de Mirabeau, *Dénonciation de l'agiotage au Roi et à l'Assemblée des notables* (1787); "PV[al] et capture du noe Gastel, perquisition chez les Srs Duflos au sujet d'imprimés," "PV[al] de perquisition chez la Fe Vaufleury, libraire au Palais-Royal," March 15, 1787 (Com. Chénon père), AN: Y 11430; Bachaumont, *Mémoires secrets*, 34:283, 293–94, 297–98, 310–13, 315–16 (March 12, 16, 18, 22, 23, 1787); Barbara Luttrell, *Mirabeau* (Carbondale: Southern Illinois University Press, 1990), 84–86; Robert Lacour-Gayet, *Calonne: Financier, réformateur, contre-révolutionnaire, 1734–1802* (Paris: Hachette, 1963), 214–17.

11. Joseph-Nicolas Barbier-Vémars, *Lettre d'un Anglois à Paris* ("London," 1787); Bachaumont, *Mémoires secrets*, 34:345–46 (April 1, 1787); Quérard, *Les supercheries littéraires dévoilées*, vol. 1, col. 354.

12. "Perquisition chez les libraires au Palais-Royal," April 5, 1787 (Com. Chénon père), AN: Y 11430; Bachaumont, *Mémoires secrets*, 34:343–45, 348–49, 351–52, 359–60 (March 31, April 2, 3, 6, 1787); Lacour-Gayet, *Calonne*, 232–35; Egret, *French Prerevolution*, 22–23; Adolphe Mathurin de Lescure, ed., *Correspondance secrète inédite sur Louis XVI, Marie-Antoinette, la cour et la ville de 1777 à 1792* (Paris: Plon, 1866), 2:125; Charles-Alexandre de Calonne, *Début du discours prononcé par M. le contrôleur-général dans l'Assemblée des notables, le lundi 12 mars 1787* (Versailles: Pierres, 1787); Calonne, *Collection des mémoires présentés à l'Assemblée des notables par M. de Calonne, contrôleur-général des finances* (Versailles: Pierres, 1787), iii–viii; *Extrait de l'avertissement placé à la tête de la collection des mémoires présentés à l'Assemblée des notables* (Versailles: Pierres, 1787).

13. "Perquisition chez la D[e] Vaufleury et autres," August 6, 1787 (Com. Chénon père), AN: Y 11431; "Ing[re] de la F[e] Vaufleury, prisonnière à La Force," August 8, 1787 (Com. Guyot), AN: Y 13579. Born Marie-Françoise Dupressoir, Vaufleury was estranged from her husband, Jean Vaufleury, and sometimes falsely referred to herself as "Veuve" Vaufleury.

14. Egret, *French Prerevolution*, 103; "Procès-verbal de capture et interrogatoire des femmes Goriot et Porcher," September 11, 1787 (Com. Chénon père), AN: Y 11431; "Procès-verbal constatant la capture de la femme Goriot, colporteuse munie d'imprimés sans approbation, et son élargissement," September 11, 1787 (Com. Leroux), AN: Y 14482; "Interrogation et emprisonnement de la Veuve Guillaume, libraire," November 16, 1787 (Com. Chénon père), AN: Y 11431.

15. "Polytype," October 8, 1787 (Com. Chénon père), AN: Y 11431; Bachaumont, *Mémoires secrets*, 36:93 (October 8, 1787); Augustin-Martin Lottin, *Catalogue chronologique des libraires et des libraires-imprimeurs de Paris: Depuis l'an 1470, époque de l'établissement de l'imprimerie dans cette capitale jusqu'à présent* (Paris: Lottin, 1789), part 2, 80, 87.

16. Sarah Maza, *Private Lives and Public Affairs: The Causes Célèbres of Prerevolutionary France* (Berkeley: University of California Press, 1993), 263–311. For documents concerning the suits and countersuits generated by the Kornmann affair, see AN: Y 11604[B] (July 8, August 21, September 17, October 3, 1787); Y 15400 (August 3, 30, 1787); and Y 16002[A] (August 19, September 18, 1787).

17. Jean-Yrieux de Beaupoil, marquis de Saint-Aulaire, *Histoire d'une détention de trente-neuf ans, dans les prisons d'État* (Amsterdam, 1787); Honoré-Gabriel de Riquetti, comte de Mirabeau, *Lettre remise à Frédéric-Guillaume II, roi régnant de Prusse, le jour de son avènement au trône* (Berlin, 1787).

18. "Perquisition chez Denné, Petit, F[e] Vaufleury et saisie de brochures chez les S[rs] Du Senne, Gattey et Devaux au Palais-Royal," June 5, 1788 (Com. Chénon père), AN: Y 11432; "Procès-verbal de perquisition et capture du Sr Lacloye," July 12, 1788 (Com. Chénon père), AN: Y 11433; *Histoire du siège du Palais, par le capitaine d'Agoult, à la tête de six compagnies de Gardes françoises et deux compagnies de Gardes suisses, sous les ordres du maréchal de Biron, ou, Récit de ce qui s'est passé lors de l'enlèvement de Mm. Duval Deprémesnil et Goëslard de Monsabert, conseillers au parlement, siégeans aux chambres assemblées, les pairs séans* (1788); *Mémoire remis à M. le comte de Thiare, le 26 mai 1788, par les membres de la noblesse qui se trouvoient à Rennes, et qui l'a souscrit pour être remis au roi* (1788). On the history of the May edicts, see Egret, *French Prerevolution*, 144–78.

19. "Interrogatoire et emprisonnement des nommés Pajot et Jardin à l'Hôtel de la Force," July 19, 1788, "Procès-verbal de perquisition, interrogatoire et capture de la De Vve Pailly," July 29, 1788, "Procès-verbal de capture et perquisition chez Daguin," August 9, 1788 (Com. Chénon père), AN:

Y 11433; *Mon coup d'œil: Cela tiendra-t-il, cela ne tiendra-t-il pas?* (1788); *Les mânes de Madame la présidente Le Mairat à M. de Lamoignon, quatrième président du Parlement, et Garde des sceaux* (1788).

20. Egret, *French Prerevolution*, 184–90; Hardy, "Mes loisirs," 8:111 (October 10, 1788).

21. Luttrell, *Mirabeau*, 115–16; untitled police report, May 21, 1789 (Com. Chénon fils), AN: Y 11518ᴬ; Mirabeau, *Lettre du comte de Mirabeau à ses commettans: 10 Mai 1789* (1789). I consulted the *Lettre du comte de Mirabeau* at the University of Washington, Seattle, spec. col. 944.04.C834, vol. 1, where it is bound together with both issues of *Etats-Généraux*, dated May 2 and 4 (no. 1), and May 5 (no. 2), 1789.

22. Anonymous to Charles-François du Périer Dumouriez, April 30, 1789, AN: F7 4691, plaq. 7, no. 213.

23. On Sieyes and his influence, see especially William H. Sewell, Jr., *A Rhetoric of Bourgeois Revolution: The Abbé Sieyès and "What Is the Third Estate?"* (Durham: Duke University Press, 1994).

24. Bachaumont, *Mémoires secrets*, 34:132 (February 11, 1787). The *Mémoires secrets* does not give the title of the pamphlet.

25. "Perquisition chez les brocheurs de livres et saisie de brochures," "Perquisition chez les différents libraires," June 10, 1789 (Com. Chénon père), AN: Y 11434; Antoine-Louis-Léon de Saint-Just, *Organt: Poème en vingt chants*, 2 vols. ("Au Vatican," 1789).

26. Mirabeau, *Lettre remise à Frédéric-Guillaume II*, 27–28; Mirabeau, *Sur la liberté de la presse, imité de l'anglois, de Milton* (London, 1788), 1. The text of *Sur la liberté de la presse* is dated December 4, 1788.

27. On the vicomte de Mirabeau's *Lanterne magique*, see Luttrell, *Mirabeau*, 120.

28. Police reports filed by the *commissaires* of the districts and sections of revolutionary Paris are found in series AA at the Archives de la Préfecture de Police (hereafter cited as APP). The earliest reports of book seizures in the district of Saint-Germain-l'Auxerrois/Louvre are dated December 19, 1789. At the district of Saint-Jacques-l'Hôpital, the earliest is January 13, 1790. In March 2008, when I examined the police reports from the Saint-Roch/Palais-Royal district, all those dated 1789 (APP: AA 81, nos. 1–60) were missing from the carton. It was thus impossible to determine whether the first book seizure in the remaining documentation from that district, dated January 30, 1790, was in fact the earliest. APP: AA 178, nos. 184, 185, 187; AA 74, no. 14; AA 81, no. 69. For studies of these documents, see Antoine de Baecque, "Le commerce du libelle interdit à Paris," *XVIIIe siècle: Revue annuelle* 21 (1989): 233–46; and Lise Andries, "Les imprimeurs-libraires parisiens et la liberté de la presse," *XVIIIe siècle: Revue annuelle* 21 (1989): 247–61. More generally on the resurgence of censorship during the Revolution, see Charles Walton, *Policing Public Opinion in the French Revolution: The Culture of Calumny and the Problem of Free Speech* (Oxford: Oxford University Press, 2009).

PART 4

ENLIGHTENMENT IN REVOLUTION

A GRUB STREET HACK GOES TO WAR

David A. Bell

In 1971, Robert Darnton conjured from the archives, in brilliantly vivid prose, the portrait of a peculiar and compelling type of eighteenth-century French-man: the "Grub Street hack" turned radical revolutionary.[1] In some ways, the hack actually seemed more of a nineteenth-century character, for he closely resembled the heroes of more than one canonical nineteenth-century novel, particularly Balzac's *Illusions perdues.* A provincial by birth, the hack dreamed of rising into the firmament of French literary art, and early on succumbed to the intense gravitational pull of Paris, arriving there with dreams of Voltair-ean fame overflowing his meager luggage. Soon enough, however, the harsh realities of Parisian literary life ground away his well-meaning naïveté. Pub-lishers, editors, and the haughty Comédie-Française refused even to glance at his literary effusions. Invitations to elegant salons stubbornly failed to materi-alize. Genius remained unrecognized, disrespected, and penniless. In short, the elegant gates of the republic of letters had slammed in the hack's face. He was left not just hungry and resentful, but also proto-revolutionary. He "hated the Old Regime in [his] guts, ached with hatred of it," as Darnton famously put it.[2] Thus the hack took whatever literary opportunities presented themselves, and they were above all pornographic. Instead of writing stately alexandrines that infused readers' brains with awe of things eternal, he scratched out grubby prose that stimulated a different part of their anatomies with crass evocations of debauch. But wherever he could, he used his writing not merely to keep himself in beggarly food and drink, but also as a vehicle for his resentments.

Whether pornographic or political, this writing depicted the established order as a corrupt, venal sink of disgusting immorality that deserved to be swept away by cleansing waves of political change. Soon enough, of course, those waves arrived, and when they did, the liberty-capped hack swept in on their crests, swelling the chorus of radicalism and gleefully leading those who had once snubbed him up the steps of the guillotine. "It was from such visceral hatred, not from the refined abstractions of the contented cultural elite," Darnton concluded, "that the extreme Jacobin revolution found its authentic voice."[3]

In the years since Darnton's essay appeared, it has received considerable criticism. It has been suggested that to the extent Grub Street hacks existed in eighteenth-century France, they had few political convictions at all, or possibly even conservative ones. It has been proposed that to the extent they did write politically corrosive literature, they did so principally at the behest of highly placed members of the established order, who were pursuing particular vendettas and had no thought of bringing down the entire structure. It has been argued that many of the hacks in question were not actually so hack-like, and that some possessed considerable literary reputations. It has been asked why French hacks should have turned revolutionary when their antecedents in the original, London Grub Street did not. Darnton's identification of the future revolutionary leader Jacques Pierre Brissot as the primus inter pares of hacks has come in for particularly scrutiny.[4] Darnton himself has responded to some of this criticism.[5] In the years since publishing his initial essay, however, he has done relatively little to pursue the line of research opened up by his speculations on the hacks. His subsequent major works—especially *The Forbidden Best-Sellers of Pre-Revolutionary France*—have looked far more closely at the effects of illicit literature on readers than at the sociology and revolutionary careers of its authors.[6]

This change of direction is understandable, for anchoring the "authentic voice" of the Jacobin revolution in any particular prerevolutionary social conjuncture is, by nature, a difficult, perhaps even impossible task. Why should we privilege the literary frustrations of some future Jacobins over the varied professional experiences of many others? Were lawyers like Robespierre, Barère, or Danton, all of them relatively successful before 1789, less authentically Jacobin than their fellow revolutionaries who had descended into Grub Street? And why should we attribute the passions of the Terror to the prerevolutionary experience in particular, as opposed to the ferocious struggles of the Revolution itself, and the traumatic impact of events such as Louis XVI's flight to

Varennes?[7] As historians of the Revolution know, many of the most violent radicals of Year II seemed anything but violent in 1789.

Yet if Grub Street hacks do not hold the single, defining key to understanding the extreme Jacobin revolution, they remain a subject of intrinsic interest, and Darnton deserves enormous credit for bringing them so vividly to his readers' attention. Their experiences need not have been typical to be important. Nor is the extreme Jacobin revolution the only thing their experiences may have been important *to*. Both before and after the French Revolution, the patterns of social mobility and male ambition they sketched out had important effects on many sectors of French society and culture: literature, of course, but also journalism, law, politics, and, more surprisingly from our present-day perspective, the military. In this essay, I will explore these effects by examining the career of a man who not only fit the description of the Grub Street hack, but also might well stand as the Platonic ideal of the type: Charles-Philippe Ronsin.

Ronsin is by no means an unknown. To specialists in the history of the Revolution, he is a familiar if distinctly third-tier figure: a member of the Cordeliers Club and the political faction known as the Hébertistes, and a radical playwright turned war ministry official turned military officer turned commander of the Parisian *armée révolutionnaire*. Half a century ago, General Auguste Herlaut published a lucid, workmanlike biography of Ronsin. The historian Richard Cobb devoted some fine pages to him, as did Morris Slavin. Specialists of the Old Regime do not know him as well, but Gregory Brown has recently revealed a good deal about his career in the theater before 1789.[8] Yet no one has really tried to put the two halves of his life together, or tried to place him in a broader context.

Ronsin was born in Soissons, in 1751, the son of a prosperous master cooper. He most likely attended the town's *collège*. To judge by his later writings, he managed to acquire considerable literary learning. At the age of sixteen, however, he quit school to enlist as a common soldier in the Aunis infantry regiment. He spent four years there, rising to the rank of sergeant, but then left, probably because men from his background had little chance to become officers. For a time, he seemed to have worked as a tutor in a noble household near Nîmes. By the mid-1770s, he had gravitated to Paris, where he tried to set himself up as a playwright.[9]

It is from this point that we can date Ronsin's entry into Grub Street. Between 1776 and 1789, he wrote five plays, which he presented for performance to the Comédie-Française, by law the only venue in the capital for the staging

of French-language drama. The plays had their merits, and at least one—
Sédécias, which dealt with the tragic career of the last king of Judah—had some
fine moments. But despite increasingly desperate efforts, Ronsin did not succeed in having any of the plays actually performed. The Comédiens did accept
one, called *Jeanne d'Arc*, but never scheduled it for production. Ronsin's relations with the Comédie turned steadily more acerbic. At one point, the actress
Françoise Raucourt supposedly offered him 600 livres to withdraw *Jeanne d'Arc*
from the list, just so she would not have to deal with him any further. During
this time, Ronsin did manage to publish three of the plays and a slim volume
of poetry.[10] The literary journalist Charles de Lacretelle remembered him as
a "scrawny author who practiced literary begging."[11]

Ronsin's frustrations with the Comédie certainly did not mark him as a
complete failure or condemn him to a life in the gutter. For a time, he received a small pension from the future duc d'Orléans. Later, he found inter-
mittent employment writing for the boulevard theaters. If the Comédie did
not perform his plays, it at least considered them and recognized him as an
homme de lettres. Still, he complained repeatedly of being "in need," and clearly
felt sharply the theater's rejections.[12] In short, he resembled many of the Grub
Street figures described by Robert Darnton: Moses-like, he came close enough
to the promised land to see its delights, but he never managed to enter. It was
a surefire psychological recipe for alienation, *ressentiment*, and rage. Extant
sources all portray him as something of a human volcano to begin with: phys-
ically large, overbearing, with a deep, raucous voice and a ferocious, easily triggered temper.[13] His repeated literary failures and frustrations clearly intensified
his powerful sense of grievance and his anger.

And Ronsin soon gave these emotions very direct literary expression. In
1786, he composed a violent play titled *Arétaphile*, loosely adapted from Plu-
tarch, about the killing of a tyrant in ancient Libya. It thundered against the
tyrant's skill in preserving the "shadow" of a senate, accused the people of cowardly worshipping the hand that oppressed them, railed against the "prejudice"
suffered by men of low rank, and finished with loud cries for liberty. Under
the Old Regime, it was utterly unperformable and unprintable (it did, however, have a successful run during the Revolution).[14] In the late summer of
1789, he followed it up, anonymously, with a pamphlet called *La ligue aristocratique, ou les Catalinaires françoises*. It was a deeply aggressive, quasi-obscene
attack on Queen Marie Antoinette, which drew on the established repertory
of sexual calumny against her. A typical line reads, "Oui, c'est elle qui . . . se
livre aux danses les plus lascives, c'est elle-même qui s'immole aux deux Vénus,

qui fait . . . des libations à Priape, avec les Énergumènes qu'elle enrôle sous ses drapeaux sanglants" (Yes, it is she who indulges in the most lascivious danc- ing, . . . who sacrifices herself to the two Venuses, who make libations to Pria- pus, along with the helpless creatures who follow her bloody flag). The pamphlet also added a new twist, for Ronsin accused the queen of plotting to poison her husband.[15] As Robert Darnton's critics have established, not all works of this sort necessarily came from frustrated seekers after literary glory, but Ron- sin clearly fits Darnton's model. Repeated frustration and failure had left the man seething with a desire to destroy the regime.

From this point on, Ronsin's career was very much that of an "authentic voice" of the "extreme Jacobin revolution." In 1789, he joined the radical Cor- deliers Club, where he developed ties with Marat, Danton, and many of the future Hébertistes. In the first instance, Ronsin used this new influence to put pressure on the Comédie-Française, warning the troupe of possible violence from the Cordeliers unit of the National Guard if it did not put on a new play of his, one that attempted to capitalize on the success of Joseph-Marie Chénier's *Charles IX* with another politically edged portrait of a French king. The Comédie gave in and performed his cloying drama *Louis XII*. It closed after a single, disastrous performance, and predictably, Ronsin attributed this new failure to a "cabal of aristocrats."[16] But he kept writing, and subsequent plays fared better, especially after the Revolution had eliminated the Comédie- Française's previous monopoly on French-language drama. In June 1791, the Théâtre de Molière staged Ronsin's most successful work, *La ligue des fana- tiques et des tyrans.* An awkward mixture of melodrama, dance, music, and undiluted radicalism, it offered one of the first calls for France to wage a war of liberation on the entire Continent. It was well reviewed and enjoyed a run of several weeks.[17]

But Ronsin soon grew impatient with the theater. He took an increasingly active role in the National Guard and participated in the attack on the Tui- leries Palace in August 1792, afterward publishing a lachrymose eulogy to the *sans-culottes* and *fédérés* who died there.[18] The next month, he stood for elec- tion to the Convention—and lost badly. Danton then wangled him an appoint- ment as a commissioner charged with raising volunteers for the army, and from there he quickly rose to the position of civilian administrator for the entire Armée du Nord. He proved to be a surprisingly efficient administrator but quarreled incessantly with the commanders, particularly Dumouriez. By the winter of 1793, he returned to Paris, working as aide to the radical war min- ister Bouchotte.[19]

Then, in May 1793, Ronsin went on to become a civilian administrator to the Vendée, where the Catholic, royalist rebellion was gaining strength at a frightening pace, posing what seemed like a mortal threat to the Revolution. The revolutionary government's attempts to suppress it were floundering on the reefs of military incompetence and political confusion: army officers, local officials, members of the Convention, and other Parisian officials were all operating independently of one another, and often in conflict with one another.[20] Ronsin himself made this confusion worse by immediately trying to assert control over the military operations, and quickly he came into conflict with army officers on the scene, particularly General Biron. Even as the Republic's ineffective forces piled disaster on disaster, Ronsin and Biron grew obsessed with each other and began a bitter and deadly duel. It was also a highly symbolic one, for Biron was an exquisitely mannered former duke who had once enjoyed a reputation as the greatest rake and seducer in France. In a missive to the Committee of Public Safety, Ronsin denounced Biron for his supposed inertia, hostility to true patriots, "and above all his status of *ci-devant*."[21] The denunciation worked: the committee recalled Biron to Paris, put him on trial, and, at the end of 1793, sent him to the guillotine. Ronsin, meanwhile, earned a handsome reward for his victory over the supposed counterrevolutionaries in his own ranks, if not the real counterrevolutionaries in the field. He was moved from the war ministry into the army itself, his first love. Commissioned a captain on July 1, he then rose successively to the ranks of major, lieutenant colonel, colonel, and brigadier general—all in just four days. Napoleon himself had a slower time of it.[22]

Brigadier general was still not a very high rank, but Ronsin's influence with the war ministry gave him much greater real importance. The *sans-culotte* generals Rossignol and Léchelle, whose political reliability well outstripped their experience and abilities, were widely considered his puppets. One of his theater cronies, the actor François Robert, became chief of staff to General Turreau. So while Ronsin himself left the Vendée department in the early autumn of 1793, he continued to help determine what happened there. In particular, it was François Robert who drew up the notorious plan for sending the "hell columns" to crisscross the Vendée region, which Turreau put into effect with hideous result in the winter and spring of 1793. Incidentally, Turreau would later marry Ronsin's widow (whom he beat, savagely, while serving as Napoleon's ambassador to the United States).[23]

Meanwhile, after the *journée* of September 5, 1793, Ronsin was named commander of the Parisian *sans-culotte armée révolutionnaire*, and so became the leading military figure on the extreme Left of the Revolution. His short career in the position is well-known, thanks to Cobb and Slavin, but it is worth recalling, in particular, his mission to Lyon with Jean-Marie Collot d'Herbois, after the repression of the Federalist Revolt there in the winter of 1793–94.[24] In the city, Ronsin helped organize the notorious mass executions by grapeshot, one of the worst crimes of the Terror. He sent hundreds, perhaps thousands, of prisoners before firing squads. He also wrote a letter back to the Cordeliers Club, which its members printed up as a poster. "The bloodstained Rhône," he declared, "should wash up on its banks, all the way down to the sea, the corpses of those cowards who murdered our brothers. . . . In this town of 120,000 inhabitants, there are . . . scarcely 1,500 men who did not take part in the rebellion."[25] Ronsin had now become not merely an authentic voice of the extreme Jacobin revolution, but also a leading figure of the Terror.

With his letter to the Cordeliers, though, Ronsin made a grave tactical error that would help end his career, for it set him up as an easy target for the emerging faction in the Convention known as the Indulgents, who denounced him as a new Cromwell. As commander of the *armée révolutionnaire*, he did in fact contemplate an insurrection in the winter of 1794, in order to eliminate both the Indulgents and the Robespierristes and bring his own radical faction to power. But he never acted on the idea or entered into any sort of real conspiracy. His opponents acted first. He was imprisoned, then freed, and then arrested again in late winter, after Robespierre intervened decisively against the so-called ultrarevolutionaries. On the sixth of Germinal, Year II, Ronsin went to the guillotine in the company of his allies Hébert, Vincent, and several others.[26]

This, very briefly, is the life of Charles-Philippe Ronsin. What are we to make of it? Most historians who have studied the man have portrayed him as crude, bloodthirsty, and unbalanced—an example of the Revolution at its worst. Slavin judged him most sympathetically, as a committed radical defender of the *sans-culottes*.[27] Cobb, with more nuance, called him a man of integrity but also politically simplistic, violent, and "one of those people who destroy themselves by talking too much."[28] This is a plausible judgment. But if we want a full evaluation of Ronsin, we need to set his revolutionary career alongside his long, frustrating, prerevolutionary struggle to establish himself in the republic of letters. In this context, it becomes clear that Ronsin is, in fact, the perfect example of that species of eighteenth-century Frenchman that Robert Darnton sketched so vividly: the Grub Street hack turned extreme revolutionary.

But there is, perhaps, something more to say about him as well. If there is one quality of Ronsin's to which all contemporary and later observers called attention, it was his ambition. And they largely take this quality for granted, as something timeless and universal—which, in one sense, as evolutionary biologists would undoubtedly tell us, it is. But the form this ambition takes, and the meanings attributed to it, have varied widely between different societies and cultures. Experts on nineteenth-century France, with literary examples like Julien Sorel before them, have recently done interesting work on this subject.[29] But for eighteenth-century France, the subject remains remarkably unexplored, though it has been illuminated by recent work on the history of the "self" by historians like Dror Wahrman, Jan Goldstein, and Jerrold Seigel.[30]

From the point of view of social history, it is clear that the eighteenth century marked a real change in the scope of French male ambitions—female ones as well, but this is a subject that requires separate study. A whole host of factors, including increasing urban wealth, new patterns of consumption and sociability, professionalization, and the transformation of religious belief and observance challenged established notions of civil society as a seamless whole in which each individual had a predetermined, immutable place. In this new world, artisans' sons like Diderot and Rousseau could grow up to become literary celebrities. So why not a cooper's son from Soissons? This change was clearly expressed and recognized in French culture at the time. Consider one serial source, of sorts: collective biographies of "grands hommes de la nation," dozens of which appeared over the course of the eighteenth century, and which generally presented a gallery of men deemed to have given the greatest service to the French nation.[31] In the early decades of the century, the men celebrated in these books hailed almost exclusively from the high nobility and clergy: Bayard, Duguesclin, Sully, and Suger were featured most often. By the 1770s and 1780s, however, the compilers were also honoring authors, artists, scholars, even merchants and bankers, including many men of humble birth. The foremost eulogist of *les grands hommes*, Antoine-Léonard Thomas, could write of one prominent naval hero that "nature did him the favor of bringing him into the world without ancestors."[32] A nice recognition of the legitimacy of ambition—or was it?

In fact, ambition has rarely been a quality much prized, or praised, in French culture. From Pierre Charron in 1601, who defined it as "a gluttonous and excessive desire for greatness," to the nineteenth-century doctors who called it a disease that induced premature aging, it has most often been judged with suspicion.[33] Even the *Encyclopédie* labeled it the "passion that leads us *with excess* to better ourselves."[34] One might also quote perhaps the single foremost expert on the subject from the late eighteenth century, Napoleon Bonaparte, in his 1791 submission to a Lyon essay contest: "Ambition, like all disordered passions, is a violent and unthinking delirium. . . . Like a fire fed by a pitiless wind, it only burns out after having consumed everything in its path."[35]

It is arguable that in some ways, French culture actually saw *greater* suspicion of ambition in the eighteenth century than in any other period—perhaps precisely because of the anxiety generated by the social changes just mentioned, as well as anxieties about the power of the imagination that have been explored recently by Jan Goldstein and Thomas Laqueur.[36] Consider again the evidence of the collective biographies of "great men." Jean-Claude Bonnet shows us that just as the canon of great men broadened out in the eighteenth century, so the criteria for honoring them changed as well. Earlier collections had mostly praised their subjects as "illustrious," a quality associated with great deeds. Eighteenth-century ones preferred "greatness," which they equated largely with virtue: inner qualities of goodness, patriotism, and dedication to duty. If the quintessential "illustrious men" of the age of Louis XIV were military heroes like Bayard, the late eighteenth century preferred supposedly selfless servants of humanity like Fénelon or d'Aguesseau. If worldly success was to come from emulating the subjects of these books, as the authors hoped, then ambitious men faced the paradox of being able to satisfy their ambition only by denying it, by sacrificing themselves to the interests of the *patrie* and humanity.[37]

There was one prominent exception to this rule, one generic figure widely held up for admiration that did not fit into this category of bland virtue. This was the "genius," the figure of *exceptional* imagination, who, as the *Encyclopédie* expressed it, broke rules and laws of taste to "leap to the sublime, the pathetic, the great," and who "seems to change the nature of things." In keeping with the prevailing suspicion of ambition, the author (Jaucourt) could not resist decrying the destructive effects of genius in the realms of politics and war, but he praised them in art and literature.[38] In eighteenth-century France, by far the most significant goad to male ambition was that provided by the example of men who seemed to fill the role of genius and great man simultaneously: above all, Voltaire and Rousseau. Both were praised, not least by themselves, as geniuses who changed the nature of things, but both were also seen (despite abundant evidence to the contrary) as men of great personal virtue and dedicated to the service of humanity.

As Robert Darnton recognized in his early essay, men like Ronsin did not necessarily seek out literary careers because of a particular affinity for literature, but rather because of a more generalized ambition: "To become a Voltaire or d'Alembert, that was the sort of glory to tempt young men on the make."[39] Few other career paths offered young men of low birth and fortune the chance to leap up the social ladder. Literature had its own, complex relationship to Old Regime social hierarchies, and writers could not escape having to negotiate a relationship with worldly society (*le monde*).[40] Yet literary life still offered remarkable mobility to a happy few. No other career path offered young men the same chance to rise quickly to a position of public prominence, or to earn recognition from posterity for "greatness." Few others offered them acknowledgment of the unique, original personal qualities that, as Dror Wahrman has recently argued, drawing on Charles Taylor, were central to new ideas of selfhood.[41] In the late Old Regime, the career of barrister came to offer something of the same quick mobility, and even the same sort of chance for personal expression, thanks to the way political and cultural issues played out in a series of spectacular causes célèbres. But a career at the bar required a law degree and still fell under the control of powerful Orders of Barristers, with the result that many Grub Street figures (Brissot and Linguet, most famously) angrily left the profession.[42]

If late Old Regime literary culture offered young men this quick path to the satisfaction of ambitions, it also, as Darnton noted, threw countless obstacles in their way. And the resulting frustrations could easily lead to rage of the sort that Ronsin poured into his obscene pamphlet against Marie Antoinette and expressed so bloodily in the Vendée and Lyon. Yet the story is more complicated. Ambition did not turn entirely into rage. It did not transform men like Ronsin into nihilists, bent only on destruction. After all, the Jacobins—including men like Ronsin—were motivated by much more than simple hatred of the Old Regime. What happened to ambitions like Ronsin's after the Old Regime had been destroyed? In some ways, the response is obvious. The Revolution opened up, suddenly and dramatically, two vast new fields for ambition, namely, politics and political journalism. But the story of ambition in revolutionary politics is riven by the same paradox I have described for the prerevolutionary period: the more scope that opened up for ambition, the more ambition was denounced and condemned. Few revolutionary epithets were as wounding as that of "ambitieux," few accusations more deadly than that of having excessive aspirations. It is no surprise that the history of the Revolution is littered, both figuratively and literally, with the bodies of the ambitious. It is no surprise that Maximilien Robespierre rose to the heights of French revolutionary politics precisely by presenting his own self as "incorruptible" and wholly dissolved into the greater cause of the people—by struggling, for a time quite successfully, to appear as a man without personal ambition.

But the Revolution did offer another path for ambition, and this was the military. Indeed, where the military was concerned, the Convention in 1793/94 effectively renounced and overturned the Enlightenment preference for inner virtue over great deeds, and tried to redefine the canon of national heroes yet again. This shift is evident in the title of the popular newspaper published by Bourdon, *Collection of Heroic and Civic Actions of French Republicans*, whose print runs ranged from 80,00 to a spectacular 150,000, and which focused on particular deeds more than general virtue.[43] It is evident in the steady parade of war heroes, many of them gruesomely wounded, across the floor of the Convention.[44] It is evident, above all, in the extraordinary rewards and promotions lavished on successful officers: consider Hoche, Marceau, and Bonaparte, who were all made generals at age twenty-four. In this one realm, then, the Revolution positively encouraged male ambition, while also redefining it, making military success less a matter of aristocratic performance than of romantic self-expression.

For this reason, Charles-Philippe Ronsin does not just provide an excellent example of the dynamics of the prerevolutionary Grub Street; he also illuminates these rapidly shifting channels of revolutionary culture. In 1789, he did not give up his dream of theatrical success; indeed, he achieved it, thanks to the help of political pressure from his Cordelier allies. But by 1792, he saw that the opening up of new fields of ambition was discounting the value of the old ones. The age of the philosophes was over. So despite his success, Ronsin turned restless. He thought of politics but could not win election to the Convention. And in any case, as early as August 18, 1792, he was already referring to himself in speeches as a "soldier," in reference to his service in the National Guard.[45] This was where his ambitions now returned: the sergeant of 1771 became the general of 1793. But he did not entirely renounce his previous literary achievements. Charles Lacretelle recalled that one evening, when his revolutionary bona fides were challenged in the revolutionary committee of his Paris section, Ronsin did not recall his deeds on behalf of the Revolution, but rather recited scenes from his tragedies.[46] Nonetheless, his ambitions had fundamentally shifted.

He was not the only one who followed this path. Today, we tend to think of literary and military ambitions as very different species of desire, but in the eighteenth century they fit together much more closely. Choderlos de Laclos, Lambert, and Sade are just three of the more prominent French literary figures from the period who also had military backgrounds. Consider the mixture of literary and military enthusiasm that is so visible in the young Stendhal. Or consider the backgrounds of men like Marshal Gouvion Saint-Cyr, a struggling artist before the Revolution, or Marshal Guillaume Brune, a failed poet, printer's assistant, and another Grub Street hack of sorts. And think, above all, of a certain young artillery officer who, before the Revolution, himself contemplated life as a philosophe. He corresponded with Raynal, submitted essays to competitions, took copious notes on Montesquieu and Rousseau, and wrote drafts of stories, philosophical dialogues, political treatises, and historical essays: none other than Napoleon himself. Where Charles-Philippe Ronsin failed, Napoleon succeeded, and in doing so, transformed our understanding of ambition forever.[47]

NOTES

1. Robert Darnton, "The High Enlightenment and the Low-Life of Literature," in *The Literary Underground of the Old Regime* (Cambridge: Harvard University Press, 1982), 1–40. The essay originally appeared in *Past and Present* 51 (May 1971): 81–115.

2. Ibid., 40.

3. Ibid.

4. See particularly Jeremy Popkin, "Pamphlet Journalism at the End of the Old Regime," *Eighteenth-Century Studies* 22, no. 3 (1989): 351–67; Frederick A. de Luna, "The Dean Street Style of Revolution: J.-P. Brissot, *Jeune Philosophe*," *French Historical Studies* 17, no. 1 (Spring 1991): 159–99; Elizabeth Eisenstein, "Grub Street Abroad," in *Grub Street Abroad: Aspects of the French Cosmopolitan Press from the Age of Louis XIV to the French Revolution* (Oxford: Clarendon Press, 1992), 131–63; Darrin M. McMahon, "The Counter-Enlightenment and the Low-Life of Literature in Pre-Revolutionary France," *Past and Present* 159 (May 1998): 77–112; Leonore Loft, *Passion, Politics, and Philosophie: Rediscovering J.-P. Brissot* (Westport, Conn.: Greenwood Press, 2002); and Simon Burrows, *Blackmail, Scandal, and Revolution: London's French Libellistes, 1758–92* (New York: Manchester University Press, 2006). See also the essays in Haydn Mason, ed., *The Darnton Debate: Books and Revolution in the Eighteenth Century* (Oxford: Voltaire Foundation, 1998), especially those by Jeremy Popkin, Elizabeth Eisenstein, and Daniel Gordon.

5. Robert Darnton, "The Brissot Dossier," *French Historical Studies* 17, no. 1 (Spring 1991): 200–218; Robert Darnton, "J.-P. Brissot and the Société typographique de Neufchâtel (1779–1787)," *Studies on Voltaire and the Eighteenth Century* 10 (2001): 26–50.

6. Robert Darnton, *The Forbidden Best-Sellers of Pre-Revolutionary France* (New York: W. W. Norton, 1995). Darnton recently focused on one author, Anne Gédéon Lafitte, marquis de Pelleport, in *Bohemians Before Bohemianism* (Wassenaar, The Netherlands: NIAS, 2006).

7. See Timothy Tackett, *When the King Took Flight* (Cambridge: Harvard University Press, 2003).

8. Gregory Brown, *A Field of Honor: Writers, Court Culture, and Public Theater in French Literary Life from Racine to the Revolution* (New York: Columbia University Press, 2005); Richard Cobb, *The People's Armies: The Armees Revolutionnaires, Instrument of the Terror in the Departments, April 1793 to Floreal Year II*, trans. Marianne Elliott (1961; trans. New Haven: Yale University Press, 1987); Auguste-Philippe Herlaut, *Le général rouge Ronsin (1751–1794): La Vendée, l'armée révolutionnaire parisienne* (Paris: Clavreuil, 1956); Morris Slavin, *The Hébertistes to the Guillotine: Anatomy of a "Conspiracy" in Revolutionary France* (Baton Rouge: Louisiana State University Press, 1994).

9. See Herlaut, *Le général rouge Ronsin*, 3–13.

10. See Brown, *Field of Honor*, chap. 6; and Herlaut, *Le général rouge Ronsin*, 3–13. Ronsin's plays were published as *Théâtre de M. Ronsin* (Paris: Cailleau, 1786). See also Ronsin, *La mort de Maximilien Jules Léopold, duc de Brunswick-Lunebourg, poème* (Paris: Royez, 1787).

11. Quoted in Herlaut, *Le général rouge Ronsin*, 210.

12. Ibid., 5–7; Brown, *Field of Honor*, chap. 6; Cobb, *People's Armies*, 62.

13. See discussion in Herlaut, *Le général rouge Ronsin*, 3–13.

14. Charles-Philippe Ronsin, *Arétaphile, ou la révolution de Cyrène* (Paris: Guillaume, 1793), 4, 9, 43, 71. The title page claimed that the play was composed in 1786, but it was almost certainly rewritten before its first performance in 1792 and its first printing in 1793. Notably, the heroine states at its conclusion, "Je meurs en citoyenne," whereas the word "citoyenne" was unknown before 1789.

15. [Charles-Philippe Ronsin], *La ligue aristocratique, ou les Catalinaires françoises* (Paris: Josseran, 1789), 9–10. On the demonization of Marie Antoinette, see Darnton's "High Enlightenment" and *Forbidden Best-Sellers*; Chantal Thomas, *La reine scélérate: Marie-Antoinette dans les pamphlets* (Paris: Seuil, 1989); Lynn Hunt, *The Family Romance of the French Revolution* (Berkeley: University of California Press, 1992); and the essays in Dena Goodman, ed., *Marie Antoinette: Writings on the Body of a Queen* (New York: Routledge, 2003).

16. Herlaut, *Le général rouge Ronsin*, 9; Brown, *Field of Honor*, chap. 6.

17. Charles-Philippe Ronsin, *La ligue des fanatiques et des tyrans: Tragédie nationale* (Paris: Guillaume, 1791); Herlaut, *Le général rouge Ronsin*, 12.

18. Charles-Philippe Ronsin, *Discours prononcé par Ch. Ph. Ronsin, le 18 août 1792 à la section du Théâtre François à l'occasion de la cérémonie funèbre ordonnée en l'honneur de nos frères d'armes morts à la journée du 10, pour la défense de la liberté et de l'égalité* (Paris: Pougin, 1792).

19. See Herlaut, *Le général rouge Ronsin*, 16–68.

20. See David A. Bell, *The First Total War: Napoleon's Europe and the Birth of Warfare as We Know It* (Boston: Houghton Mifflin, 2007), 175–78.

21. Ibid., 87–112; quote from Gaston Maugras, *The Duc de Lauzun and the Court of Marie-Antoinette* (London: Osgood, McIlvaine, 1896), 453. See also Bell, *First Total War*, 175–78.

22. Herlaut, *Le général rouge Ronsin*, 102.

23. Bell, *First Total War*, 175–78; "Trivia," *William and Mary Quarterly*, 3rd series, 9, no. 4 (1954): 633–34.

24. Cobb, *People's Armies*, and Slavin, *The Hébertistes to the Guillotine*.

25. Quoted in Herlaut, *Le général rouge Ronsin*, 184.

26. See Cobb, *People's Armies*, 567–617, and Herlaut, *Le général rouge Ronsin*, 180–261.

27. Slavin, *The Hébertistes to the Guillotine*.

28. Cobb, *People's Armies*, 573.

29. See especially Kathleen Kete, "Stendhal and the Trials of Ambition in Postrevolutionary France," *French Historical Studies* 28, no. 3 (2005): 467–95; and Kete's forthcoming book on the subject.

30. Jan Goldstein, *The Post-Revolutionary Self: Politics and Psyche in France, 1750–1850* (Cambridge: Harvard University Press, 2005); Jerrold Seigel, *The Idea of the Self: Thought and Experience in Western Europe Since the Seventeenth Century* (Cambridge: Cambridge University Press, 2005); Dror Wahrman, *The Making of the Modern Self: Culture and Identity in Eighteenth-Century England* (New Haven: Yale University Press, 2005).

31. On this subject, see David A. Bell, *The Cult of the Nation in France: Inventing Nationalism, 1680–1800* (Cambridge: Harvard University Press, 2001), 107–39.

32. Antoine-Léonard Thomas, "Eloge de Duguay-Trouin," in René Duguay-Trouin, *Mémoires de M. Duguay-Trouin, lieutenant général des armées navales* (Rouen, 1785), 275.

33. Pierre Charron, *De la sagesse, trois livres* (1601; repr., Paris: Chaignieau Aîné, 1797), 135; Kete, "Stendhal and the Trials of Ambition in Postrevolutionary France," 468–69.

34. Denis Diderot and Jean Le Rond d'Alembert, eds., *Encyclopédie, ou dictionnaire raisonné des sciences, des arts et des métiers*, 16 vols. (Paris: Briasson, 1751–65), sv "Ambition," accessed July 10, 2009, at http://artfl.uchicago.edu/cgi-bin/philologic31/getobject.pl?c.2:562.encyclopedie1108.

35. Napoléon Bonaparte, *Œuvres littéraires et écrits militaires*, ed. Jean Tulard (Paris: Claude Tchou, 2001), 1:227.

36. Goldstein, *Post-Revolutionary Self*; Thomas Laqueur, *Solitary Sex: A Cultural History of Masturbation* (New York: Zone Books, 2003).

37. Jean-Claude Bonnet, *Naissance du Panthéon: Essai sur le culte des grands hommes* (Paris, 1998).

38. Diderot and d'Alembert, *Encyclopédie*, sv "Génie," accessed July 10, 2009, at http://artfl.uchicago.edu/cgi-bin/philologic31/getobject.pl?c.52:146.encyclopedie1108.

39. Darnton, "High Enlightenment," 3.

40. See Brown, *Field of Honor*; and Antoine Lilti, *Le monde des salons: Sociabilité et mondanité à Paris au XVIIIe siècle* (Paris: Fayard, 2005).

41. Wahrman, *Making of the Modern Self*; Charles Taylor, *Sources of the Self: The Making of the Modern Identity* (Cambridge: Harvard University Press, 1989).

42. See David A. Bell, *Lawyers and Citizens: The Making of a Political Elite in Old Regime France* (New York: Oxford University Press, 1994).

43. [Thomas Rousseau, et al.], *Recueil des actions héroïques et civiques des Républicains français*, 5 issues (Paris, 1793–94). See Dominique Julia, *Les trois couleurs du tableau noir* (Paris: Belin, 1981), 208–13.

44. See Antoine de Baecque, *The Body Politic: Corporeal Metaphor in Revolutionary France, 1770–1800*, trans. Charlotte Mandell (Stanford: Stanford University Press, 1997), 280–308.

45. Ronsin, *Discours prononcé*, 3.

46. Herlaut, *Le général rouge Ronsin*, 210.

47. On the question of military and literary ambitions in the eighteenth century, see Bell, *First Total War*, 26–27, 201–7.

NINE

READING *IN EXTREMIS:*
REVOLUTIONARIES RESPOND TO ROUSSEAU

Carla Hesse

> One might count the number of references to Rousseau; but would such a count serve to weigh the influence of Rousseau on the [Jacobin] clubs?
> —CRANE BRINTON, *The Jacobins: An Essay in the New History*

Concerning the Jacobin Republic, the eminent American historian Robert R. Palmer wrote in 1941, "The new state, so far as it came from books, was to draw its inspiration from *The Social Contract.*"[1] This essay addresses the parenthetical, "so far as it came from books" part of this statement. Studies of the influence of Rousseau's thought on all aspects of the French Revolution—politics, law, civic ritual, and social moeurs—are too numerous to cite in their entirety. There were already at least three hundred works—taking into account only those written in French—devoted to Rousseau and his ideas published during the revolutionary decade (1789–99) alone.[2] A full bibliographic survey of such studies up to the present would run into the multiple thousands. More important, Palmer's 1941 thesis (already heir to a distinguished nineteenth-century lineage) has been reinvigorated in recent years by a generation of scholars in the orbit of Keith Michael Baker and the late François Furet. And it is generally accepted, now as much as then, that Rousseau (and above all *The Social Contract*) "wrote the script" (Keith Baker's formulation) of the Revolution, or at least the Jacobin version of it.[3] My question concerning the Jacobins and Rousseau, then, is not "What did they learn from Rousseau?" (I take this question to have been sufficiently answered; in short, almost everything), but rather "How so?" What I am proposing, to put it otherwise, is a phenomenological, as opposed to a hermeneutical, approach to the problem of revolutionary reading practices, and in particular, the revolutionary practices of reading Rousseau.

Let me observe from the outset that the compatibility of reading and rev-olution is not self-evident, and that of reading Rousseau and revolution even less so. The man who made the greatest leap forward for interiority since Augustine of Hippo, and who (along with Diderot) essentially invented mod-ern self-reflexivity, though very partial to the emphatic, was not at all at home in the imperative. As Robert Darnton so vividly recaptured in his remarkable essay "Readers Respond to Rousseau," Rousseau, above all other French phi-losophes, was not only the author of the most widely read books of the late eighteenth-century philosophical canon (*La Nouvelle Héloïse* and *Émile*); he was, through these works, also the inventor of a new form of intensive read-ing—the rhetorical construction of a private communion between two indi-vidual souls through the fulcrum of a published text.[4] As Darnton observes, it was the *Nouvelle Héloïse* that most exemplified this new form of intimate com-munion between reader and writer: "It is thus that the heart speaks to the heart," Saint-Preux writes to Julie.[5] This idealized figuration of intensive, private read-ing was elsewhere more systematically elaborated and advocated by Rousseau as a path to moral regeneration. "In moral matters," Rousseau states, "I hold that there is no reading that can be of use to socialites [*gens du monde*]. . . . The further one moves away from business, big cities, crowded social gather-ings, the more the obstacles [to effective reading] diminish. At a certain point, books can have some usefulness. When one lives alone, one does not hurry through books in order to parade one's reading. One varies them less and med-itates on them more. And as their effect is less mitigated by outside influ-ences, they have greater influence within."[6] And this was not merely a theory espoused by Rousseau. As Darnton shows, readers of Rousseau came to feel an intimate connection to the author that was without equal among contem-porary writers. In hundreds of letters sent to the author, they poured out their feelings of devotion and admiration for his works, and they sought his advice for the most personal of their struggles. Rousseau's contemporaries—Chardin and Fragonard, most famously—visually elevated this form of intensive, roman-tic reading to iconic status.[7] And so the question: What happened to these solitary, Rousseauist reading practices after 1789?

First, the most obvious change: Reading Rousseau as a revolutionary (rather than as a prerevolutionary, Enlightenment dissident) meant reading him in public rather than in private—that is, it meant bringing Rousseau out of the literary underground where his works had circulated under the Old Regime, and exposing him to the light of day—testifying to him and claiming his pres-ence. It also meant reading him collectively rather than in solitude.

A. Duplessis, *La Révolution française*, ca. 1790 (detail). Photo: Musée de la Révolution française, Vizille, France

The Paris publisher Claude Poinçot rose to the task of making Rousseau public with remarkable alacrity—and entrepreneurial savoir faire—in the wake of the Bastille's fall on July 14, 1789, by demanding immediate restitution from the Paris Commune of his edition of Rousseau's *Oeuvres complètes* that had been "embastillée" before 1789.[8] And with equal strategic acuity, he promptly donated a copy of the edition to the newly constituted French National Assembly.[9] After 1789, editions of Rousseau's works—large and small, complete, individual, and selected, lavish and modest—flooded the nation. There were at least as many copies of *The Social Contract* published in the decade of the Revolution as there had been in the twenty-five years preceding it.[10] I have been able to identify forty-four separate editions of *The Social Contract* published between 1789 and 1799, and the number of copies of Rousseau's works, more generally, published in some form or another over the revolutionary decade ran into the hundreds of thousands.[11] Several grand editions of Rousseau's *Oeuvres complètes* consecrated his works as a summa of modernity, but more novel were the rapidly multiplying and increasingly modest editions of *The Social Contract* in small format—the original "little red book"—and the many abridgements of his words and ideas into simple maxims for everyday life.

The burgeoning Jacobin clubs and popular societies of 1789–91 made a natural home for these editions, not least because, as Michael Kennedy has shown, a large share of the revolutionary clubs were in fact reincarnations of the literary societies and backroom *cabinets de lecture* of the Old Regime.[12] What remains of their subscription lists and loan books amply attest to the presence of the citizen of Geneva in their libraries and reading rooms. Many revolutionary clubs held weekly study groups, seminars, and short courses, most famously the one led by Claude Fauchet at the Société des amis de la vérité in Paris on *The Social Contract* and *Émile*.[13] Jacobin clubs throughout France regularly gave away copies of *The Social Contract* as prizes in essay competitions and in recognition of acts of exceptional civic virtue.[14]

The educated revolutionaries had, almost to a person, read some Rousseau before the Revolution. But after 1789, encounters with Rousseau's texts, in fact, occurred *least* frequently through reading books (even those by Jean-Jacques), which, as Brissot famously put it later, "no one had time to read."[15] The well-documented explosion of the periodical press and political ephemera after 1789 makes clear that the most *revolutionary* modes of textuality were anti-bibliographic at heart.[16] Thus Camille Desmoulins reminded some of his more elitist comrades in the Paris Jacobin Club in 1791 that the Revolution may have been prepared by "a path that had been cleared by Mably and Rousseau, but [it] had been made by these three words alone: con artist, aristocrat, and lynching."[17] And therein lay the challenge to revolutionary Rousseauism: to transform the "first author of the French Revolution," as Louis-Sébastien Mercier had dubbed him, from a bookish philosophe into a revolutionary propagandist.[18]

The solution, to borrow from the Italian literary scholar Armando Petrucci, lay in the translation of Rousseau's texts from bibliographic into epigraphic forms.[19] And the epigraphic meant, first and foremost, the epigrammatic— *sloganizing*. The opening phrase of book 1, chapter 1 of *The Social Contract*— "Man is born free . . ."—rapidly appeared as an epigrammatic devise on everything from revolutionary identity cards, processional banners, and public podia to paper money and festive altars. The Cordeliers Club, the most popular and radical of the Paris revolutionary clubs, published excerpts of the *Considérations sur le gouvernement de Pologne* in broadside form and plastered them throughout the capital in December 1790.[20] The Jacobin Club of Paris lent its support to one of its members' proposal that "Platière Street should be renamed J.-J. Rousseau Street, because then sensitive hearts and ardent souls can invoke in their minds, while crossing this street, that Rousseau lived here." Through an ensuing series of acts of renaming the city streets, Charles Villette imagined that "Paris, from one end to the other, will be blazoned with the great book of the Rights of Man."[21] The capital was to become a book, and the text to be read from it was Rousseau.

The apogee of the epigraphic Rousseau came with his apotheosis: the reburial of his remains in the Pantheon on October 11, 1794. In the wake of that great festival in Paris, provincial cities followed suit, and the Committee of Public Safety paid special attention, through its representatives on mission, to the festival in Lyon two days later.[22] Here, Rousseau's apotheosis was of particular political sensitivity because it became the occasion to restore both the name of Lyon to the once-rebel city and full political and civil rights to its citizens. Nonetheless, the Lyon festival followed a formula that had been carefully orchestrated in Paris and adapted to local circumstances throughout France. In Lyon, the ceremonial cortege was assembled as follows: "A group of young men, under a banner that read, 'He gave us *Émile* as a model.' A group of young girls, under a banner where it was written, 'You see among you the candor of Sophie.' A group of mothers nursing their children, under a banner bearing these words: 'He restored women to their duties and happiness to children.'" These were to be followed by a group of Lyonnais who had met the great man, a group of citizens of Geneva, and not least, a group of city fathers, artists, and public officials, "in the midst of whom was carried in full pomp and circumstance the book of *The Social Contract* from which the following words have been extracted and emblazoned on a banner above: 'Man is born free. To remove his freedom is to renounce his humanity, his right to humanity, and his duty to be human.'"[23] The text was thus literally extracted from the book and displayed above it, in order to be read publicly and collectively, rather than individually and privately.

The cortege processed to the peninsula formed by the confluence of the Rhône and the Saône Rivers, where a simulacra of the island tomb of Rousseau at Emmenonville, replete with a draping willow, had been set up as the site for a statue of the philosophe embracing two adoring children with one arm and bearing a "tablet of the laws" (presumably the Declaration of Rights) in the other.[24] In his appreciation of Rousseau as the first author of the French Revolution, Mercier had applauded the absence of epigrams in Rousseau's writings—the epigram of the Old Regime smacked of learned affect, artificial cleverness, and elitism.[25] But the epigraphic mode of the Republic demanded epigrams, and revolutionary textual editing, epigraphy, and oratory produced just that. As Jean-Jacques Régis de Cambacérès intoned to the crowd gathered at the Pantheon to celebrate the apotheosis in October 1795, "The essence of his immortal writings is found in this maxim: Reason deceives us more often than nature."[26]

The revolutionary reading of Rousseau after 1789 was not only a public and a collective affair—it was a profession of faith to the brethren and an act of proselytizing to the unconverted, and thus it was, above all, out loud, à haute voix. When Camille Desmoulins famously harangued the crowd in the Palais Royal on July 12, 1789, it was said that he read to them from Rousseau. The national deputy Claude Fauchet read him aloud to enraptured audiences at his revolutionary seminars.[27] Throughout France, members of popular societies were treated to regular disquisitions by the professors among them on the lessons of the master.[28] And remaining records indicate that Rousseau was widely invoked and quoted by even the most modest of speakers at popular societies in the smallest of villages.[29]

The invocation of Rousseau, in both speech and writing, came to have a kind of talismanic effect. On formal ceremonial occasions and in official trans-actions, he was "J.-J. Rousseau." But in everyday speech, he alone among the philosophes was referred to by his first name—and this public profession of intimacy with "Jean-Jacques" was the sign of a true disciple, the citizen who not only had read Rousseau, but also had taken him into his heart. Invocation functioned as a password among strangers and legitimated a speaker among friends. The members of the Committee of Public Safety noted, for example, that Citizen Billard, a lowly volunteer in the Army of the Rhine and Moselle, declared "himself to be a disciple Jean-Jacques Rousseau" when seeking a private audience with the representative on mission in his letter to the committee.[30]

There was invocation of the man, and then, most important, there was citation from the texts—everywhere—in the debates of the National Assem-bly and the Convention, in sectional meetings and popular societies, and in petitions to local and national authorities.[31] But the citation of authority was more than talismanic. Over the course of debates in the Jacobin Club of Paris between 1791 and 1794, the question of revolutionary hermeneutics—of how to get the text right—reared its head and provoked sustained discussion about the virtues and limits of reading Rousseau in times of Revolution. Three de-bates were key: (1) those over the first law against the emigration (February 28, 1791; December 12, 1791); (2) those over federalism (September 10, 1792); and (3) those over purging moderate Dantonists (January 7, 1794).

In his coverage of the debate in the Jacobin Club on February 28, 1791, in his *Révolutions de France et de Brabant*, Camille Desmoulins reported one Citizen Duport's denunciation of the liberal aristocratic deputy Mirabeau as a traitor, because of his opposition in the National Assembly to a law pro-posed by Le Chapelier against emigration in the wake of the departure of the

Mesdames de France (the king's aunts). Desmoulins speculated, cynically, that Le Chapelier had presented the law against his own conscience, and that he, along with a third deputy, Demeunier, had secretly conspired with Mirabeau to subvert the law. Desmoulins imagined the following secret conversation for his readers:

> —*Deputy Le Chapelier*: Have you forgotten that J.-J. Rousseau says that in moments of trouble emigration can be outlawed?
> —*Deputy Demeunier*: To be honest, Rousseau's authority really isn't that great. But since you sponsored the law, you will be compromised if you now oppose it. Let's turn to Mirabeau . . .
> —*Deputy Mirabeau*: Okay, my dear Chapelier; I'll try to save you from embarrassment by opposing the law. I'll say that it is detestable and atrocious. Some will cite *The Social Contract* in support of it, but I will respond with a letter I wrote to the king of Prussia. In truth, my authority isn't that great, but reputation isn't like a bad law on emigration—mine has a retroactive effect.[32]

By 1791, cynicism about the authority of Rousseau was already profound. More interesting, however, are the multiple plays on the liberal doctrine of the non-retroactivity of the law and the retroactive authority of Mirabeau's letter. Mirabeau, in this imagined scene, and Desmoulins, as its author, are both aware that the lesser philosophe (Mirabeau) has, through his revolutionary deeds, accrued greater retroactive textual authority than the greater philosophe and first author of the French Revolution, Rousseau, who has played no living role in the revolutionary events.

The problem of reading and interpreting Rousseau became a question of assessing the status and authority of textual models in a moment that revolutionaries increasingly recognized to be without precedent. Could there be a script for a "scriptless" event? Louis-Sébastien Mercier certainly thought so in 1789, and he continued to believe so at least until 1791, when he published his famous, two-volume *De J.-J. Rousseau, considéré comme l'un des premiers auteurs de la Révolution*.[33]

But with the fall of the monarchy in August 1792, reading Rousseau as a script for the Revolution became increasingly problematic. In the session of the Jacobin Club of September 10, 1792, Citizen Terrasson gave the following speech: "In this moment, when the National Convention is turning its attention to the means of giving France the best possible form of government, it is the duty of every good citizen to lend the nation whatever enlightenment he possesses. For my part, having studied the truths to be grasped in Jean-Jacques concerning the different forms of government, I request that we debate the following question: What is the best means of perfecting a federalist form of government?"[34] Objection was raised immediately that the speaker had pre-judged the question in favor of federalism. Why not simply set the question as follows: "What form of government is best suited to France?" Terrasson replied, "I don't know what objection one can raise to the philosopher Jean-Jacques when he explicitly states in his *Considérations sur le gouvernement de Pologne* that the federal form of government is the only form suited to people united in a large empire." To which, another member (unnamed in the record) responded, "I request that in entering into this discussion we resolve to rely first and foremost on our own experience, on the knowledge that four years of revolution to those of us capable of reflection, rather than on the authority of a philosopher, however great he may be."[35]

The debate escalated over the value of precedents. An unnamed member opined that the Revolution had broken with the past and that no script, even one taken from Rousseau, should be blindly followed. The club should debate what is best for France "in the present moment." Another observed that it is dangerous to reason from present circumstances alone; models are important when one hopes to create a new government not only for the present: "It is necessary to act in light of the future, in light of eternity, if possible."[36] He was rejoined by yet another (unnamed) deputy, who repeated that it was better to find a good government "without citing authorities against the facts." If we were to use only Rousseau as a guide, "the aristocracy could easily find in his works citations that they can quote to their advantage." Finally, M. Camille intervened: "[Rousseau] also said that the only way to liberate a great empire is to burn a capital city as great as Paris. And so I ask you, messieurs, do you want to burn Paris?"[37] With this, the conversation ended. If Rousseau had written a script for the Revolution, by the time that the National Convention convened in October 1792, no Jacobin believed he was following it. And this is why, a bit more than a year later, when Robespierre ordered the destruction of Desmoulins's printing presses, the journalist's famous response—"Well done Robespierre, but I respond with Rousseau—to burn is not to answer—could not save him."[38] The Rousseauist text had already been burned, or at least laid to the wayside, in order to save the capital.

Lionello Strozzi, in his study of counterrevolutionary uses of Rousseau, per-ceptively noted that—albeit with some notable exceptions—counterrevolu-tionary Rousseauists were the more careful textualists; their citations were more exact, they footnoted, and they did so accurately.[39] The Jacobins, by contrast, were prone to paraphrase, to tailoring Rousseau's concepts and ideas to the immediate context without respect for his exact wording (as in the speech by Cambacérès at the Pantheon, quoted above). Accordingly, not one of the citations from the debate above can be found in Rousseau's works. But it is equally true that the careful textualism of the counterrevolutionaries did not produce the most faithful reading of Jean-Jacques.

It was a problem, as Antoine Lilti has recently observed, that Rousseau, especially in *Juge de Jean-Jacques*, anticipated only too fully. The problem with texts is that they can be readily manipulated by readers and put to nefarious purposes. "Do you know how much they can be disfigured?," Rousseau asked. "All these collections—expanded by insulting criticisms, venomous libels, and crafted for the unique purpose of disfiguring the author's production, altering his maxims and changing their spirit little by little—have been falsified with great artistry to that end."[40] For Rousseau, the happiest examples of reading his works were those where he read the works aloud, face-to-face with his audience—a scene such as he describes at the end of the *Nouvelle Héloïse*. This kind of sentimental communion gave readers direct access to the author's sentiments and, in turn, gave the author control over the effects produced by his words. Things were otherwise in the world of print, where readers were strangers and perhaps enemies.

Counterrevolutionaries were exactly these kinds of bad-faith readers. They may have been more faithful to the word, but they betrayed the spirit, taking citations out of context, pedantically twisting meanings, and over-reading the parts instead of taking in the whole: Rousseau the monarchist, Rousseau the federalist, Rousseau the defender of religious orthodoxy. Counterrevolutionaries reasoned; revolutionaries drew on their natural moral sentiments. Cambacérès had gotten it exactly right: "The essence of his immortal writings is found in this maxim: Reason deceives us more often than nature."[41]

Thus we may speak of a revolutionary hermeneutics of reading Rousseau. To cite the text exactly was to keep the text at a distance, to make oneself master over it. To paraphrase, by contrast, was to be mastered by it, to internalize the text, and to let its meaning speak through one's own words. Far from sloppiness or usurpation, it was an act of letting the text shape the speaker. To paraphrase was to embody the spirit of the author—to bring Rousseau back to life. For the truly revolutionary reader, it was not a question of what Rousseau *had* said, but rather what Rousseau *might have said* were he here. In their oration at the festival for the apotheosis of Rousseau at the Pantheon, the delegates of the Paris Jacobins thus described themselves as "sectarians, professors, and *elaborators* of the doctrines of the immortal Jean-Jacques."[42] With Rousseau no longer living, the only faithful reader was the reader who *became*—rather than interpreted—him.

This distinction between revolutionary and nonrevolutionary styles of reading Rousseau—between paraphrasing and citation; between empathetic, sentimental enactment and exact reference—was precisely the one that Georges Auguste Couthon, the most ruthless of Jacobins, tried to get at in his crucial May 1794 speech announcing the Committee of Public Safety's embrace of the Cult of the Supreme Being. "True Jacobins," he wrote, "are those who profess out loud his principles; principles that should not be regarded as religious dogma, but rather as social sentiments, without which, Jean-Jacques said it is impossible to be a good citizen."[43]

This sentimental Rousseauist communitarianism was no mere figment of the Parisian Jacobin's imagination: it was the lifeblood of Republic.[44] As a representative of the popular society Section de la Fontaine-de-Grenelle in the Auxerre put it, well before Couthon, "The true patriot keeps nothing to himself. He shares everything with the community: his pleasures, his unhappy feelings. Everything is delivered into the hearts of his brothers. This is the kind of public life that distinguishes fraternal—which is to say, republican—government."[45] Revolutionary reading was orthopractic. Through empathetic public enactment of the spirit, rather than the word, came regeneration of both self and society. This is why a delegate from the Jacobin Club in Bordeaux, upon arrival at the mother club in Paris, explained that his report on the state of the countryside should carry weight because "I traveled to do this as Jean-Jacques would have—that is, on foot."[46] It was not enough to read the words; the true citizen inhabited them.

Silent, solitary, romantic readers of the sort that Robert Darnton uncovered in his study of Rousseau's fan mail could, of course, be found in France at the height of the Terror—in prison, in hiding, or in exile. Madame Roland turned back to the *Nouvelle Héloïse*, yet again, while awaiting the guillotine.[47] The abbé Sieyès not only "lived" through the Terror, according to his shoemaker, he read his way through it.[48] In that year, Madame de Staël, too, dug deep into renewed study of the Genevan philosophe with her coterie in Coppet.[49] These dissident Rousseau readers of the Revolution indelibly marked solitary reading practices with their darker cast of mind for the century to come.[50] But the revolutionary reader of Rousseau was a creature of another order. Through epigraphy, epigram, paraphrasis, and orthopraxis, Rousseau's works saturated both the body and the world—the citizen and the nation. The Revolution thereby transformed reading Rousseau, albeit fleetingly, from an exercise in romantic individualism into an elusive quest for romantic sociability—a quest for something that one might call public intimacy.

NOTES

1. Robert R. Palmer, *Twelve Who Ruled: The Year of the Terror in the French Revolution* (Princeton: Princeton University Press, 1941), 310.

2. See Pierre Coulon's 1981 bibliography, which, now thirty years old, is far from definitive: *Ouvrages français relatif à Jean-Jacques Rousseau: Répertoire chronologique, 1751–1799* (Geneva: Droz, 1981).

3. Keith Michael Baker, *Inventing the French Revolution* (Cambridge: Cambridge University Press, 1990), esp. chap. 4, "A Script for the French Revolution: The Political Consciousness of the Abbé Mably," 86–106.

4. Robert Darnton, "Readers Respond to Rousseau: The Fabrication of Romantic Sensitivity," in *The Great Cat Massacre, and Other Episodes in French Cultural History* (New York: Basic Books, 1984), 215–56.

5. Cited in ibid., 233.

6. Cited in ibid., 231.

7. See Michael Fried, *Absorption and Theatricality: Painting and Beholder in the Age of Diderot* (1980; repr., Chicago: University of Chicago Press, 1988). See also Roger Chartier, *Lectures et lecteurs dans la France de l'Ancien Régime* (Paris: Seuil, 1987); and Guglielmo Cavallo and Roger Chartier, eds., *Histoire de la lecture dans le monde occidental* (Paris: Seuil, 1997).

8. For his negotiations with the Paris Commune, see Sigismond Lacroix, ed., *Actes de la Commune de Paris pendant la Révolution (1789–1791)*, 1st ser. (Paris: Le Cerf, 1895), 2:656–57, 671–72; 4:13, 385; 5:60. For a list of some of his *livres embastillés*, see his declaration of bankruptcy: Archives départementales de la Seine, fond faillite, ser. D4b6, carton 109, doss. 7739, Claude Poinçot, March 16, 1789.

9. For Poinçot's overtures to the assembly, see Jérôme Madival and Emile Laurent, eds., *Archives parlementaires de 1787 à 1860*, 1st ser. (Paris: Dupont, 1875–1913), 25:94; 45:43; 46:324; 52:688.

10. Carla Hesse, "Revolutionary Rousseaus: The Story of His Editions After 1789," in *Media and Political Culture in the Eighteenth Century*, ed. Marie-Christine Stuncke (Stockholm: Kungl. Vitterhets Historie Och Antikvitets Akademien, 2005), 107–28.

11. Ibid.

12. Michael L. Kennedy, *The Jacobin Clubs in the French Revolution: The First Years* (Princeton: Princeton University Press, 1982), 1:9.

13. See ibid., 2:103–4; and Isabelle Bourdin, *Les Sociétés populaires à Paris pendant la Révolution* (Paris: Sirey, 1937), 229.

14. Kennedy, *Jacobin Clubs*, 1:105–6.

15. Jacques Pierre Brissot de Warville, cited by Louis Eugène Hatin, *Histoire politique et littéraire de la presse* (Paris: Poulet-Malassis, 1859–61), 5:22–23.

16. See Jeremy Popkin, Jean Sgard, Carla Hesse, and the catalog published by the Musée de la Révolution française at Vizelle, *Affiches en Révolution.*

17. Camille Desmoulins, *Discours sur la situation politique de la nation, à l'ouverture de la seconde session de l'assemblée nationale, prononcé à la Société des Amis de la Constitution dans la séance du 21 octobre par Camille Desmoulins* (Paris, 1791), in *La Société des Jacobins, recueil de documents pour l'histoire du club des Jacobins de Paris*, ed. Alphonse Aulard (Paris, 1889–97), 3:202–17.

18. Louis-Sébastien Mercier, *De J.-J. Rousseau, considéré comme l'un des premiers auteurs de la Révolution*, 2 vols. (Paris: Buisson, 1791).

19. Armando Petrucci, *Public Lettering: Script, Power, and Culture*, trans. Linda Lappin (Chicago: University of Chicago Press, 1993).

20. Bourdin, *Les Sociétés populaires à Paris*, 245–46. See also Roger Barny, *L'éclatement révolutionnaire du rousseauisme* (Paris: Belles Lettres, 1988).

21. Letter from Charles Villette to the Paris Jacobin Club, April 13, 1791, in Aulard, *La Société des Jacobins*, 3:318.

22. Letter from the representatives on mission (Charlier and Pocholle) to the Committee of Public Safety, 26 vendémiaire, an III (October 17, 1794), in *Recueil des actes du Comité de salut public, avec la correspondance officielle des représentants en mission et le registre du Conseil exécutif provisoire*, ed. Alphonse Aulard et al. (Paris: Imprimerie nationale, 1893–1964), 18:492–93.

23. The *procès-verbal* of the fête is kept in the Bibliothèque municipale de Lyon; see Hippolyte Buffenoir, "L'image de J.-J. Rousseau dans les sociétés de la Révolution en Province," *La Révolution française* 71 (1918): 50–54.

24. The sculpture, by Chinard, has never been located; see ibid.

25. Mercier, *De J.-J. Rousseau*, 1:3.

26. Cambacérès, *Discours prononcé par le Président de la Convention nationale, lors de la translation des cendres de Jean-Jacques Rousseau en Panthéon, le 20 vendémiaire de l'an III de la République* (Paris: Imprimerie nationale, an III), 2.

27. Bourdin, *Les Sociétés populaires à Paris*, 229.

28. See, for example, *Éloge de J.-J. Rousseau, citoyen de Genève, prononcé dans la nouvelle salle des séances de la société populaire de Montpellier, le 20 floréal, l'an second de la Révolution française* (Montpellier: Imprimerie révolutionnaire, an II).

29. Michael L. Kennedy, *The Jacobin Clubs in the French Revolution, 1793–1795* (New York: Berghahn Books, 2000), 172, 264.

30. Letter from Merlin de Douai, on behalf of the Committee of Public Safety, to the representative on mission to the Army of the Rhine and Moselle, 15 Germinal, an II (April 4, 1795), in Aulard et al., *Recueil des actes du Comité de salut public*, 21:520. For Billard's letter, see Jean-Jacques Rousseau, *Correspondance complète de Jean-Jacques Rousseau*, ed. R. A. Leigh (Oxford: Voltaire Foundation, 1965–98), 48:205.

31. For uses of Rousseau in formal political debate and in political pamphlets, see James Swenson, *On Jean-Jacques Rousseau: Considered as One of the First Authors of the French Revolution* (Stanford: Stanford University Press, 2000); and Barny, *L'éclatement révolutionnaire du rousseauisme*; for popular citation of Rousseau, see Albert Soboul, "Audience des lumières: Classes populaires et rousseauisme sous la Révolution," *Annales historiques de la Révolution française* 34 (1962): 421–38.

32. Session of February 28, 1791, in Aulard, *La Société des Jacobins*, 2:99.

33. Mercier, *De J.-J. Rousseau*.

34. Session of September 10, 1792, in Aulard, *La Société des Jacobins*, 4:273.

35. Ibid, 4:274.

36. Ibid, 4:275.

37. Ibid., 4:279.

38. Camille Desmoulins, debate in the Jacobin Club, Session of January 7, 1794, cited in Palmer, *Twelve Who Ruled*, 267.

39. Lionello Strozzi, "Interprétations de Rousseau pendant la Révolution," *Studies on Voltaire and the Eighteenth Century* 64 (1968): 187–223.

40. Jean-Jacques Rousseau, *Rousseau: Juge de Jean-Jacques*, in *Oeuvres Complètes de Jean-Jacques Rousseau* (Paris: Gallimard, 1959), 1:958, cited in Antoine Lilti, "The Writing of Paranoia: Jean-Jacques Rousseau and the Paradoxes of Celebrity," *Representations* 103 (Summer 2008): 53–83.

41. Cambacérès, *Discours prononcé par le Président de la Convention nationale*, 2.

42. Reported in the *Moniteur*, no. 26 du 26 vendémiaire, an III (October 17, 1794), réimpression, xxii, 237, found in Leigh, *Correspondance complète de Jean-Jacques Rousseau*, 48:106.

43. Convention nationale, *Adresse lu au nom des Jacobins de Paris, par Marc Antoine Jullien, membre de la Commission exécutive de l'Instruction public à la barre de la Convention nationale, dans la séance du 27 floréal: Discours prononcé par le citoyen Couthon, représentant du peuple: Imprimés et envoyés aux*

communes, sociétés populaires, et armées de la République, par ordre de la Convention nationale (Paris: Imprimerie nationale, s.d.), 8. Couthon's address is reproduced in Aulard, *La Société des Jacobins*, 6:135–37.

44. On Jacobin sentimentalism, see Patrice Higonnet, *Beyond Goodness and Virtue: Jacobins During the French Revolution* (Cambridge: Harvard University Press, 1998).

45. Bibliothèque nationale Lb40 1831, cited in Albert Soboul, "L'An Deux," *Le Mouvement Social*, no. 79, *La Commune de 1871: Actes du Colloque Universitaire pour la Commémoration du Centinaire Paris, les 21–22–23 mai 1971* (April–June, 1972), 18.

46. Session of May 25, 1792, in Aulard, *La Société des Jacobins*, 3:607.

47. Marie-Jeanne Phlipon Roland, *The Private Memoirs of Madame Roland*, ed. and trans. Edward Gilpin Johnson (Chicago: McClurg, 1900), 272–74. See also Gita May, *Madame Roland and the Age of Revolution* (New York: Columbia University Press, 1970), 245–47.

48. Charles-Augustin Sainte-Beuve, "Sieyès," in *Causeries du Lundi* (Paris: Garnier, 1926–49), 5:216.

49. Simone Balayé and Daniel Candaux, eds., *Groupe de Coppet: Actes et documents du deuxième colloque de Coppet* (Geneva: Slatkine, 1977).

50. Victor Brombert, *La prison romantique* (Paris: J. Corti, 1975).

✒ TEN

LES GRAINES DE LA DISCORDE:
PRINT, PUBLIC SPIRIT, AND FREE MARKET POLITICS IN
THE FRENCH REVOLUTION

Charles Walton

In his *The Forbidden Best-Sellers of Pre-Revolutionary France*, Robert Darnton showed how the booming market of book-length libels eroded the Old Regime's legitimacy.[1] Often written as histories of the Bourbon monarchy, these illegal books combined Enlightenment epistemology with slander, creating a potent mix that deprived the government of respect and credibility. But if print was powerful enough to delegitimize the Old Regime, was it powerful enough to legitimize the new one after 1789? What kinds of printed messages did revolutionaries think would be effective in bolstering support for the new order? How were those messages diffused, and how did contemporaries respond to them?

These questions open onto vast areas of research. In this essay, I focus on one area, the spread of government propaganda during a short but critical phase of the Revolution: the first year of the First Republic. Between the overthrow of the monarchy on August 10, 1792 (the Republic was declared in September) and the heightened phase of judicial Terror a year later, the government ran nationwide propaganda campaigns in an effort to win hearts and minds over to republicanism. But disagreements emerged over what kinds of messages were best suited to achieving this task. Among the many matters of contention, distributive justice—that is, the "just" way a society organizes the distribution of goods and wealth—was frequently raised. While some believed that the

I would like to acknowledge Yacine Khezzari (1974–2009), who suggested the title for this essay.

I would like to acknowledge Yacine Khezzari (1974–2009), who suggested the title for this essay.

Republic should be based on free markets and civic morality (that is, on classical economics and classical republicanism), others insisted that its legitimacy
depended on regulating subsistence markets and providing charity. In the struggle between these liberal and social conceptions of republicanism, embattled
revolutionaries invoked the concept of "virtue" and Rousseauian ideas about
the "general will." At the same time, they took up the Old Regime tactic of
demonizing political adversaries through libels. Thus high Enlightenment
philosophy—or certain political, economic, and moral strands of it—and low
Enlightenment slander came together in the government propaganda of 1792
and 1793. Under conditions of weak political legitimacy, both contributed to
radicalizing the Revolution.

A week after Louis XVI's arrest on August 10, 1792, the Legislative Assembly accorded Jean-Marie Roland, minister of the interior, 100,000 livres to
promote "public spirit."[2] A prominent figure among the "Brissotin" faction of
the Jacobin Club (later known as the Girondins), Roland established a Bureau
of Public Spirit within his ministry's Division of Public Instruction. He, along
with his wife, Marie-Jeanne Phlipon (Madame Roland), and a longtime
friend, François-Xavier Lanthenas, assembled a team of "patriotic missionaries"
to spread republican propaganda throughout France and to report back on its
impact. The correspondence between these agents and the bureau gives insight
not only into the propaganda that was being circulated, but also into how it
was received. It shows revolutionaries struggling over what principles and
communication tactics would best help them legitimize the new Republic.

What publications did the Bureau of Public Spirit circulate? The Legislative Assembly instructed the minister to disseminate copies of laws (with added
pedagogical explanations), publications endorsed officially by legislators, and
whatever else Roland thought would strengthen public spirit. The bureau's
records show that he diffused many circulars and addresses, often in the form
of placards to be posted in cities and towns. The bureau subsidized inspira-
tional texts, such as patriotic hymns, republican catechisms, and celebratory
histories of revolutionary *journées*.[3] It provided updates on the war and the
situation of the imprisoned king, often through newspapers produced by the
Cercle Social, the Paris-based publishing house and intellectual vanguard of
the Revolution that published tracts such as Jacques Pierre Brissot's *Patriote
français* and Jean-Baptiste Louvet de Coudray's fiery antiradical broadsheet
La Sentinelle.

The Bureau of Public Spirit also spread a good many libels against royalists
and radicals. Sometimes the two categories were fused into blanket anathemas.

In October 1792, for example, the bureau circulated a pamphlet denouncing Robespierre and Marat as royalists, or, at the very least, as anarchists serving the royalist cause by discrediting the Revolution.[4] Despite the fact that some of Roland's own agents fashioned themselves as sansculottes ("anarchists," according to their adversaries), after the September prison massacres, the minister began portraying radicals as misled at best, bloodthirsty at worst. In reprisal, radicals in the Jacobin Club expelled Roland and Brissot and mounted a counter-libel campaign, accusing the "Brissotins" and "Rolandistes" of perpetuating aristocracy and despotism, of lying and calumniating, and of starving the people for the benefit of wholesale merchants (*négociants*).[5] This libel war did much to extend Paris-based factionalism into the provinces, further polarizing them. By late 1792 and early 1793, the Revolution had succumbed to the culture of calumny. Inherited from the Old Regime but amplified after freedom of expression was declared in 1789, this culture of demonization, insults, and slander envenomed revolutionary politics.[6]

But the Bureau of Public Spirit spread more than libels. It also disseminated treatises on rights, republicanism, and civic morality. Among such tracts figured French translations of Thomas Paine's *Rights of Man* and *Common Sense* (Paine himself was elected to the National Convention in September 1792). Roland's assistant Lanthenas, who had translated Paine's texts, had his own treatise, *De l'influence de la liberté sur la santé, la morale et le bonheur*, published with bureau funds. The bureau also diffused a revised, republican edition of the perennial *Code conjugal*, which instructed readers in how to be civic spouses while informing them that divorce was now legal. Roland saddled his agents with the works of Rousseau, Mably, and Condorcet, and later sent them new ones by Cercle Social authors, such as Antoine-Jean-Thomas Bonnemain's *Instituts républicains* and Henri Bancal's *Du nouvel ordre social*. All told, in the five months of its existence, Roland's bureau spent nearly a third of its allotted 100,000 livres, mostly on a mix of news, libels, philosophy, and civic tracts.[7]

The bureau's propaganda was shot through with republican and Rousseauian language. "Virtue" and the "general will" were frequently invoked. Some historians of the Enlightenment and the French Revolution have considered these principles to have been utopian, unrealizable, and consequently destabilizing. During the Cold War, Rousseau was often singled out as the Enlightenment's most insidious thinker. His prescription in *The Social Contract* that opponents of the general will should be purged as enemies of society, his belief that citizens may have to be "forced to be free," and his commitment to equality have been read as formulas not only for the Terror of the French

Revolution, but also for the left-wing revolutionary excesses of the twentieth century. Overlooked in this interpretation is the fact that French revolutionaries invoked Rousseau to advance the cause of economic liberalism. The "general will" was, indeed, indeterminate. It could be pressed into the service of free markets and inviolable property rights as readily as market controls and wealth redistribution.

Roland was an economic liberal. He had written several tracts on manufacturing, commerce, and agriculture before the Revolution, and as minister of the interior he vigorously sought to deregulate grain markets. Although he, along with other Girondins, claimed to be protectionist (thus rejecting Adam Smith's views on the benefits of international trade), he did little to enforce the Revolution's ban on exports and nothing to revoke the "free port" status of Dunkirk and Bayonne, which the National Assembly had confirmed in 1791.[8] His free market views were not new. Ever since the 1760s, the monarchy, counseled by Physiocrats, had tried intermittently to deregulate the domestic grain trade. It sought to eliminate not only trade barriers and tolls within France, but also government inspections of grain supplies and interventions in subsistence markets during times of dearth. Old Regime ministers often deployed force to implement such policies, but when prices soared and communities rebelled, they frequently found themselves backpedaling into paternalistic regulation.[9] Despite this history of failures, revolutionaries renewed liberalization efforts in 1789. On August 29, 1789, two days after completing the Declaration of the Rights of Man and of the Citizen, the Constituent Assembly passed one of the most liberal economic measures to date. It deregulated entirely domestic grain markets (exports were banned, but to no avail), and it authorized off-market trading, thereby raising fears about speculation, hoarding, and exportation.[10] Given the drive toward democratization and the fracture of policing institutions, coercion was even less viable now than it had been when Physiocratic ministers resorted to it. From the perspective of free market republicans like Roland, if citizens were to be empowered and markets freed, the masses would have to be trained to think about their interests and duties in a new way. Securing both free markets and a more democratic government would require nothing less than moral regeneration. "Such is the kind of revolution still needed," Roland declared to the National Convention in a speech in which he complained about free market obstructionists.[11]

Already during his first brief tenure as minister of the interior in spring 1792 (Louis XVI dismissed him in June), Roland made his economic agenda clear to departmental administrators. He instructed them to complete a questionnaire, the sixth question of which inquired, "Is the circulation of grain free?" Many took the occasion to enumerate what they took to be the reasons for the dearth of grain in their local markets. Some attributed it to the free market itself.[12] One advanced an apolitical explanation, pointing to three years of poor harvests.[13] But several blamed rebellious crowds, who, in imposing ad hoc price ceilings, were scaring away merchants from the marketplace.[14] Roland sided with this last group. In April, he instructed local administrators to post an address in which he called on the educated elite to use their moral authority to enlighten ordinary citizens about their true interests and to dissuade them from revolt. "Good learned citizens and magistrates elected by the people," Roland wrote, "should hasten to instruct [the people] through readings and explanations appropriate to the simplest of minds."[15] Roland rejected the "poor harvest" thesis. Repeating a common refrain of Physiocrats, he insisted that grain was aplenty and that the real problem was distribution. Lifting all fetters to trade, he sermonized, would equalize grain supplies throughout the Republic. All citizens would benefit equally.

But for many, the free market's invisible hand was delivering invisible benefits. The price of grain was soaring for several reasons, including the plummeting value of the revolutionary currency, the assignat. During his second ministry, just as France was being invaded by foreign troops, Roland continued trumpeting the virtues of the free market, tethering it to the general will. He entrenched himself in his liberal economic views and grew paranoid about the forces opposing them. In an address on September 1, he announced his suspicions that "enemies of the Revolution" were stirring up fears about the free market to advance their "particular" interests at the expense of the general interest: "A league similar to the one formed against you in 1789 is plotting against you today. . . . They stir up imaginary fears [of famine] to distract us from the evil they are preparing for us. . . . [They seek to] weaken us by provoking internal quarrels, from which they profit."[16] Roland discounted the widespread belief that it was wealthy farmers and merchants who were plotting against the people by hoarding and exporting grain: "Could farmers and the owners of grain supplies, who have made such great profits in recent years, calculate so coldly in the pursuit of even greater profits?"[17] Many thought that they were, and reports from border regions and from abroad confirmed that exports of staples were going unstopped, despite laws banning them.[18] But Roland's question was rhetorical, and he did not bother answering it. Instead, he turned to what he took to be the real problem: free market obstructionists. These "enemies of the public weal [*la chose publique*]," he insisted, were to be "punished terribly!"[19]

The alternative to punishment was persuasion. Later that autumn, Roland urged patriotic and popular societies throughout France to instruct the people about their true interests and duties: "Friends of the Constitution, teach people SUBMISSION TO THE LAW; teach them how its yoke is sweet and honorable under a free Constitution that secures the general will. Through your example and discourse, ensure that grain circulates freely."[20] Roland's adversaries in the Jacobin Club had little difficulty exploiting popular discontent over Roland's economic policy. Yet even supporters of deregulated grain markets were troubled by the practical and moral implications. In a joint report to the National Convention, the Committees of Agriculture and Commerce noted that the penury of grain in many local markets was the fault not only of merchants—who were hiding and exporting it for fear of seeing it looted or sold at a loss—but also of local administrators—who, often wealthy farmers and merchants, were using their authority to manage grain movements in order to drive up prices.[21] While supporting free markets in theory, the committees recommended regulations, specifically, obliging grain merchants to sell in times of scarcity while reinforcing the protection of granaries from pillage. These measures, they maintained, would establish a climate of trust, reassuring the people that their fate was not left to the mercy of greedy speculators, while reassuring farmers and merchants that their property would be safe from spoliation.

Less than two weeks later, however, the Executive Council, on which sat Roland and Étienne Clavière (international financier, minister of finances, and adept of Adam Smith), issued a proclamation calling for totally free subsistence markets.[22] Unlike Roland's public-spirit propaganda, which put the general interest before particular ones, the proclamation insisted on giving particular interests free rein, or at least the particular interests of *négociants*: "If domestic commerce in France is free, if *négociants* are not disturbed in the purchase or transport of grain, they will be spurred by their interest to send grain to areas where prices are high and supplies low. [With these shipments,] prices will begin to drop, and individuals, no longer afraid of starving, will be able to return to work."[23] In early December, the Convention passed a raft of laws enforcing free market policies, including one that imposed the death penalty on anyone found obstructing grain movements or even provoking such obstruction through alarmist speech.[24]

Roland's views on political economy found philosophical elaboration in several treatises subsidized by the bureau. A cursory reading of these tracts suggests Rousseauian inspiration, but upon closer inspection, one finds John

Locke at the core. In his *Instituts républicains*, for example, Antoine-Jean-Thomas Bonnemain devoted several pages to the concepts of equality and the general will, citing Rousseau repeatedly. But unlike Rousseau, who believed that wealth imbalances were created by society, Bonnemain attributed them to nature, specifically, differences in strength and intelligence: "Men, equal in their right of action, are not equal in the means they have to act: people are strong or weak, intelligent or inept. . . . It is from these differences that disproportions of wealth and happiness [*jouissances*] are derived."[25] Bonnemain echoed Scottish Enlightenment theory, which held that individuals, in seeking their own interests in society, are compelled to treat others with respect and civility: "The result of a society in which each individual desires and seeks his reciprocal utility [i.e., interests] is that all members have the same interest in respecting and helping each other."[26] This happy state of affairs, presented as the natural tendency of social relations, nevertheless required making people understand their rights and duties. Among those duties figured respect for the sanctity of property: "The social body must maintain each member in the plenitude of his physical and moral faculties. Such is the principle of ensuring the inviolability of property, which follows from civil rights and duties."[27] Bonnemain folded these liberal principles into Rousseau's social contract: "What could the social pact be other than the consensus of free wills? This pact necessitates unanimous consent from each member. Should someone oppose the social contract, he cannot invalidate it; he is simply to be excluded."[28]

Roland received enthusiastic support for his propaganda from some quarters. Many local administrators were delighted to see national leadership on the issues of economic liberalization and social discipline. The mayor and municipal officials of Neufchâtel (department of Seine-Inférieure) applauded Roland "for all your efforts to enlighten your fellow citizens about their true interests and their duties."[29] Members of the Club of Friends of the Republic in Pontivy (department of Morbihan, Brittany) waxed rhapsodic. They composed a verse honoring Roland and his patriotic missionary, Claude Guérin:

> Roland is like a beneficent star,
> Who spreads his light everywhere . . .
> Guérin deserves credit as well
> For seconding his generosity
> By his patriotism and ability to attach hearts
> To the Republic . . . [30]

The minister received sober praise as well. Emmanuel Guillemeau, a member of the district administration in Niort (Deux-Sèvres), wrote a long letter elaborating on Roland's economic principles and explaining the main obstacle to their realization: ignorance. According to Guillemeau, "I am a victim of the ease with which ignorant people can be alarmed by anything that differs from their ordinary ideas."[31] He believed that education was the Republic's most urgent task, even more urgent than securing food. Acknowledging the poor's plight, he nevertheless saw acts of charity as so many sterile bribes. At any rate, they would not bring about the nation's much-needed moral regeneration: "The goods that are given to the poor only affect them as long as the goods are given. The poor are disposed to rally to the cause of those who provide [this charity] only for the day that it is provided. The next day, the benefactor is forgotten." Heartened by this kindred spirit, Roland returned a warm letter of appreciation: "France would be better off if more people thought like you. Your ideas are the ones I most cherish. One obeys laws not because they are imposed but because they are inscribed in one's heart."[32] Roland asked Guillemeau to provide the names of potential public instructors in the countryside around Niort to whom he could send "good ~~readings~~ food."[33]

Roland found support also among local observers and public instructors. These men were recruited by his itinerant public-spirit agents or appointed directly by the minister on the recommendation of provincial administrators. Some individuals took the liberty of appointing themselves, furnishing Roland with reports on local opinion and writing tracts on his behalf, though not always with his blessing. Regardless of how they ended up proselytizing and observing for the minister, these men often tried to parlay their loyalty into patronage. A departmental official in Ille-et-Vilaine (Brittany), M. Gilbert, sent Roland sample surveillance reports on public opinion in his department, hoping to obtain a position in the ministry of the interior: "While waiting for this happy moment [when I would receive] a position making 1,500 livres [per year] for my family of six children . . . I would like to take the liberty of corresponding with you about all that relates in some way to the public happiness of the department."[34] A schoolmaster in Régny (department of the Loire), M. Depierre, served as a local instructor for a couple of months before beseeching Roland for a position in the coming education system.[35] He also requested a leave of absence for his son, a soldier in the army near Verdun, which had come under much enemy fire in recent months. In Paris, a hack living in the rue Saint-Jacques took the initiative to compose libels against Roland's enemies. He hoped that his loyalty would be rewarded with a job:

"It was principally the indignation your enemies inspired in me and my interest in seeing your success that prompted me to take up my pen. . . . I hope that your civic spirit prompts you to find a position for me as a secretary in one of your [ministerial] departments. . . . You can do this, if you wish."[36]

Roland thus garnered support from provincial administrators who agreed with his moralizing, free market principles and individuals seeking favors or patronage. His public-spirit agents, on the other hand, were less obsequious. These twenty-one men who left Paris on horseback with reams of propaganda in August and September were on the front lines of the republican conversion. Often confronting hostile, polarized communities, they had a sharper sense of the kinds of messages that would inspire attachments to the Republic. They did not refrain from advising Roland to adopt different socioeconomic policies or propaganda strategies. Clément Gonchon, a well-known orator from the working-class faubourg Saint-Antoine (just outside Paris), told Roland flat out that the bureau's shipments of political philosophy were entirely unhelpful: "I have just received a shipment from the Cercle Social Messieurs, and I must say that this is not at all the kind of writing appropriate for the present circumstances." He continued, "I cannot simply distribute instruction books about how to be an apostle of liberty and equality; I need short, energetic readings." He specified which kinds: "Please send me collections of writings about the treason of the court."[37]

Several agents observed that news about the monarchy's perfidy was effective in winning adherents to the Republic. Such tracts helped canalize widespread rage onto a consensual and safely controlled target (since the king was imprisoned). The agent Vassant, a professor of rhetoric from the Ardennes, wrote, "I can never have enough writings dealing with Louis's crimes . . . to advance the cause of the Republic, the very idea of which alarms citizens here."[38] Proselytizing in Pontoise, Victor Féron remarked that public spirit was so low that the best he could do was to alarm people about "the plots of our enemies, the counterrevolutionary massacres they provoke, and the bankruptcy that they are about to cause us to suffer."[39] Public spirit was apparently stronger in the department of La Manche (Normandy). The agent working there, Jean-Robert Buhot, attributed this fortunate situation to the newspapers he was receiving, which "made known the crimes of Louis XVI."[40]

To be sure, the monarch was guilty of conspiring against the Revolution, but from the agents' point of view, his actual culpability mattered less than the need to publicize it in order to manage the groundswell of rage sweeping across France. On his way to Lyon, Guillaume Bonnemant informed the bureau about his encounter with battalions of National Guardsmen headed toward Paris to volunteer for the war. He offered them propaganda, but they rejected it. He concluded that people had been manipulated and misled for so long that they no longer trusted anyone. He noted that they "often had on the tips of their tongues the word 'vengeance' . . . 'yes, we'll go to war, but we'll also purge the interior!'"[41] He was not sure whom they wanted to purge, which is why he requested propaganda that would identify royalist culprits. But when the bureau failed to deliver fresh news about counterrevolutionary conspiracies, agents grew anxious. Begging the bureau to send more newspapers quickly, François Enenon explained, "I am convinced that the people have thus far shown patience to put up with misery only because these papers flatter them with the hope of seeing the destruction of those whom they believe are the authors of their misfortune. . . . It is thus important to inform them; otherwise insurrections are to be feared."[42]

Agents found that people were often receptive to the Minister's propaganda when it was accompanied by food, clothes, even small change. Numerous reports speak of such spontaneous acts of generosity. The agent Gadol worked on converting radicals in the faubourg Saint-Antoine to Roland-style republicanism with dinners and drinks at a neighborhood tavern; Gonchon took two destitute and wayward soldiers out for dinner and gave them ten francs each; Pierre Lalande gave the poor parents of seven children a meal and five livres.[43] Roland did not complain about such informal acts of charity, but he reprimanded his agent Enenon when he insisted that such generosity be institutionalized, constituting a fundamental component of republicanism. After weeks without receiving new propaganda shipments and fearing insurrection, Enenon began dispensing small sums to people in the department of Vienne. In his words, "The misery of some individuals, combined with the zeal of others, necessitates the greatest generosity."[44] He was, indeed, generous. The items enumerated under the rubric "dépenses et charités" of his four-page expense report for the months of September and October amounted to 1,002 livres and 5 sous, much of it charity.[45] In early September, Enenon explained, "The people are forced to turn to a charitable hand for subsistence, and this hand determines their opinion. . . . I can think of no more powerful way to transform the masses corrupted in the name of the divinity than to alleviate the misery of the working class. . . . The least bit of charity performs miracles!"[46] Lanthenas, Roland's assistant at the bureau, agreed: "Your reflections on the ways to attach people to the Revolution by relieving it of its misery are just and sound. . . . Nothing is more imperative now than to convey that a government *by* the people must also be *for* the people . . . that the aid people can expect to receive will be greater and less humiliating than the insolent charity handed out by their former tyrants."[47] Once Roland became aware of this conversation, he scolded Enenon: "Your mission is purely moral. Its aim is to instruct and inspire patriotism through the simple means of persuasion, zeal, and example. It does not authorize you to spread liberalities. . . . Such alms are on your personal account since I did not authorize you to hand them out. They tend to distort your mission, buying sentiments that cannot be bought."[48]

But could republican sentiments not be bought? Modest farmers and National Guardsmen in the department of Seine-Inférieure certainly thought so. In January 1793, they sent the minister a letter stipulating the terms of their loyalty to the new order: "Bread, wine, good meat—[securing] these resources will most certainly secure our favorable disposition. . . . Without them, [our opinion] becomes marred, errant, and prey to the will of those who provide us aid in our state of need."[49] They continued by outlining the "most certain measures" that the government should adopt "to attach us [to the Republic]." The measures included the regulation of staple markets.

These struggles over distributive justice were dramatically demonstrated by the failed mission of two public-spirit agents, Louis Prière and Jean Alexandre. These "apostolic missionaries," as they referred to themselves, arrived in Orléans in October to spread the republican word, but they ended up embroiled in a battle between municipal officials, who favored deregulating the grain trade, and sectional militants, who opposed it.[50] "Republicanism everywhere is in derision," the agents observed, attributing the situation to the lack of trust between administrators and citizens. Locals doubted the authenticity of a letter sent by Roland insisting on free grain markets, which municipal officials were publicizing to justify their position. Obliged to attend a contentious town meeting, the agents tried to strike a compromise between the two camps. They proposed a motion that "cast contempt on rich egoists" while also "recommending the maintenance of respect for persons and private property." The next day, they found themselves forced to explain the merits of the free market before angry crowds gathered to thwart the sale of grain to commissioners from Tours. (The authorities, too terrified to address the crowds on their own, pressured Prière and Alexandre to speak on their behalf.) When someone in the crowd put a knife to Prière's chest, Prière cried out (or so he claimed), "If my blood can bring peace to this city, go ahead, stab me!" Hardened elements on both sides of the grain controversy undermined the agents' efforts to secure public spirit. Instead of enlightening the locals about the principles of republicanism and economic liberalism, Prière and Alexandre ended up fleeing the city in the middle of the night, chased by "brigands."

Throughout the fall and winter of 1792/93, tensions between social and liberal conceptions of distributive justice began tearing the Republic apart. Focus on the king's perfidy may have helped forestall civil war; and the law of December 4, 1792, which criminalized calls for a return to the monarchy, can be seen as giving expression to this fragile republican consensus. It was in this spirit that some deputies sought to blame the king for bread shortages. "The source of our troubles [famine] . . . is in the prison of the Temple," asserted one deputy. "Cut off the king's head, and we'll have bread!"[51] Four days later, however, the National Convention declared the obstruction of free grain movements to be a capital offense. Complicating matters, exports of grain were again banned.[52] Citizens were thus called on to closely monitor the movement of grain to make sure none was leaving France, but they were forbidden to raise fears about dearth upon seeing carts of grain roll out of town. In the end, the contradiction mattered little since neither law was enforced. But in the absence of a consensual and enforceable policy, tensions over distributive justice increased, contributing to political radicalization. Upon Louis XVI's execution on January 21, 1793, the main scapegoat vanished. Revolutionaries were left pitted against themselves.

Two days after the execution, Roland, under attack from Parisian radicals and Montagnard deputies, resigned.[53] (The Convention had just withdrawn his propaganda funds.) A month later, Jean-Paul Marat—radical journalist, national deputy, and sansculotte spokesman—helped foment bread revolts in Paris through his newspaper. Many deputies, especially the Girondins, were furious, but Marat's street support prevented the Convention from taking immediate action against him. On March 29, in the course of establishing revolutionary tribunals, the Girondins persuaded the Convention to add a new clause to its reiteration of the December 4 law. Now, calls for a return to the monarchy *and incitement to anarchy* were declared capital offenses.[54] A few days later, the Convention indicted Marat. No sooner was he acquitted than the Convention indicted Brissot and launched an investigation into Roland's propaganda bureau, uncovering evidence of partisanship and corruption. On June 2, the Convention, besieged by pike-fisted sansculottes a few days earlier, arrested twenty-nine Girondin deputies. Roland went into hiding and eventually fled to Rouen, where he committed suicide in November, two days after Madame Roland was guillotined in Paris.

The purge of the Girondins from the Convention did not end efforts to advance liberal economic ideas, but Roland's successors in the ministry of the interior—Dominique-Joseph Garat (January to August 1793) and Jules-François Paré (August 1793 to April 1794)—proceeded more discreetly. Even as the Convention, under intense pressure, imposed price ceilings on May 4, 1793 (a precursor to the General Maximum of September), and included new social and economic rights in the republican constitution promulgated in June (which was circulated throughout France for a referendum in August), Garat sent surveillance agents into the provinces, armed with translated copies of Adam Smith's *An Inquiry into the Nature and Causes of the Wealth of Nations* and Arthur Young's *Journeys in France* (Young was a Smithian). He instructed them to calibrate their observations in light of the perspectives in these books.[55] Some agents expressed enthusiasm for these ideas. Others, while subscribing to free market principles, were puzzled by evidence showing that prices were lower and grain supplies more abundant in places where authorities were regulating markets. Still others rejected Smith's economic principles outright.[56] In his report from the Midi in September 1793, for example, the observer Gabriel Feydel explained:

> In Nîmes, as elsewhere, aristocracy has taken hold of, not the "rich"— that would be erroneous—but of *négociants*, these [speculating middle-] men who have undermined all sound ideas of a healthy political economy for quite some time, accustoming the public to conflate their own success with the prosperity of commerce, of which they are, in fact, the bane. . . . As long as these men place themselves between the producer and the consumer . . . the French Republic will exist only in name. Please excuse this short digression, but I believe it is more valuable than the royalist sophisms of Smith and Young, which are dangerous.[57]

The divergent views of the ministry of the interior's agents in 1792 and 1793 with regard to liberal economic principles reflect broader disagreements over the terms of distributive justice in the First Republic. As historians well know, these disagreements were expressed in faction fighting in Paris and other cities (where radical sansculottes waged war against "greedy," "egotistical" aristocrats), in controversies over the revolutionary armies (which sought to control staple markets and terrorize hoarders), and in the policing machinery of the Terror, which struck at both liberal *négociants* and sansculotte levelers.[58] The problem of distributive justice continued to polarize France after the Terror.

Although police forces became more effective, their ability to prevent revolts was never more than tenuous.[59]

This brief study of Roland's Bureau of Public Spirit has shown how the Enlightenment, high and low, figured in the French Revolution. Whereas many historians have attributed the Revolution's radicalization to disagreements over the terms of sovereignty (representation versus direct democracy), my evidence suggests that struggles over distributive justice—over how the Republic would deal with resources—greatly contributed to creating a climate of distrust, animosity, and instability, at least according to the agents observing public opinion. In debating the terms of distributive justice, Rousseauian rhetoric was invoked by liberals and radicals alike. That society should be based on civic morality and a general will was not disputed; that it should be based on unregulated staple markets, however, was hotly contested. The bureau's promotion of free markets and civic virtue, we have seen, had only limited purchase with the public. Aware of this, Roland's "patriotic missionaries" proposed alternatives. Some called for reassuring the public that the government was committed to regulating subsistence markets and providing charity; for them, political legitimacy depended on material security, not abstract philosophy. Others advised the bureau to circulate more tracts denouncing counterrevolutionary conspiracies; they were convinced that support for republicanism depended on identifying enemies who could be blamed for all the Republic's woes, including grain shortages. After Louis XVI's execution, distributive justice loomed as one of the most explosive issues dividing revolutionaries, and the demonization tactics hitherto deployed against "royalists" were now more fully deployed by revolutionaries against one another.

Thus high Enlightenment philosophy and low Enlightenment libels came together in the French Revolution. In the context of weak political legitimacy, their combination proved to be especially noxious. Discord over liberalizing the grain trade, intolerance reinforced by the concepts of virtue and the general will, and hatreds fueled by relentless slander intensified the punitive impulses unleashed by democratic transition. Together they helped push the Revolution toward the proscriptive politics of the Year II.

NOTES

1. Robert Darnton, *The Forbidden Best-Sellers of Pre-Revolutionary France* (New York: W. W. Norton, 1995).

2. M.-J. Mavidal and M.-E. Laurent, eds., *Archives parlementaires de 1787 à 1860: Recueil complet*

des débats législatifs et politiques des Chambres françaises (hereafter cited as *AP*) (Paris: Dupont, 1867–1913), 48:348.

3. The titles the Bureau of Public Spirit subsidized and circulated can be found in the Bibliothèque nationale de France (hereafter cited as BnF), manuscrits, nouv. acq. fr., 22423. Later, when the bureau came under investigation, Roland publicized a list of titles (doc. 136, a poster, "J.-M. Roland à ses Concitoyens"). For an analysis of the bureau's partisan subsidies, see Claude Perroud, "Roland et la presse subventionnée," *La Révolution française* 62 (1912): 206–13, 315–32, 396–419.

4. Jean-Baptiste Louvet, *À Maximilien Robespierre et à ses royalistes* (Paris: Cercle social, 1792). For Roland's 1,000-livre subvention of this tract, see BnF, manuscrits, nouv. acq. fr., 22423, doc. 41.

5. See, for example, Maximilien Robespierre, *Discours de Maximilien Robespierre sur l'influence de la calomnie sur la révolution, prononcé à la Société dans la séance du 28 octobre 1792* (Paris: Duplain, 1792).

6. For a discussion of the libel campaigns of the Girondins and Jacobins and their obsessions with calumny, see my *Policing Public Opinion in the French Revolution: The Culture of Calumny and the Problem of Free Speech* (New York: Oxford University Press, 2009), esp. 128–36, 207–9.

7. Perroud, "Roland et la presse subventionnée," 319.

8. Marcel Dorigny, "Recherche sur les idées économiques des Girondins," in *Actes du colloque: Girondins et Montagnards*, ed. Albert Soboul (Paris: Société des études robespierristes, 1980), esp. 83–93.

9. Steven L. Kaplan, *Bread, Politics, and Political Economy in the Reign of Louis XV*, 2 vols. (The Hague: Martinus Nijhoff, 1976); Cynthia Bouton, *The Flour War: Gender, Class, and Community in Late Ancien Régime France* (University Park: Penn State University Press, 1993).

10. Judith A. Miller, *Mastering the Market: The State and the Grain Trade in Northern France, 1700–1860* (Cambridge: Cambridge University Press, 1999), 125.

11. [Jean-Marie Roland], *Le ministre de l'intérieur aux corps à la Convention nationale, du 30 septembre 1792* (Paris: Imprimerie nationale, [1792]), 8.

12. "Extraits des réponses des directeurs de département à la circulaire de 20 mai 1792," in BnF, manuscrits, nouv. acq. fr., 22422. See especially the responses from Oise and Eure.

13. Ibid. The response of the departmental administration of Lozère.

14. Ibid. The responses from Seine and Oise, Seine and Marne, and Haute-Saône.

15. Roland, *Aux corps administratifs, municipalités et citoyens: De Roland, [nouveau] ministre de l'intérieur*, poster from the Cher department, BnF, fol. Lb41.5364(2).

16. [Roland], *Le ministre de l'intérieur aux corps administratifs, et, par eux, à tous les citoyens* (September 1, 1792), 1.

17. Ibid., 2.

18. See the report written by Citizen Cusset concerning the exportation of grain by French farmers in the department of Le Nord to the generals of enemy troops, *Réimpression de l'ancien "Moniteur," seule histoire authentique et inaltérée de la Révolution française depuis la Réunion des États-Généraux jusqu'au Consulat (mai 1789–novembre 1799* (hereafter cited as *Moniteur*) (Paris: Plon, 1850–54), vol. 14, no. 342 (December 7, 1792), p. 663. The public-spirit agent Louis-Guillaume Régnier reported that wholesale merchants in Bayonne were regularly exporting to Spain, England, and Holland. See his report dated December 12, 1792, in Archives nationales de France (hereafter cited as AN), fonds anciens, series H¹ "Administration locales et comptabilités diverses," carton 1448. A Frenchman in Holland by the name of "Monsieur Fouscuberte" informed the minister of the navy in spring 1792 (after exportations had been banned) that staples from the French colonies, initially imported to the interior of France, were being redirected as exports to Holland, thus driving up the prices for these staples in France. See AN, H¹ 1439, "Extrait d'une lettre écrit au Ministre de la Marine par M. Fouscuberte . . . à Rotterdam, le 9 avril 1792." Claude Fauchet reported to the Legislative Assembly in February 1792 that the royal government was secretly authorizing the sale of grain to England and then reimporting it with public funds to deal with subsistence crises. See *Moniteur* 11, no. 50 (February 19, 1792): 411.

19. [Roland], *Le ministre de l'intérieur aux corps administratifs*, 2–3. Roland also called for punishing landowners who threw in their lot with the enemy and farmers who purposely withheld staples to drive up prices.

20. Roland, "À mes Concitoyens," AN, H¹ 1439, doc. 107 (penciled). An asterisk note attached to the title reads, "Particulièrement à ceux qui réunissent en société patriotique." Also in BnF, fol. Lb-41-5364(5).

21. *Moniteur* 14, no. 309 (November 4, 1792): 377–78.

22. Clavière's interest in Smith was conveyed to Jean-Baptiste Say, who collaborated with Clavière in the late 1780s. See Jacob H. Hollander, "Adam Smith, 1776–1926," *Journal of Political Economy* 35, no. 2 (April 1927): 193.

23. *Moniteur* 14, no. 319 (November 14, 1792): 462.

24. Miller, *Mastering the Market*, 142–43. See especially the law of December 8, 1792, in *AP*, 54:688. Debate in the National Convention indicates that "provoking obstruction" encompassed alarmist speech and writing.

25. Antoine-Jean-Thomas Bonnemain, *Instituts républicains, ou Développement analytique des facultés naturelles, civiles et politiques de l'homme* (Paris: Cercle social, 1792), 6.

26. Ibid., 8.

27. Ibid.

28. Ibid., 9.

29. AN, fonds modernes: F¹ᶜ III, Seine-Inférieure, carton 15, doc. 162.

30. AN, H¹ 1448, Georgetin (or Georgelin?), membre du Club des amis de la République française séant à Pontivy aux Citoyens Rolland et Guérrin [sic], October 17, 1792.

31. AN, F¹ᶜ III, Vendée, carton 7, doc. 26, letter dated August 21, 1792.

32. Ibid. Roland's response is joined with the original letter.

33. It is difficult to discern whether the strikethrough of "bonnes lectures" and insertion of "bonne nourriture" indicates Roland's sincere use of a metaphor for public instruction or the ironic protest of an assistant, such as the more socially minded Lanthenas, who left the bureau in November and distanced himself from the Rolands, his longtime friends. In any case, the modifications were written in the same hand as the rest of the letter.

34. AN, H¹ 1439, doc. 122, letter by Gilbert, président du département d'Ille-et-Vilaine, n.d.

35. Ibid., doc. 120ᵇⁱˢ, letter by Depierre, maître de l'école à Régny, January 1, 1793.

36. AN, H¹1448, letter by Philoclès Sidney Sanchamau, September 27, 1792.

37. Ibid., report sent from Bar le Duc, September 14, 1792.

38. Ibid., report sent from Sédan, October 5, 1792.

39. Ibid., report sent from Pontoise, September 6, 1792.

40. Ibid., report sent from the department of La Manche, December 31, 1792.

41. Ibid., report of September 11, 1792.

42. Ibid., report sent from Poitiers, October 24, 1792.

43. Gadol's methods were revealed in a public investigation of the bureau in April 1793, *Rapport fait par le citoyen Brival au nom du Comité de sûreté générale, relativement aux papiers trouvés chez le citoyen Roland et inventoriés par les commissaires de la Convention* (Paris: Imprimerie nationale, 1793). Gonchon's generosity was described in his report sent from Bar le Duc on September 14, 1792. Lalande's charity was recounted in his report from Civray, dated October 30, 1792. The latter two reports can be found in AN, H¹ 1448.

44. AN, H¹ 1448, report dated October 31, 1792.

45. Ibid. "État des dépenses que j'ai faites depuis le premier septembre jusqu'au 31 octobre" included with the report written on this date.

46. Ibid., report sent from Poitiers, September 3, 1792.

47. Ibid., letter of September 1792 (no date specified), my italics.

48. Ibid., letter by the minister of the interior to Enenon, November 25, 1792.

49. AN, F¹ᶜ III, Seine-Inférieure, carton 15, undated but grouped with documents of January 1793.

50. AN, H¹ 1448, reports dated October 9, 10, and 15, 1792. The term "apostolic missionaries" is in the October 9 report. Most of what is recounted here is found in the lengthy report of October 15.

51. *Opinion of S.-B. Lejeune, député de l'Indre, sur les subsistances*, in *AP*, 54:692. The king's involvement in grain speculation was discussed in a Convention debate on December 8, 1792; see *AP*, 54:668–88.

52. Miller, *Mastering the Market*, 142–43; *AP*, 54:688.

53. Roland explained his reason for resigning in a letter drafted on the eve of leaving office. See "Le ministre de l'intérieur aux corps administratifs, aux sociétés populaires et à tous ses concitoyens, le 22 janvier, l'an 2 de la République," *Moniteur* 15, no. 25 (January 25, 1793): 262.

54. *AP*, 60:700.

55. The recommendation to order copies of these two works was approved on May 12, 1793; see AN, F¹ᵃ 551, dossier "Franqueville." Interestingly, subsequent documents in this dossier stress the importance of maintaining free markets for subsistence staples, despite the legal regulations passed on May 4.

56. Many of the reports furnished by the agents of Garat and Paré can be found in AN, F¹ᵃ 550 and 551. Substantial excerpts can also be found in Pierre Caron, ed., *Rapports des agents du ministre de l'intérieur dans les départements (1793–an 2)*, 2 vols. (Paris: Imprimerie nationale, 1913).

57. Caron, *Rapports des agents*, 1:345–46.

58. Albert Soboul, *The Parisian Sans-culottes and the French Revolution, 1793–94*, trans. Gwynne Lewis (Oxford: Clarendon Press, 1964); Richard Cobb, *The People's Armies: The Armees Revolutionnaires, Instrument of the Terror in the Departments, April 1793 to Floreal Year II*, trans. Marianne Elliott (1961; repr., New Haven: Yale University Press, 1987).

59. Howard Brown, *Ending the French Revolution: Violence, Justice, and Repression from the Terror to Napoleon* (Charlottesville: University of Virginia Press, 2006). For liberal economic arguments during the Directory, see James Livesey, *Making Democracy in the French Revolution* (Cambridge: Harvard University Press, 2001), esp. 107–9. On government vacillation on the issue of regulating grain markets, see Miller, *Mastering the Market*, 163–94; for government regulation of industry, see Jeff Horn, *The Path Not Taken: French Industrialization in the Age of Revolution, 1750–1830* (Cambridge, Mass.: MIT Press, 2006), esp. 169–210.

PART 5

ENLIGHTENMENT UNIVERSALISM AND
CULTURAL DIFFERENCE

ELEVEN

THE LIMITS OF TOLERANCE:
JEWS, THE ENLIGHTENMENT, AND THE FEAR OF PREMATURE BURIAL

Jeffrey Freedman

La mort est certaine, et elle ne l'est pas. Elle est certaine, puisqu'elle est inévitable, elle ne l'est pas, puisqu'il est quelquefois incertain qu'on soit mort.

—JEAN-JACQUES BRUHIER, *Dissertation sur l'incertitude des signes de la mort et l'abus des enterrements et embaumements précipités*

In 1798, a little-known German journal, the *Schlesische Provinzialblätter*, published a report about a case of narrowly averted tragedy. It concerned a young Jewish boy in Breslau who had been pronounced dead in November of the previous year. Actually, the boy was not dead, he only seemed to be, and since Jewish ritual law required rapid burial—within twenty-four hours at the latest unless the Sabbath intervened—he was at great peril of being buried alive. He escaped that fate because the misdiagnosis of death occurred late in the afternoon—too late in the afternoon to permit a burial before nightfall. The burial had to be postponed until the following morning, and by then, the boy was showing signs of life. Had it not been for the late hour of his apparent demise, it is quite possible that he would have awakened to find himself entombed beneath the earth. Instead, he awoke, as if after a long sleep, in his bed.[1]

All's well that ends well? Not according to a small coterie of Jewish reformers in Breslau, a group comprising some doctors and a handful of like-minded allies. The reformers were well aware that for roughly a half century, doctors in Europe had been calling attention to the difficulty of distinguishing between "seeming death" and real death, and the consequent danger of premature burial. Hardly any educated reader in Germany or France could have been unaware of it, so vast was the accumulated body of literature dealing with the subjects of seeming death and premature burial—treatises, pamphlets, and journal articles in both French and German, nearly all of which sounded the same alarms and made the same basic points: that the absence of such vital signs as respiration and arterial pulsations proved nothing in itself, that the only infallible sign of death was the putrefaction of the corpse, and that unless burial were postponed until the onset of putrefaction, untold numbers of innocent victims would suffer the horrible torture of being buried alive.[2] For the reformers in Breslau, the case of the young Jewish boy seemed to confirm the wisdom of the medical warnings. In their view, the appropriate response to such a case was action, not complacency—prompt and coordinated action to protect the Jews of Breslau against the danger of being buried alive. Shortly after the revival of the boy in November, the reformers launched a bold initiative: the creation of a new burial society (*Beerdigungsgesellschaft*). The new society elected officers and printed statutes, which it submitted for approval to the Prussian authorities, and in which it stipulated that no one should ever be dispatched to his grave until the body showed signs of decomposition.

But what authority did the reformers have to launch such an initiative? Within the traditional structure of the Jewish community, none whatsoever. The new burial society had no official standing, and there already was an official institution responsible for looking after the dead and the dying, the burial confraternity, which was one of the pillars of the Jewish community. The creation of a rival burial society was an open challenge to the corporate organization of the Jewish community, so brazen and provocative a challenge that it tore the community apart.

The reformers and their adversaries became embroiled in a bitter conflict, an intra-communal battle of words that grew increasingly poisonous until it finally came to a head in mid-April 1798, following the real death of a young boy, the infant son of a certain Doctor Zadig. As it happened, Zadig was one of the founding members of the new burial society, so the body of his infant son was treated in accordance with the statutes of the group: corpse watchers observed it night and day until the first signs of decomposition began to appear, at which point Zadig made a request to the directors of the confraternity for a burial plot in the Jewish cemetery. The request was denied. Then a second request was denied. And, eventually, after several more days had gone by and the corpse had reached a state of advanced decomposition, Zadig became so desperate that he decided to appeal to the Prussian state for help against his own coreligionists. He submitted a petition of grievance to the Prussian minister, Privy Councilor von Osten, who issued an official order requiring the confraternity to grant a burial plot. That did the trick. Soon afterward, Zadig's infant child was indeed laid to rest in the Jewish cemetery of Breslau, the burial watched over by the lieutenant general of police and four other police inspectors, who were there to ensure compliance with the government order.

And so ended the burial controversy in Breslau. In retrospect, it seems to have prefigured much of the future course of German-Jewish history in the nineteenth century: the battle between modernizers and traditionalists within the Jewish community, the victory of the modernizers, and the gradual erosion of communal autonomy under pressure from an expanding sovereign state.[3] By way of comparison, however, consider how it appeared to a contemporary, the journalist writing in the *Schlesische Provinzialblätter.* He viewed the burial controversy as a momentous event—less because of its significance for German Jews than because of its significance for the eighteenth century as a whole:

> The remarkable events and the staggering revolutions in the thinking and the behavior of mankind which in the short time span of the past nine years [i.e., since the outbreak of the French Revolution] have followed one another in rapid succession have made the eighteenth century seem remarkable; but the century could with justification be called the most extraordinary [in all of history] if before it comes to an end, it witnesses a general revolution in the thinking and behavior of the Jewish nation, a salutary and wise reform of a religion that has been totally perverted by rabbinical hair-splitting [*Rabbinerschnitzelei*].
>
> In general, however, one cannot expect this religious revolution, whose consequences for all the Jews and for the states in which they live would certainly be very beneficial, since the entire Jewish nation will not, of its own free will and from a rational conviction, undertake to reform its antiquated and useless dogmas, and since the state, constrained by the principles of justice, will not force it to do so. But the already enlightened [*erleuchtet*] part of the Jewish nation can take advantage of the contemporary climate of opinion and the enlightened attitude [*helle Denkungsart*] of princes to work for the realization of a proposal that will lay the foundations for and consolidate the civil well-being of themselves and their coreligionists for all eternity.
>
> And truly, if one considers how in the short span of six months a small society of Jews here in Breslau managed to overthrow one of the oldest Jewish practices—or rather abuses—which had endured down to the present despite the attacks against it from Jewish scholars and famous physicians and despite the conviction of the government, which held that the practice was not a matter of religion and that it was outrageous

and inhumane—[if one considers all of these things], one requires no special illumination and need make no claim to the art of divination in order to foresee that before the end of this century the better part of the Jews will indeed bring about the aforementioned reform [in the thinking and behavior of the Jewish nation].[4]

A local dispute among Jews in a remote province of Prussia the crowning event of the eighteenth century? A more significant turning point than the storming of the Bastille or the execution of Louis XVI? A harbinger of world historical change? The claim seems so extravagant that the historian may be tempted to dismiss it as nonsense. But that temptation should be resisted. "The most promising moment in research can be the most puzzling," Robert Darnton has argued.[5] And Darnton's dictum can be applied to a seemingly extravagant claim about a burial controversy in Breslau no less than to the joke of a cat massacre in Paris. If we can solve the puzzle of why the Silesian journalist ascribed such enormous significance to a movement for burial reform in Breslau, then other pieces of his contemporary culture are likely to fall into place, too.

But first a general point about being buried alive. All of us can conjure up in our minds the terrors of such a fate: the immobility, the confinement, the solitude, the unrelieved silence, the sense of utter helplessness. Those terrors were not at all peculiar to the eighteenth century. One finds them depicted in gothic literature of the nineteenth century—in the works of Edgar Allan Poe, for example—as well as in horror movies today—most recently, in the Dutch film *Spoorloos (The Vanishing)*. So also in documents of much earlier ages—the tragedy of *Antigone*, for example, where Creon condemns the heroine to be walled up inside a cave, or early modern plague chronicles, which evoke the horror of the plague by describing how the ailing and the dead were thrown together pell-mell and consigned to the same mass graves for burial. Premature burial has inspired dread in so many times and places that one could describe it as one of the archetypal fears of the human imagination, like drowning at sea or falling into an abyss, and yet to describe it in that way, sub specie aeternitatis, does not help us in the least to grasp the historical significance of burial reform among the Jews of Breslau in 1798. Even archetypal fears, after all, have a history. They wax and wane; and, most important, they change shape. For our purposes, the important question is not whether the fear of premature burial has always existed. Rather, it is what people *did* with that fear in the eighteenth century.[6]

Take the treatise of the French physician Jean-Jacques Bruhier, *Dissertation sur l'incertitude des signes de la mort* (1742–49), the first of the many French works on the danger of premature burial to be published in the eighteenth century. To impress on his readers just how serious the danger was, Bruhier told stories, 181 gripping, lurid tales of torture or narrowly averted torture, many of which played variations on a single necrophilic theme. A young woman has been given up for dead and is called back to life by the ardent embrace of her lover, just in time to escape the fate of expiring in her grave. It looks like a timeless theme, the myth of love conquering death, which traverses the ages from the Christian Gospels to Sleeping Beauty to Pedro Almodóvar's *Habla con ella (Talk to Her)*. But Bruhier was not using it that way. In his telling of the tales, love does not conquer death because the women are not dead to begin with—they only *seem* to be dead. The difference is crucial, and it gives the tales an admonitory meaning. Beware of inferring death from the usual outward signs. When people wake up in their graves, Bruhier implied, it is simply because some ignorant fools made a misdiagnosis of death. There is nothing the least bit mysterious about it. Indeed, once one takes account of the phenomenon of seeming death, all kinds of mysteries dissolve, like the supposed resurrection of Lazarus in the New Testament, which Bruhier dismissed as a religious hoax.[7]

Bruhier, in short, was a man of his age: a scientist who wrote like a philosophe. He treated the reported cases of premature burial in the manner of Voltaire, by stripping them of their mystery and explaining them in naturalistic terms; then he forged them into critical weapons, to be wielded, rapier-like, for the skewering of superstition and credulity. Other writers who discussed cases of premature burial after Bruhier treated them in much the same way. Why had so many people testified to having heard horrible, bone-chilling screams in cemeteries during the night?, asked an anonymous author in a German journal of the 1770s. Not, he answered, because those people had stumbled on a witches' Sabbath—the hoary legends about witches and their nocturnal gatherings in cemeteries had no basis in reality. The most likely explanation of the screams was that they came from victims of premature burial who were crying out to be released from their subterranean prisons.[8] That explanation did not make the screams any less terrifying; quite the contrary. But at least it removed them from a supernatural frame of reference. The writers of the eighteenth century who sounded the alarm about the danger of premature burial were men of the Enlightenment.

I say "the" Enlightenment, knowing that some readers will object to the use of the definite article. And there are good reasons for objecting to it. The Enlightenment, after all, did not take the same form in France as it did in Germany, and in neither country did it stand for a set of fixed and immutable beliefs. But it did cohere as a process, as an open-ended debate revolving around certain central topics of concern—for instance, that of prejudice. The most radical Enlightenment authors, like Paul-Henri Thiry Baron d'Holbach in France, condemned prejudice categorically; the more moderate ones, like Moses Mendelssohn in Germany, were prepared to concede that certain prejudices contained moral truths and were therefore useful—at least for the uneducated classes, which had not yet learned to apprehend those truths rationally. But the question of how to deal with prejudices—whether to combat them, and if so, by what means, or to tolerate them, and if so, under what circumstances— was a recurrent subject of discussion in the European Enlightenment. It was also one of the main reasons why reported cases of premature burial took on such great significance: those cases exemplified prejudice in both of the senses in which that concept was understood in the eighteenth century—prejudice as precipitate or "overhasty" (*übereilt*) judgment and prejudice as uncritical attachment to tradition (the prejudice in favor of authority).[9] To send someone to his grave before the evidence warranted a definitive pronouncement of death was to be guilty of prejudice in the first sense; to follow the traditional practice of rapid burial, simply because that practice was traditional or because it enjoyed the sanction of religious authority, was to be guilty of prejudice in the second sense. Either way, victims of premature burial were victims of prejudice. And so a great deal was at stake for the Enlightenment in the reform of burial practice—the elimination not just of any evil but of an evil that epitomized the harmfulness of prejudice.

The obstacles to reform, however, were every bit as formidable as the stakes were high. To begin with, there was the sheer scarcity of doctors and their physical distance from the actual sites of death. In the eighteenth century, the vast majority of people did not die with doctors anywhere near their bedsides. If they were lucky enough to die "well"—which is to say, in their native villages, rather than destitute and on the road—then they would, in most cases, have been attended at their deathbeds by family members, some of their fellow villagers, the local vicar or parish priest, and perhaps some traditional healers like the village cunning man or wise woman—but not by doctors. The "medicalization" of death, like the "professionalization" of medicine, was a development more of the nineteenth than the eighteenth century.[10] Therefore, it was not enough for doctors alone to grasp just how easily life could counterfeit death. The general population had to grasp it, too, and many people were bound to balk at the idea of keeping unburied bodies lying around in their houses or cottages for days on end. As an alternative to keeping bodies in homes, the German physician Christoph Wilhelm Hufeland advocated the construction of a new kind of public health institution: waiting mortuaries (*Leichenhäuser*), in which bodies would be laid out and monitored by specially trained corpse watchers before burial. Hufeland was one of the most renowned and respected figures in German medicine, as well as the court physician of Karl August, Grand Duke of Weimar, and with the backing of the duke, he was able to bring his project to fruition: the first German *Leichenhaus* opened its doors in Weimar in 1791, followed over the next two decades by *Leichenhäuser* in Berlin, Brunswick, Ansbach, Kassel, Mainz, and Munich. The German medical establishment embraced Hufeland's project enthusiastically; the public, on the other hand, much less so. Working-class Germans in towns proved reluctant to surrender the bodies of their loved ones to the tender mercies of the corpse watchers. The *Leichenhäuser*, therefore, were rarely filled to capacity, and some of them sat practically empty, notwithstanding Hufeland's tireless propagandizing. In 1791, he published a short work about the public health benefits of the *Leichenhäuser*, and then, seventeen years later, he published a second, much longer work in which he tried to win support for his project by repeating many of the same horror stories that had originally appeared in Bruhier's treatise more than a half century earlier. But even if Hufeland's project had caught on with the public, it would only have affected town-dwellers, and most Germans in the late eighteenth century lived in the countryside.[11]

In order to promote the reform of burial practices in rural areas, the Prussian government launched a small public health initiative of its own. It allocated monies from the royal coffers to underwrite the printing of short and simple books on the subject of seeming death. In their form, the books were modeled on religious catechisms; ideologically, they belonged to what Germans called the "popular enlightenment" (*Volksaufklärung*), which was a kind of philanthropic publishing campaign whose chief goal was not to make peasants into philosophers so much as to convey practical information to the "common man" (*gemeiner Mann*)—in this particular case, practical information about reanimation techniques, diagnosing death, and the importance of observing waiting periods before burial.[12] It was one thing, however, to print and disseminate such books, and quite another to ensure that their message would get across. By the second half of the eighteenth century, most German states had introduced laws requiring some schooling for the whole population, but the laws were not always enforced, and in any case, most village schools were so ill equipped and poorly run that one could have attended those schools and still not had sufficient literacy to decipher even so simple a book as a medical catechism. In practice, the message of such a book was unlikely to reach its intended audience unless some literate intermediary like the local vicar or schoolmaster transmitted it verbally.[13]

It is easy to understand, therefore, why educated Germans would have been pessimistic about the prospects for successful burial reform. And yet the degree of pessimism is remarkable all the same. For several decades, beginning in the 1770s, German journals repeatedly issued gloomy pronouncements about the futility of efforts to eliminate the scourge of premature burial. In one journal, for example, an author began his article about seeming death and premature burial by announcing that he planned to discuss "our mishandling of the dead," which he held to be a subject of the greatest importance. In the very next sentence, he went on to say that he did not believe his article would be the least bit useful: "To believe such a thing, I would have to be ignorant of the force that traditional practices have on human minds and the slowness with which improvement occurs in such cases where the power of reason has to triumph over common prejudice."[14] Another author writing about the danger of premature burial admitted that the "common people" (*das Volk*) were not even aware of the existence of the journal in which his article was being published.[15] So why bother? The question was inescapable, and it hung over the discussions of premature burial like a dark cloud. To all appearances, the cause of burial reform was trapped in a closed circle: the already enlightened speaking to the already enlightened. The problem of how to break out of that circle looked well-nigh insoluble.

And if the problem seemed so difficult to solve for the German population in general, then how much more so in the specific case of the Jews. Jewish communities defied the medical consensus about the danger of same-day burial not out of lethargy or fatalism or ignorance, but because it contradicted their religious law. To them, same-day burial was a commandment and a way of showing respect for the dead; to the partisans of burial reform, it was an abomination. German journals fulminated against the "inhumanity" and "cruelty" of same-day burial, a practice all the more intolerable as it also provided a camouflage for the most dastardly crimes—poisoning, for example, which was likely to go undetected because the bodies of the victims were dispatched to their graves before autopsies could be performed. Under the cover of same-day burial, it was alleged, Jews were able to murder their own coreligionists with impunity.[16] Those allegations made the Jews seem perfidious and depraved at the very moment, it should be noted, that Germans were also debating the issue of Jewish emancipation, which the Prussian official von Dohm had launched with the publication in 1781 of his pamphlet "On the Civic Improvement of the Jews" ("Über die bürgerliche Verbesserung der Juden").[17] Given that Jewish burial practice and Jewish emancipation were being discussed simultaneously, it would be natural to suppose that those who denounced Jewish burial practice were hostile to Jewish emancipation—but it was not that simple.

Anton Büsching, a writer who made some particularly nasty comments about the Jewish practice of same-day burial, presented himself with some plausibility as a friend of the Jews. It was only because enlightened Christians regarded Jews as fellow human beings, Büsching argued, that they felt duty bound to speak out against Jews murdering their own coreligionists. Had they said nothing, their silence would have bespoken indifference to Jewish suffering.[18] And yet speaking out did not do any good, either, if the Jews were not listening. "It is futile to present to the Jews the most vivid depictions of the terrifying consequences of rapid burial and to refute their erroneous religious scruples. It is futile to persuade them that their treatment of the dead is indecent and that it violates the rights of man," another German author concluded bitterly in a journal article of the early 1790s. "As long as the rabbi remains what he now is, the all-powerful of the nation, capable of grinding into the dust with complete impunity whomever he wishes, . . . all efforts to enlighten the Jewish nation, to instill in it true feelings of humanity and self-worth and to suppress the old national prejudice in favor of rapid burial, will be totally useless."[19] By clinging to their "old national prejudice" and ignoring the voice of reason in the matter of burial reform, the Jews seemed to dramatize one of the weightiest problems of the late eighteenth century: the impediments to the spread of Enlightenment.

So what was to be done? The German commentators were convinced that some Jews harbored secret misgivings about same-day burial but dared not say so for fear of incurring the wrath of their all-powerful rabbis. The solution, therefore, was to curtail the power of the rabbis. Governments, it was argued, would have to adopt laws mandating waiting periods before burial, then enforce those laws in the teeth of rabbinic opposition, by coercive means if necessary.[20] And that was precisely what German governments did. Gradually, laws calling for waiting periods before burial were enacted in the major states of the old Reich: the Habsburg lands of Austria and Bohemia (1786–87), electoral Saxony (1792), and, finally, following the events in Breslau mentioned earlier, Prussia (1798). The laws caused tremendous turmoil in Jewish communities, but the German commentators were absolutely right that some Jews harbored misgivings about the wisdom of same-day burial, not least Mendelssohn, the most famous Jew in all of Europe, who argued as early as 1772, in a letter to the Jewish community of Mecklenburg-Schwerin, that the Jews would do well to heed the warnings of doctors. A conciliator by nature, Mendelssohn blunted the sharp edge of his argument by wrapping it in exegesis— he endeavored to show that the practice of same-day burial was based on a misreading of the relevant sources and that Jews could abandon the practice without abrogating Jewish law.[21]

Mendelssohn's followers in the next decade, however, were not nearly so circumspect. For Marcus Herz, a Jewish physician writing in the 1780s, the authority of doctors trumped the authority of Jewish law, and that was that.[22] When German governments acted against the power of the rabbis, therefore, they did enjoy the support of a minority of self-styled "enlightened" Jews. David Friedländer, one of the leaders of the Jewish Enlightenment in Germany, went so far as to publish an article in a Berlin journal hailing the emperor Joseph II for having outlawed same-day burial in Bohemia: "My enlightened brothers recognize with gratitude this paternal concern for our well-being [which] marks a new victory over an old prejudice that inspires feelings of indignation."[23] For anyone who felt frustrated at the apparent tenacity of traditional prejudices, the mere existence of Jews like Friedländer and Herz, or the reformers in Breslau who challenged the burial confraternity, was a source of hope. It made it possible to argue that Jews, too, had the capacity to heed the voice of reason, and therefore that the chief obstacle to the spread of Enlightenment among the Jews was not any intrinsic flaw in the Jewish character, it was institutional—the organization and autonomy of Jewish communities— and as such removable through political action. Our Silesian journalist did not spell out that argument precisely, but something like it was clearly implied in his comments about the burial controversy in Breslau.

And so the pieces of the puzzle have finally fallen into place. Why would anyone regard the burial controversy in Breslau as the crowning event of the eighteenth century? In the first place, because premature burial epitomized the iniquity of prejudice and because the Enlightenment, in whatever form it appeared, was deeply concerned about the problem of prejudice. But also, and most important, because the prejudice in favor of rapid burial proved so difficult to root out. With the Jewish resistance to burial reform, the Enlightenment seemed to have reached an impasse—there was much hand-wringing among the already enlightened about the power of prejudice but little progress toward the goal of eliminating same-day burial. Then, suddenly, at the very end of the "century of Enlightenment," there was progress—at least in Breslau—and it pointed a way out of the impasse. The way out lay in a new kind of alliance: an enlightened minority of educated Jews and the enlightened Prussian officialdom marching together to reform Jewish rituals.

With all the pieces of the puzzle in place, our work of historical reconstruction might seem to be at an end. But there is a problem with applying the metaphor of puzzle solving to the work of historical reconstruction: the pieces of a puzzle are designed to fit together whereas the elements of a culture are not. Different value systems, for example, will often coexist within a single culture, even within a single individual, and it would be a mistake to suppose that they can always be so neatly fitted together. By way of conclusion, therefore, it may be instructive to go back over some of the same ground we have already covered, this time with a view not to solving the puzzle but to highlighting certain unresolved tensions.

Consider, first, the recurrent use of fear in the campaign for burial reform. From Bruhier to Hufeland, nearly all the authors involved in the campaign appealed openly to fear, describing the horrible suffering of being buried alive so as to raise public awareness of the need to delay burial. As we have said, however, those same authors were also men of the Enlightenment, committed to understanding the universe in rational terms; and it was one of the core convictions of Enlightenment authors that rational understanding would diminish the terrors of human existence. "The more Enlightenment [*philosophie*, in French; *Aufklärung*, in German], the less fear" was practically a definition of Enlightenment. All the *philosophes* and *Aufklärer* would have endorsed it, just as most of them would have endorsed the proposition "the less prejudice, the better." And, of course, fear and prejudice were closely linked, for prejudices led to fear—notably, religious prejudices, like the beliefs in hell or purgatory, which caused humanity to fear the prospect of death. In the campaign for burial reform, however, that link had been severed. Instead of exposing prejudice in order to banish fear, authors like Bruhier and Hufeland incited fear in order to combat prejudice.[24]

Fearmongering to advance the cause of the Enlightenment? Clearly, the means and the ends were in tension. But how deep did that tension go? And what are we to make of it? Of course, it was never in the Enlightenment's power to banish fear completely. Some old fears were bound to survive, like the fear of famine, which burst into the open during *la grande peur* of the French Revolution. This incident derived from the widespread belief in an aristocratic plot to starve the French people, and apart from the fact that the supposed villains were aristocrats rather than, say, witches, something very like it could have broken out in the seventeenth century, too. All the myth bashing of Enlightenment authors could not dent the fear of famine for the obvious reason that famine was not a myth. It was grounded in real conditions of material scarcity. There was only one effective cure for the fear of famine, and it was not philosophy. It was an increase in agricultural production, which was, in fact, occurring during the second half of the eighteenth century, but not fast enough to guarantee adequate food supplies for the entire population when harvests failed.[25] Within the conditions of the eighteenth century, the fear of famine made eminently good sense. The fear of premature burial, however, belonged to a different category. It did not survive *despite* the Enlightenment, it flourished *because* of it. The publications on seeming death and premature burial contributed to reactivating an ancient fear, and there is no question that some of the readers of those publications were really frightened. One example is Mme. Necker, the salon hostess and wife of the French finance minister, who lifted a long list of reanimation techniques and precautionary measures against premature burial from Bruhier's treatise and wrote them into her last will and testament.[26] During the last years of her life, Mme. Necker dreaded the prospect of her own death just like any believing Christian of an earlier period, except that the suffering she dreaded pertained to the body rather than the soul and was situated in an in-between state this side of the divide between life and death: the grave as this-worldly purgatory.

And yet the fear of being buried alive was not the same thing as the fear of languishing in purgatory or burning in hell, either. In the latter case, the fear was of something belonging to the domain of religious dogma. Purgatory was a reality because the Catholic Church said it was. So, too, with hell, except that hell was dogma for all Christians and not just Catholics. One could not question the reality of purgatory or hell from within the discourses of Catholic or Protestant orthodoxy, only from without—by subjecting the dogma to rational critique. The fear of being buried alive was different. It was a fear of something that belonged to the domain of scientific "fact," and the Enlightenment never conferred unimpeachable authority on scientific fact; quite the contrary.[27] In the eighteenth century, at a time when scientists had not yet withdrawn behind the protective walls of professional journals and technical jargon, scientific facts were open to critique in the public sphere, and so, too, were the fears those facts supported.

In 1776, for example, the magistrates in Zurich became convinced that someone had poisoned the communion wine in the main cathedral of the city. The evidence for the crime came from a team of eminent physicians who performed a chemical analysis on the wine and concluded that it contained arsenic. The crime, therefore, was a scientific "fact," and it reactivated the ancient fears of poisoning and sacrilege, which found a wide echo in the press coverage of the event. To contemporary observers, it seemed one of the worst crimes imaginable—until Friedrich Nicolai, a prominent figure of the Berlin Aufklärung, published an article in a leading Berlin journal in which he argued that the evidence was flawed and that the wine had never been poisoned. Nicolai retrospectively declared the "fact" to be a nonfact, and, as far as one can tell, most people agreed with him, including some of his bitterest enemies.[28] In the case of premature burial, the outcome was the other way around: the fearmongers defeated the doubters. Or so it would appear from the published record, for most of those who wrote on the subject of premature burial took the view that a great many people were, in fact, being buried alive. But the doubters made their voices heard, too.

In 1792, for example, a German author published a journal article in which he took issue with another author who had claimed, in the pages of the same journal, that throughout history one in thirty people had been buried alive. How could anyone claim to know such a thing?, he asked. Only by performing an experiment of first burying and then exhuming thousands of bodies, he answered. No such experiment had ever been tried; therefore, the claim was nothing but "theory and hypothesis"—"an arbitrarily adopted proposition . . . beyond the reach of any possible experience." The author did not go so far as to affirm that no one had ever been buried alive; he could not have done so without violating his own empiricism—the phrase "beyond the reach of any possible experience" was a nod in the direction of Kant's *Critique of Pure Reason*—but he was convinced that the fear of premature burial was overblown and that all the talk about it was doing more harm than good: "The otherwise-praiseworthy condemnation of rapid burial that is now widespread in Germany and that has prompted governments in many regions to enact edicts on the subject has also caused much anguish among the common people, especially among those who have lost loved ones and who now torment themselves night and day with the thought that they may have buried their loves ones too soon. I shall not conceal my view, therefore, that we have gone a little too far—a little too far, that is, in our damning remarks about frequently occurring premature burials."[29]

Or consider the physician writing in a medical journal in 1790 (a medical journal, however, that was clearly addressed to both doctors and nondoctors alike). He was prepared to admit that it was sometimes possible to mistake seeming death for real death, but only in those cases where the outward signs of death appeared suddenly and no previous indication of illness had been present, as after strokes, seizures, fainting, or suffocation, and such cases were too rare to justify the shrill alarmism of the campaigners for burial reform. "The terrors of life and death are for the most part only imaginary. Why then do we wish to multiply and enlarge them without cause?," the physician concluded.[30] Or, finally, consider the Jewish physician M. J. Marx, who published an article in support of the Jewish practice of same-day burial. Whatever the danger of premature burial, Marx argued, it paled beside the public health danger that resulted from leaving dead bodies unburied: better to run the infinitesimal risk of premature burial than to expose whole populations to the threat of contagion. The argument was clever and well designed to impress other physicians; eighteenth-century physicians were greatly concerned about the noxious effects of the "miasmatic vapors" that decomposing bodies were thought to emit, no less concerned than they were about the danger of premature burial.[31] On the advice of physicians, laws mandating the removal of cemeteries from areas of dense habitation were being enacted at the same time as the laws mandating waiting periods before burial. The two sets of laws contradicted each other, and Marx deftly exploited the contradiction in order to mount a rational, medically sound defense of a traditional Jewish ritual.[32]

So what can we conclude? Certainly not that Marx or the other doubters made much difference in the end. The important point is simply that they had the opportunity to challenge the consensus, that there was a debate, however lopsided, and that the fear of premature burial had to withstand the test of critical scrutiny in the public sphere. As it existed in the eighteenth century, therefore, the fear of premature burial could well be described as a rational fear. But whether rational or not, it was still a fear, and fear tends to create an environment inimical to tolerance—a point that brings us to the final unresolved tension in the campaign for burial reform.

To anyone who feared premature burial, the Jewish practice of same-day burial posed a stark choice: either tolerate the practice and thus accept the suffering of innocent Jews, or accept coercive measures to end the practice and thus violate the principle of religious tolerance. Our Silesian journalist tried to evade the choice by emphasizing that the original impetus for burial reform had come from within the Jewish community. In that way, he was able to make it seem that the Jews of Breslau were reforming their "antiquated" ritual on their own, with just a little help from the Prussian state. But, in fact, the Jews as a whole were doing no such thing; only a small minority of them were. And how did the reform appear to those Jews in Breslau who did not belong to that minority? To some of them at least, it must have seemed coercive and intolerant. David Friedländer, who represented the view of the Jewish minority, saw this position quite clearly. To him, it was obvious that one had to make a choice between two incompatible options. Hence his support of Joseph II's decision to outlaw same-day burial in Bohemia, an opinion worth citing at length because it presented the two options without any attempt to soften the opposition between them:

> Praised be the Eternal One that the antiquated abuse of burying the dead beneath the earth on the same day as their demise has finally been abolished forever among my coreligionists in this land. My enlightened brothers recognize with gratitude this paternal concern for our well-being. It marks a new victory over an old prejudice that inspires feelings of indignation. . . . To be sure, this hard-won victory was not of the noblest sort. It was won not through persuasive reasoning [*überzeugenden Gründen*] but through force [*Gewalt*] and not without encountering resistance. But the prejudice that had to be overcome was itself of such an ignoble and harmful sort that it had to be eliminated root and branch without delay and consideration.[33]

Here it is also worth pointing out that Friedländer's article was published in the *Berlinische Monatsschrift*, the same journal in which Kant had published his famous essay "What Is Enlightenment?" just a few years earlier. By framing the opposition in the way that he did, "persuasive reasoning" on the one hand and "force" on the other, Friedländer was echoing and, to some extent, challenging Kant's conception of Enlightenment, which revolved around exactly the same opposition but which repudiated the use of force as a means of spreading Enlightenment. As an ideal defined by Kant, Enlightenment could only spread through the free "public use of reason." To impose it by force was to violate it as an ideal—and as far as the ideal went, Friedländer agreed with Kant, which was why he admitted that outlawing same-day burial was "not a victory of the noblest sort." Friedländer, however, was writing as a social reformer, which Kant never did. Kant's philosophy did not bother with the messy business of reforming social institutions, nor did it concern itself with human beings as they really existed in eighteenth-century society. The person for whose dignity the categorical imperative commanded respect was an abstraction from social reality: the self-legislating individual who determined the ends of his own existence. An eighteenth-century social reformer had to deal with human beings as they really were—in other words, as members of communities, groups that imposed their own forms of coercion and determined the ends of human existence on behalf of their members. And as with human beings, so with their prejudices. The prejudice in favor of same-day burial was not the prejudice of free-floating, autonomous individuals who just happened to be Jews; it was the prejudice of the Jewish community. With all the weight of a community and an ancient tradition behind it, such a prejudice could not be dislodged through the force of argument alone. To the force of argument, one had to join force tout court.

Or so it appeared to Friedländer—but not just to Friedländer. As already mentioned, non-Jews, too, argued that German governments should take action to end the practice of same-day burial among the Jews. That practice did not affect them directly, so why did they care? Of course, one cannot discount the possibility that they did not really care about the well-being of the Jews, and that, on the contrary, they disliked Jews and merely wanted to see them discomfited by laws that compelled them to change their traditional customs. Such an interpretation would fit nicely with the current scholarly fashion to look for anti-Semitism and intolerance of cultural diversity in the Enlightenment.[34] The textual evidence alone, however, does not support it. When a German commentator said the following—"Oh, Princes! Remove from these bearded priests [i.e., the rabbis] their antiquated power, their unlimited authority, their freedom to subject anyone to their heavy ecclesiastical yoke according to their pleasure and fancy, and the Jew will bless your memory and will bury his dead just like Christians only after he has exhausted all possible means of reviving the body and only after having waited several days"—his professed motive was to benefit the Jews by freeing them from the authority of their rabbis.[35] Why assume that the professed motive had to conceal one darker and more sinister? It is just as likely that the German commentator was reasoning empathically: what if I were a Jew and had to be exposed to the torture of being buried alive? To reason in that way, by imagining oneself in someone else's skin, was to perform a mental operation that could, in some cases, lead to tolerance of other cultures; it is just that same-day burial was not one of those cases. It was a prejudice whose consequences seemed so dreadful as to make tolerance intolerable.

Were the consequences really so bad? That question is difficult to answer, for we have no way of knowing just how widespread premature burial was in the late eighteenth century—the most we can say is that a great many people believed it to be widespread.[36] Whatever the *objective* fact, however, most of us will have no difficulty grasping the *subjective* moral dilemma. Where to draw the boundary between tolerance as respect for other cultures and tolerance as indifference to human suffering is a problem that the Enlightenment bequeathed to the whole tradition of modern liberalism, and it has reappeared in various guises throughout the modern era, from widow burning in the British raj to female genital mutilation in contemporary Africa. It is a genuine problem even if the idea of stamping out "native" customs for the good of the "natives" has sometimes been used to nefarious ends, to provide ideological cover for British imperialism or to buttress the notion of Western superiority. For the Western liberal, the question is still, more or less, the same: what if *I* were a Hindu widow, or an African Muslim girl—or, for that matter, a Jewish boy in eighteenth-century Breslau? To see the similarity of such cases is not to deny the cultural differences between the early twenty-first, the mid-nineteenth, and the late eighteenth centuries, it is merely to identify a connecting thread, and of course that thread is only visible in retrospect—our Silesian journalist was bound to see things differently. To him, the elimination of same-day burial in Breslau was the crowning event of the eighteenth century because it signaled the victory of the Enlightenment over prejudice. To us, looking back, that same episode seems to point beyond its own epoch to one of the enduring dilemmas of the modern liberal conscience.

APPENDIX

The work that inaugurated the concern about "seeming death" and premature burial in the second half of the eighteenth century was *Dissertation sur l'incertitude des signes de la mort* by the French physician Jean-Jacques Bruhier—a work based loosely on a Latin treatise, *Morte incertae signa*, published two years earlier by an expatriate Danish physician living in Paris named Winslow.

Bruhier's French version appeared in one volume in 1742, a second volume came out in 1746, and, finally, the two volumes were published together in 1749, the first volume having been considerably revised in the meantime. The publication of Bruhier's work was then followed by a spate of other works in French: H. Le Guern, *Rosaline, ou les mystères de la tombe: Recueil historique d'événements nécessitant qu'on prenne des précautions pour bien constater l'intervalle qui peut s'écouler entre la mort imparfaite et la mort absolue* (Paris, n.d.); M. Pinot, *Mémoire sur le danger des inhumations précipitées, et sur la nécessité d'un règlement pour mettre les citoyens à l'abri du malheur d'être enterrés vivants* (Paris, n.d.); M. B. Durande, *Mémoire sur l'abus des ensevelissements des morts* (Strasbourg, 1789); Thiery, *La vie de l'homme respectée et défendue dans ses derniers moments* (Paris, 1787); Marin Bunoust, *Vues philanthropiques sur l'abus des enterrements précipités* (Arras, n.d.); Janin, *Réflexions sur le triste sort des personnes qui sous une apparence de mort one été enterrés vivantes* (The Hague, 1772); J.-J. Gardanne, *Avis au people sur les morts apparentes et subites* (Paris, 1774). These works echoed Bruhier's main thesis on the matter of seeming death. One French author, however, did take issue with Bruhier and challenged the credibility of his evidence: Antoine Louis, *Lettres sur la certitude des signes de la mort* (Paris, 1752). In the second half of the eighteenth century, German booksellers were quick to publish translations of successful French works, and a German translation of Bruhier's work was published in 1754. To the body of translated literature, however, Germans made their own original contributions, among them an anonymous collection of horror stories, *Wiederauflebungs-Geschichten scheintodter Menschen* (Berlin, 1798); H. F. Köppen, *Achtung des Scheintodtes*, 2 vols. (Halle, 1800); H. V. C., *Wirkliche und wahre mit Urkunden erläuterte Geschichten und Begebenheiten von lebendig begrabene Personen, welche wiederum aus Sarg und Grab erstanden sind* (Frankfurt and Leipzig, 1798), and two works by the famous Weimar physician C. W. Hufeland, *Über die Ungewissheit des Todes und das einzige untrügliche Mittel sich von seiner Wirklichkeit zu überzeugen: Nebst der Nachricht von der Errichtung eines Leichenhauses in Weimar* (Weimar, 1791) and *Der Scheintod* (Berlin, 1808). In the latter work, Hufeland noted that no fewer than twenty-six German books and pamphlets had been published on the subject of seeming death and premature burial in the seventeen years since the publication of his first work on that subject in 1791. Finally, there was also a widespread discussion of seeming death and premature burial in German journals of the second half of the eighteenth century, including *Berlinische Monatsschrift, Journal von und für Deutschland, Deutsches Museum, Neues Hamburgisches Magazin, Historisch-politisch-literarisches Magazin,*

Orientalische Bibliothek, Ephemeriden der Menschheit, Hannoverisches Magazin, Lausizisches Wochenblatt, and *Almanach für Ärzte und Nichtärzte.*

NOTES

1. In English, the epigraph reads, "Death is certain, and it is not. It is certain because inevitable; not certain because it is sometimes uncertain whether one has died." On the Breslau boy nearly buried alive, see "Darstellung der Vorgänge und Resultate wegen der aufs neue in Anregung gebrachte frühen Beerdigung der Juden, bey der jüdischen Gemeinde in Breslau; vom November 1797 bis Ende May 1798," *Schlesische Provinzialblätter* 28 (1798): 21–53. For historical accounts of events in Breslau, see Max Freudenthal, "Die ersten Emancipationsbestrebungen der Juden in Breslau," *Monatsschrift für Geschichte und Wissenschaft des Judenthums* (1893): 565–79; and Michael Edward Panitz, "Modernity and Mortality: The Transformation of Central European Responses to Death, 1750–1850" (Ph.D. diss., Jewish Theological Seminary, 1989), 146–50.
2. For a list of publications dealing with "seeming death" and premature burial, see the appendix at the end of this essay.
3. On German-Jewish history, but without any mention of burial practices, see Amos Elon, *The Pity of It All: A Portrait of the German-Jewish Epoch, 1743–1933* (New York: Holt, 2002).
4. "Darstellung der Vorgänge . . . ," 21–23.
5. Robert Darnton, *The Great Cat Massacre, and Other Episodes in French Cultural History* (New York: Vintage, 1985), 262.
6. On the fear of premature burial, see Martina Kessel, "Die Angst vor dem Scheintod im 18. Jahrhundert: Körper und Seele zwischen Religion, Magie und Wissenschaft," in *Hirntod: Zur Kulturgeschichte der Todesfestsellung,* ed. Thomas Schlich and Claudia Wiesemann (Frankfurt: Suhrkamp, 2001), 133–66; Jan Bondeson, *Buried Alive: The Terrifying History of Our Most Primal Fear* (New York: W. W. Norton, 2001); and Ingrid Stoessel, *Scheintod und Todesangst: Äusserungen der Angst in ihren geschichtlichen Wandlungen (17.–20. Jahrhundert)* (Cologne: Forschungsstelle des Instituts für Geschichte der Medizin der Universität zu Köln, 1983). Bondeson cites examples of the fear from antiquity to the eighteenth century, including the descriptions of premature burial in early modern plague chronicles; see *Buried Alive,* 32–34.
7. Bruhier, *Dissertation sur l'incertitude des signes de la mort* (Paris, 1749), 522–53. Cited in Bondeson, *Buried Alive,* 59. One version of the necrophilic theme concerned a randy monk who impregnated and thereby revived a woman in a state of seeming death. That story and the reactions to it are discussed in Thomas Laqueur, *Making Sex: Body and Gender from the Greeks to Freud* (Cambridge: Harvard University Press, 1990), 1–4.
8. *Deutsches Museum* 1 (1778): 445. An almost identical explanation of screams in cemeteries appeared a decade earlier in *Hannoverisches Magazin* 82 (October 10, 1768): 1302.
9. In the German debate on the question, what is Enlightenment?, Moses Mendelssohn took the position that some prejudices contained truths necessary to morality, and that in certain instances the "virtue-loving [*Tugendliebender*] Aufklärer . . . would do better to tolerate the prejudice than to drive out the truth with which the prejudice was so closely intertwined." See Moses Mendelssohn, "Über die Frage: Was heisst Aufklären?," *Berlinische Monatsschrift* 4 (1784): 198–99. In his *Essai sur les préjugés* (1770), D'Holbach denounced prejudices unconditionally, arguing that they were ipso facto harmful and incompatible with virtue and happiness. Compared to D'Holbach's position, Mendelssohn's looks quite moderate. But Mendelssohn's formulation, "better to tolerate the prejudice" (*lieber das Vorurteil dulden*), implied that it would have been better still if the truths necessary to morality were grounded in reason rather than apprehended in the form of prejudice. Even for Mendelssohn, therefore, the tolerance of prejudice was merely a provisional concession, not an ideal. On the concept of prejudice in the German Enlightenment, see Hans-Georg Gadamer, *Truth and Method,* rev. ed., trans. Joel Weinsheimer and Donald G. Marshall (New York: Continuum,

1989), 271–85; and Werner Schneiders, *Aufklärung und Vorurteilskritik: Studien zur Geschichte der Vorurteilstheorie* (Stuttgart: Frommann-Holzbook, 1983).

10. On eighteenth-century German medicine, see Thomas Broman, *The Transformation of German Academic Medicine, 1750–1820* (Cambridge: Cambridge University Press, 1996); Claudia Huerkamp, *Der Aufstieg der Ärtze im 19. Jahrhundert: Vom gelehrten Stand zum professionellen Experten: Das Beispiel Preussens* (Göttingen: Vandenhoeck & Ruprecht, 1985), 23–45; Ute Frevert, *Krankheit als politisches Problem: Soziale Untersichten in Preussen zwischen medizinischer Polizei und staatlicher Sozialversicherung* (Göttingen: Vandenhoeck & Ruprecht, 1984), 11–83; and Mary Lindemann, *Health and Healing in Eighteenth-Century Germany* (Baltimore: Johns Hopkins University Press, 1996). None of these works, however, devotes any attention to the issue of seeming death and premature burial.

11. See C. W. Hufeland's *Über die Ungewissheit des Todes und das einzige untrügliche Mittel sich von seiner Wirklichkeit zu überzeugen: Nebst der Nachricht von der Errichtung eines Leichenhauses in Weimar* (Weimar, 1791); and *Der Scheintod* (Berlin, 1808). On the public reaction to the *Leichenhäuser*, see Bondeson, *Buried Alive*, 100–110.

12. *Katechismus der anscheinenden Todesfälle oder sogenannten Pulslosigkeiten: Wodurch der gemeine Mann unterrichtet wird, wie er bey den verschiedenen Arten anscheinender Todesfälle verfahren soll: Auf Befehl Sr. königlichen Hoheit des Prinzen Heinrich von Preussen zum Druck befördert* (Berlin, 1787); *Unterricht vom Scheintode und dem sichersten Mittel das Lebendigbegraben zu verhüten für Ungelehrte* (Breslau, 1798). On the *Volksaufklärung* in general, see the discussion in Jonathan B. Knudsen, "On Enlightenment for the Common Man," in *What Is Enlightenment? Eighteenth-Century Answers and Twentieth-Century Questions*, ed. James Schmidt (Berkeley: University of California Press, 1996), 270–90.

13. On literacy and the circulation of the printed word among the laboring classes in late eighteenth-century Germany, see Rudolf Schenda, *Volk ohne Buch: Studien zur Sozialgeschichte der populären Lesestoffe, 1770–1910* (Frankfurt: Vittorio Klostermann, 1970).

14. *Neues Hamburgisches Magazin* (1778): 23.

15. *Lausizisches Wochenblatt* (1792): 327.

16. See, for example, "Abscheuliche Vergiftung in einer jüdischen Familie in Hamburg," *Historisch-politisch-literarisches Magazin* 8 (1790): 357–59.

17. On the debate about Jewish emancipation, see Gerda Heinrich, "' . . . man sollte itzt beständig das Publikum über diese Materie en haleine halten': Die Debatte um 'bürgerliche Verbesserung' der Juden 1781–86," in *Appell an das Publikum: Die Öffentliche Debatte in der deutschen Aufklärung, 1687–1796*, ed. Ursula Goldenbaum (Berlin: Akademie Verlag, 2004), 814–95.

18. Anton Friedrich Büsching, "Über die frühe Beerdigung der Juden," *Berlinische Monatsschrift* 5, no. 2 (1785): 112. On the other hand, the Christian Hebraist Johann David Michaelis, who wrote a lengthy article in his *Orientalische Bibliothek* (6 [1789]: 51–77) on the subject of Jewish burial practice, was indeed a staunch opponent of von Dohm.

19. "Über die frühe Beerdigung der Todten und über die Ungewissheit der Kennzeichen des wahren und falschen Todes," *Almanach für Ärzte und Nichtärzte* (1790): 182–83.

20. Such an argument was advanced in "Abscheuliche Vergiftung," 358–59, and "Über die frühe Beerdigung der Todten und über die Ungewissheit der Kennzeichen des wahren und falschen Todes," 183.

21. Originally written in Hebrew, Mendelssohn's letter to the Jews of Mecklenburg-Schwerin was translated into German and published after his death. See "Schreiben des Herrn Moses Mendelssohn an die achtbare Gemeinde zu Schwerin," *Berlinische Monatsschrift* 9 (1787): 325–29. When Jacob Herschel, the rabbi of the Jewish community in Altona, learned of Mendelssohn's position, he wrote an angry letter to him in which he castigated Mendelssohn for his "pride" and "arrogance." See M. Kayserling, *Moses Mendelssohn: Sein Leben und seine Werke* (Leipzig: Hermann Mendelssohn, 1862), 276–80.

22. Marcus Herz, *Über die frühe Beerdigung der Juden* (Berlin, 1788).

23. David Friedländer, "Über die frühe Beerdigung der Juden: Ein Brief aus Prag an die Herausgeber, nebst einigen Urkunden," *Berlinische Monatsschrift* 9 (1787): 318.

24. On the Enlightenment and fear in general, see Christian Begemann, *Furcht und Angst im Prozess der Aufklärung: Zu Literatur und Bewusstseinsgeschichte des 18. Jahrhunderts* (Frankfurt: Athenaeum, 1987); Hartmut Böhme and Gernot Böhme, *Das Andere der Vernunft: Zur Entwicklung von Rationalitätsstrukturen am Beispiel Kants* (Frankfurt: Suhrkamp, 1983); and Jean Deprun, *La philosophie de l'inquiétude en France au XVIIIe siècle* (Paris: J. Vrin, 1979). The generally accepted thesis is that the Enlightenment inaugurated an historical shift from "fear" (*Furcht*), which has a specific object—for example, witchcraft or hell—to "anxiety" (*Angst*), which is a defuse state of disquiet. The fear of premature burial, however, does not fit that thesis for the obvious reason that it did, in fact, have a precise object: awakening to find oneself entombed beneath the earth. On the traditional, pre-Enlightenment fears of early modern Europe, see Jean Delumeau, *La peur en Occident (XIVe–XVIII siècles): Une cité assiégée* (Paris: Fayard, 1978).

25. On famine in eighteenth-century Germany, see Wilhelm Abel, *Massenarmut und Hungerkrisen im vorindustriellen Deutschland*, 2nd. ed. (Göttingen: Vandenhoeck & Ruprecht, 1977).

26. On Mme. Necker's obsessive fear of being buried alive, see Antoine de Baecque, *La gloire et l'effroi: Septs morts sous la terreur* (Paris: B. Grasset, 1997), 217–51. Another French historian, Jean-Louis Bourgeon, has tried to track the fear of being buried alive by using the quantitative methods of the Annales school. He compared Parisian wills during fifteen-year periods from the first and second halves of the eighteenth century in order to determine whether there was any increase in the number of wills requesting safeguards against premature burial, and, in fact, there was an increase. In the period from 1710 to 1725, only two out of a thousand wills prescribed safeguards; in the period from 1760 to 1775, the number was thirteen out of a thousand, and additional thirty-four requested delays in burial for unspecified reasons. Bourgeon's study does not support the conclusion that there was a widespread panic, but it does indicate some rise in the fear of premature burial, probably due to the works of Bruhier and others. See Bourgeon, "La peur d'être enterré vivant au XVIIIe siècle: Mythe ou réalité?," *Revue d'histoire moderne et contemporaine* 30 (1983): 139–53. See also Bondeson, *Buried Alive*, 77.

27. On the "fragility" of scientific facts and the "fear" of that fragility among Enlightenment authors, see Lorraine Daston, "Enlightenment Fears, Fears of Enlightenment," in *What's Left of Enlightenment? A Postmodern Question*, ed. Keith Michael Baker and Peter Hanns Reill (Stanford: Stanford University Press, 2001), 115–28.

28. Jeffrey Freedman, *A Poisoned Chalice* (Princeton: Princeton University Press, 2002).

29. The passages cited appear in footnotes to the article that was being criticized. *Lausizisches Wochenblatt* (1792): 137–38, 325.

30. "Über die frühe Beerdigung der Todten und über die Ungewissheit der Kennzeichen des wahren Todes," *Almanach für Ärzte und Nichtärzte* (1790): 215.

31. Alain Corbin, *Le miasme et la jonquille: L'odorat et l'imaginaire social, XVIIIe–XIXe siècles* (Paris: Aubier, 1982).

32. M. J. Marx, *Journal von und für Deutschland* 1 (1784): 227–35.

33. David Friedländer, "Über die frühe Beerdigung der Juden: Ein Brief aus Prag an die Herausgeber, nebst einigen Urkunden," *Berlinische Monatsschrift* 9 (1787): 318.

34. For a criticism of that scholarly fashion, see Ronald Schechter, "Rationalizing the Enlightenment: Postmodernism and Theories of Anti-Semitism," in *Postmodernism and the Enlightenment: New Perspectives in Eighteenth-Century French Intellectual History*, ed. Daniel Gordon (New York: Routledge, 2001), 93–116.

35. "Über die frühe Beerdigung der Todten und über die Ungewissheit der Kennzeichen des wahren und falschen Todes," *Almanach für Ärzte und Nichtärzte* (1790): 183.

36. Bondeson reviews the evidence and concludes that some people probably were buried alive in the eighteenth and nineteenth centuries, though many fewer than the anti-premature-burial activists alleged. But, of course, precise figures cannot be obtained. See *Buried Alive*, 238–57.

TWELVE

FROM COSMOPOLITAN ANTICOLONIALISM TO LIBERAL IMPERIALISM:
FRENCH INTELLECTUALS AND MUSLIM NORTH AFRICA IN THE
LATE EIGHTEENTH AND EARLY NINETEENTH CENTURIES

Shanti Singham

It has been fashionable during the last three decades to attack the Enlightenment. This attack has come mainly from the Left and has been associated
with the victors of the 1960s civil rights and feminist movements, which have
so changed the character of our universities and, at last, our research agendas.
This trend has taken place during a shift—some would say contingent, some
not—toward cultural history and away from Marxist paradigms, along with
the vogue for postmodernism in American academic circles in the 1980s and
1990s. Feminists such as Joan Landes and Joan Scott, and "third worlders" like
Emmanuel Eze, Michel-Rolph Trouillot, Bhikhu Parekh, and Edward Said,
have taken Enlightenment thinkers to task for their racist, sexist, and Eurocentric ideas—in short, for their inability to think in pluralistic and multicul-
tural terms.[1] In many ways a welcome challenge to a historiography that had
virtually ignored women and people of color in the eighteenth century, these
attacks nonetheless have significant shortcomings. Besides being one-sided
and failing to properly locate Enlightenment texts within their own complex
eighteenth-century context, these scholars all too easily cede the Enlightenment to a new academic Right that was intent on challenging, in the United
States, multiculturalism and affirmative action, and in France, the antiracist
movement spurred by Maghrebin, or *beur*, youth during 1980s. Leading figures
defending the Enlightenment from postmodern attacks in the U.S. culture wars
of the last two decades include Harold Bloom, Lynne Cheney, and David
Horowitz, and, in France, Alain Finkielkraut.[2]

For most of the eighteenth and nineteenth centuries, however, it was right-wing thinkers who attacked the Enlightenment. They did so precisely because of concerns that Enlightenment relativism and pluralism were undermining church and state.[3] Although Enlightenment scholars have disagreed widely about the "essence" of Enlightenment thought, in part because of its geographic spread and the generational diversity of thinkers associated with it, most would probably agree with Robert Darnton's characterization of the Enlightenment as first and foremost a movement of reform united in a common quest for knowledge, designed to dispel the evils of ignorance and superstition and to ensure individual rights and liberties.[4] As such, it was primarily a movement aimed at attacking the ideological and institutional power of the church. It was centered in France, especially in Paris, where the battle was most acute and often fought over issues such as the illegal publications of the movement, the struggle to control the Académie française and other institutions of thought and learning, and the world of the theater. Although leading philosophes such as Voltaire, Montesquieu, Rousseau, and Diderot disagreed about the most ideal form of government, in their courageous battles against religious and political authorities they not only articulated many of the ideals of nineteenth-century liberalism—religious tolerance, increased popular participation in government, freedom of thought and of the press—but they also actively engaged in the battles that were to occupy the men and women of the nineteenth century against slavery, colonialism, and imperialism, as well as in support of women's rights and greater social responsibility toward the poor.

Not surprisingly, then, these same Enlightenment thinkers were roundly condemned after World War II. The unprecedented carnage of two world wars and the unspeakable horrors of the Holocaust were attributed to the inevitable failures of liberalism and socialism. While Jewish thinkers like Arthur Hertzberg squarely blamed anti-Semitism, and even the ideology of the Holocaust, on philosophes like Voltaire, Jewish émigrés fled Europe and created the modern state of Israel based on Zionist principles that seemed to reject some important Enlightenment values.[5] In the United States and the Caribbean, decolonization and civil rights moved in the same direction, proudly championing difference—*négritude, les griots*, black power—and assailing the racist legacy of modern Western forefathers like Washington and Jefferson, Robespierre and Napoleon. More recently, the misadventures of the United States in the Middle East, combined with deeply entrenched fears of Muslims and Islamic fundamentalism in Europe and North America, have focused attention in the academic world on the West's racist and imperialist forays in that region.

Is it fair to blame the Enlightenment for the racism and nationalism of the nineteenth and twentieth centuries? To what extent is the Enlightenment guilty of originating the sins of the nineteenth century, particularly concerning the West's unfavorable attitude toward Muslims and Arabs? By looking at a few key texts from the eighteenth and nineteenth centuries, this essay seeks to weaken the ties that bind the philosophes to their liberal and even socialist descendants in the nineteenth century, and to restore a sense of their radical, Pan-European, cosmopolitan, and internationalist vision. Inspired by Robert Darnton's pioneering work on the importance of the lesser-known works of the Enlightenment—works he sometimes referred to as "gutter Rousseauian" or *libelles*—as well as by his great sympathy for the ideals of the Enlightenment, what follows is a provisional and speculative argument based on some of the new work available on France's initial forays into the Middle East during the age of Enlightenment.[6] By comparing and contrasting the eighteenth-century works of Charles-Etienne Savary and Constantin-Francois Volney on Egypt with Alexis de Tocqueville's nineteenth-century writings on Algeria, I hope to highlight the contrasting worldviews of these intellectuals while paying attention to the differing colonial and metropolitan contexts in which they were articulated.

In an important sense, the philosophes' interest in the extra-European world began in earnest in the 1770s with the illegal publication of the Enlightenment's second major collective call to arms, the *Histoire des deux Indes*.[7] Both masters of the early Enlightenment, Montesquieu and Voltaire, had in some senses initiated this interest much earlier with their sympathetic portrayals of other cultures, their commitment to a comparative approach to human history and the burgeoning social sciences, and their open denunciation of New World slavery. These issues were to become more central to the French and English public as the century wore on, as slaves in both countries used the courts to challenge their status, as Americans battled for their independence, as the French and British radicals opposed the status quo of their governments, and as more and more philosophes such as Diderot and Bernardin de Saint-Pierre traveled abroad to see the world firsthand.[8] In the 1770s, Raynal and Diderot collaborated to produce the multivolume and multiauthored *Histoire des deux Indes*.[9] Like the *Encyclopédie*, this work claimed to be objective and empirical, a documentary survey of the extra-European world as made known by European travelers and colonizers. It became an international best seller, translated into many European languages and reprinted several times in the decades preceding the French Revolution.[10] Its central message stressed the

urgent need to embrace the ongoing struggle against despotism, be it against
the dictatorial Chancellor Maupeou of France, the Ottoman overseers of Egypt,
or the French and English slave owners of Caribbean plantations.[11] The pictures and text of the many volumes of the *Histoire* strongly condemned European imperialism and espoused a vision of cultural equality. "I speak to the
most cruel Europeans," the work concluded. "There are regions of the world
that have supplied you with rich metals, beautiful clothes, delicious food. But
read this book and see at what price you have received these goods. Would
you still want these things knowing their human cost? Surely no one is evil
enough to answer—Yes, I still want these things. This same question will continue to haunt future generations with the same force and power."[12]

Soon after the appearance of Raynal and Diderot's work, two important
travel diaries of the Middle East appeared, Savary's *Lettres sur l'Égypte* (1787)
and Volney's *Voyage en Égypte et en Syrie* (1787), along with Volney's more general work on the Russo-Ottoman conflict and the Ottoman Empire, the *Considérations sur la guerre actuelle des Turcs* (1788). These works, which were to
play an important role in French involvement in Egypt and the Levant during the Napoleonic period and after, were unusual in that both Savary and
Volney not only traveled to and spent considerable time in the Middle East,
but they also learned Arabic in order to better appreciate Egypt and Syria.
Savary produced an early French translation of the Koran in 1784 that was
still being used by Tocqueville fifty years later.[13] Of the two, Volney appears
to have been more influential and more representative of the Enlightenment,
displaying a strong Voltarian antipathy to organized religions of all sorts, especially in his later work *Les ruines; ou, Méditation sur les révolutions des empires*.
Volney was to become an active revolutionary and was associated with the
Girondins. Although he had to lie low at key moments of the tumult during
the 1790s and the Napoleonic period, he struggled all his life for the creation
of a world language, designed to bring about the world harmony he thought
was on the horizon.[14]

Savary's attitudes toward Islam and Egypt were mixed. On the one hand,
he was much more sympathetic to Islam and more positive about Egypt than
Volney. "Muhammad was born a genius," Savary declaimed, "destined to change
the world, creating a language for the Arab people, allowing them to unite various tribes and arm themselves against the rest of the world."[15] In some ways,
Savary seems more of a cultural relativist than Volney. Like Montaigne before
him, Rousseau during his own lifetime, and the Romantics after him, Savary
viewed the natives he became acquainted with as archetypal noble savages,

primitive men in an unspoiled state. He certainly gave a more favorable assessment of the region as a whole, leading Volney to criticize him as misleading.[16] On the other hand, Savary tended to subscribe to stereotypes about the Egyptian people that seemed racist and unscientific. Thus Volney criticized both Montesquieu and Savary for adhering to what he considered ridiculous theories of the climate influencing the behavior of Egyptians and other "Orientals."[17] Savary had argued that laziness was an Egyptian vice, related to the hot climate, that trapped Egyptians in eternal negative typology, his positive portrayal of Islam notwithstanding.[18] In this contradictory stance, Savary displayed an attitude similar to that of Voltaire before him and a number of the Napoleonic savants after him, who were all more interested in Egypt's ancient history than its present. In fact, exposure to Egyptian antiquities helped Savary articulate a secular and enlightened theory of the rise and fall of great civilizations—one that condemned Egypt to a grand but forever lost past. Such an attitude combined great respect for early Egyptian culture and the later political and religious successes of Muhammad with dismay and contempt for the barbarous present, and this would contribute to later justifications for Western conquest as a necessary means of uplift.

Napoleon's troops reportedly found Savary's work misleading and untruthful, with its emphasis on past grandeur and exotic charm, and far preferred the accuracy of Volney's portrait.[19] The vision Volney conjured up was far less exotic and much harsher. Sharing a Voltarian antipathy to religion, Volney was unsympathetic to Muhammad and Islam, especially the impact of Islamic law on social life. His hostility is one of the reasons Volney gets such negative treatment by Edward Said in his landmark work *Orientalism*. Said argued that "Volney's views were canonically hostile to Islam as a religion and as a system of political institutions."[20] This is true, but Volney was equally hostile to Christianity and other forms of organized religion. Indeed, the entire premise of his later work *Les ruines* was to expose the similarity and inanity of all religions— Judaism, Islam, Christianity, that of the Persians, Hinduism, even Tatars—and to insist that they were the major cause of conflict and difference among the peoples of the world. In the interests of world harmony and peace, Volney advocated a strict separation of church and state.[21] Said goes on to insist that "the climax of the *Voyage* occurs in the second volume, [in] an account of Islam as a religion."[22] But, in fact, the chapter on religion is a mere nine pages, an aside about Syria. The climax of the book, I would argue, centers on the political sections describing the role of the Mamelukes in Egypt and of the Turks in Syria in oppressing the native Arabs. Unlike Savary, Volney was more interested in the Egypt of his own day, of the peoples and cultures he encountered, not with architectural relics of a former grandeur.

Even though Volney was strongly critical of Islamic laws and of the condition of the Egyptian and Syrian people, his portrayal of Muslim and Arab peoples, whom he called Orientals, was in important ways quite sympathetic. "In general, the Orientals are remarkable for a clear conception, an easy expression, a propriety of language in the things they are acquainted with, and a passionate and nervous style," he noted. "[They are] a people of a more humane and generous character, and possessing more simplicity and more refined and open manners, than even the inhabitants of European countries, as if the Asiatics, having been polished long before us, still preserved the traces of their early improvement."[23] Like many philosophes at the time, such as Diderot, d'Holbach, and Helvetius, who all had condemned the "despotism" of Maupeou, Volney attributed the problems of the Egyptian and Syrian people not to the climate, but rather to the despotic political system—namely, the Turkish empire—under which these people labored. "The government of the Turks in Syria is a pure military despotism," he concluded.[24] It is true that this rhetoric could be construed to sound Eurocentric—after all, Volney lauded European societies for having two key bulwarks against despotism (the widespread existence of printed books and of strong middle classes between the ruling oligarchs/despots and the people)—as if Europe had invented freedom.[25] In fairness to Volney, however, it is important to note that he praised only certain European societies—Greece, Italy, Holland, and Switzerland—and his criticisms of certain features of Turkish society were clearly intended as criticisms of France.[26] This was especially true of his condemnation of Turkish tax farmers, venal office holders, and the high price of Turkish justice, all issues of pressing concern in prerevolutionary France.[27]

Preoccupied with the later Napoleonic incursion, Said misses much of the meaning and nuance of Volney's works by not placing them within the international and global context of the American Revolution and the universal struggle against despotism, of which Volney and other radical philosophes considered themselves a part.[28] While critical of the government of Egypt and Syria, of the upper classes, of the condition of women, of the state of the roads, of commerce, and of the arts, Volney expressed great sympathy and respect for the poor, for the oppressed peasants, and for beleaguered women, especially those in upper-class confines.[29] Just as Raynal and Diderot anticipated Toussaint-Louverture's revolution in Saint-Domingue in the *Histoire des deux Indes*, Volney anticipated Mehmet Ali's revolt against the Ottomans at the

beginning of the nineteenth century.[30] Thus, writing about the Egyptian peasantry, he concludes,

> Besides, if any men are capable of this ardor [i.e., the courage necessary
> to overthrow their condition of slavery], it should be those whose minds
> and bodies, inured to suffering by habit, have acquired a hardiness that
> blunts the edge of pain, and such are the Egyptians. We deceive our-
> selves when we represent them as enervated by heat, or effeminate from
> debauchery. . . . All prove that their minds, when swayed by certain
> ideas, are capable of great energy. . . . The cruelties and seditions that
> have sometimes been the consequence of their exhausted patience in-
> dicates a latent fire, which waits only for proper agents to put it into
> motion, and produce great and unexpected effects.[31]

Volney was very critical of the Turks and the Mamelukes as outside con-
querors and oppressors of the Egyptian people, and he presciently predicted
their fall. In fact, his digressions on conquest show his opposition to colonization, which he thought was bad for both the conquered and the conqueror.[32]
In his *Considérations*, written several years after his trip to Egypt and after the
successful American Revolution, Volney addressed Turkish despotism once
again, but in the context of what was about to become the seat of a forthcoming Eastern war, with Russia and Austria looking on eagerly for territorial and
commercial gains. The French government, a long-standing ally and trading
partner of the Ottomans, scrambled to decide what role to play in the ensuing conflict, and Volney's writings and opinions played a significant role.[33]
Although Volney's prediction concerning the demise of the Ottomans was
premature—it took another hundred years and World War I to finally bring
about the dismantling of the Ottoman Empire—his analysis of the changing
contours of Ottoman and European powers was remarkably astute. But Volney
counseled a path neither of accommodation nor of war against the Ottomans.
Rather, he advocated a "wait and see" policy, one that would give the French
time to work behind the scenes and via the medium of a tolerant policy of
trade to help wean the Turkish people of despotic rule.[34] Most important,
Volney strongly opposed French expansionism on both moral and tactical
grounds and warned that should they attempt to invade Egypt, the French
would be met with firm resistance on the part of the native Arabs of Egypt.[35]
Napoleon clearly did not heed Volney's advice, neither in his extremely harsh
treatment of the Egyptian people nor in his relations with the armed vestiges

of the Ottoman army. Underestimating the strength of their joint resistance, unaware of the extent of British involvement in the area, and overestimating the power and impact of his hypocritical rhetorical gestures of respect for Islamic and Egyptian culture, Napoleon's brief escapade in Egypt and Syria was to end in ignoble defeat.[36] But while the Napoleonic invasion was a transitory, albeit important, early French foray into North Africa, it was soon to be surpassed by the absolutist maneuvers of Charles X into Algeria in 1830, with much more long-lasting results.[37] The nineteenth-century intellectual and traveler Alexis de Tocqueville was to have an important impact on these initiatives. Like his predecessors, Tocqueville was an engaged intellectual. But not only were his politics and personal biography radically different—Tocqueville came from a distinguished aristocratic and legitimist family that had greatly suffered during and because of the Revolution—so, too, were the avenues open to him for political praxis, avenues that were generally much expanded, even during the restored monarchy.[38] Like Volney and Savary, Tocqueville wrote of his travels to the Muslim and Arab lands of North Africa. But the contrast between Volney's account of Egypt in the 1780s and Tocqueville's account of his travels to another Arab North African land, Algeria, forty years later, is dramatic. Unlike Volney, Tocqueville did not learn Arabic before going to or during his stays in Algeria in 1841 or 1846.[39] Like Volney, he seemed to share an early predisposition to view Algerians positively and to adhere to a monogenetic understanding of the essential unity of the human race. In his second letter, written before actually going to Algeria, Tocqueville even embraced racial intermingling: "Nothing . . . indicates to me that there should be any incompatibility of temper between the Arabs and us. I see, on the contrary, that in times of peace the two races intermix without trouble. . . . There is, then, no reason to believe that time will not succeed in amalgamating the two races."[40]

Unlike Volney, however, Tocqueville's actual travels produced the opposite effect, distancing him from his initial sympathy toward Algerian Arabs. Some scholars insist on Tocqueville's non-racism, as evidenced in his early letters written in the 1830s and his long-standing disagreement with Gobineau.[41] But his increasingly hostile attitude toward Algeria, Arabs, and Islam in the 1840s— a result of his travels and of his growing nationalism, induced, in part, by his involvement in a public career in the Chamber of Deputies—reveal a hardening of opinion. Moreover, even as a young man in the 1830s, Tocqueville never questioned the validity of French colonialism. Through all the vicissitudes of his career, Tocqueville remained committed to the necessity of the

French conquest of Algeria. His reflections on the matter centered on discovering how that conquest could be most successful—be it via direct or indirect rule, military harshness and expansion, appropriation or payment for land, or the coming together or the strict separation between European settlers and Algerian locals.

Tocqueville's evolving views on Algeria were determined by his primary concern, namely, France's position in the changing configuration of world politics. "I do not think France can think seriously of leaving Algeria," he said in 1841. "In the eyes of the world, such an abandonment would be the clear indication of our decline. . . . If France shrank from an enterprise in which she faced nothing but the natural difficulties of the terrain and the opposition of little barbarous tribes, she would seem in the eyes of the world to be yielding to her own impotence and succumbing to her own lack of courage. Any people that easily gives up what it has taken and chooses to retire peacefully to its original borders proclaims that its age of greatness is over."[42] As Tocqueville matter-of-factly stated, "Africa has entered the civilized world." European dominion over Algeria, he insisted, whether direct or indirect, was going to happen. The only question was which European power would receive the spoils. "If these positions do not remain in our hands," he noted, "they will pass into those of another European people."[43] While briefly admitting the possibility of a nascent Arab power taking over, it was clear that Tocqueville's main fear was the English. Like Napoleon, Tocqueville's concern was the world struggle between France and England for dominance, one in which, after Waterloo, France found itself severely weakened. Tocqueville spent much of his time decrying Frenchmen's weaknesses, especially their disinclination for colonial adventures and economic gain. Equally to blame for France's second-class status as a colonial power, however, was Tocqueville's ultimate bête noire, the spirit of administrative centralization emanating from Paris, which was responsible for stifling European local initiative in Algeria. Governors, generals, and other emissaries from Paris gave too little power, security, or freedom to local whites, according to Tocqueville, thereby hampering their ability to successfully rule over their Arab neighbors.

Tocqueville's primary recommendation—a consistent trope in his various colonial writings—was that the French had to increase the number of local European colonists going to Algeria by improving the conditions of life for these émigrés. His recommendations as to how these Europeans were to treat the locals varied, based in part on Tocqueville's astute recommendations that French locals use divide-and-rule tactics to secure their power, favoring the lighter-skinned, more-European-like Berbers over their Arab neighbors.[44] In the 1840s, until the French conquest was complete, Tocqueville was to advocate harsh military maneuvers against the Arabs. By then, he had given up on his advocacy for a policy of assimilation, arguing instead for the need of a strict delineation between the two cultures, Arab and European.

In important ways, Tocqueville helped articulate and encourage the kind of unequal, apartheid-like regime in Algeria that was to result in a civil war of unparalleled cruelty in the twentieth century. His private thoughts in 1841 after his first visit reflect this harsh worldview. Arguing against his leftist, anticolonial colleagues, Tocqueville insisted that only "those who have been there know that unfortunately Muslim society and Christian society do not have a single tie, that they form two bodies that are juxtaposed but completely separate. . . . The Arab element is becoming more and more isolated . . . The Muslim population always seems to be shrinking, while the Christian population is always growing. The fusion of these two populations is a chimera that people dream of only when they have not been to these places. There can, therefore, and there must be, two very separate societies there."[45] Moreover, since the settlement of Europeans in Algeria necessarily entailed a war between peoples, not an old-fashioned European war between governments, Tocqueville noted that "burning harvests, seizing unarmed men, women and children . . . are unfortunate necessities" in the war in Algeria.[46] Induced starvation by commercial sanctions, ravaging of the countryside, and permanent destruction of all Arab towns, and the inhabitants therein, were the means Tocqueville advocated to secure the nation. Arguing that the colonization of Algeria and domination over the Arabs were "the two greatest interests France has in the world today," Tocqueville shows us just how important the French, even liberals like Tocqueville, considered imperialism to be. "Our preponderance in Europe, the order of our finances, the lives of part of our citizenry, and our national honor are engaged [in Algeria]," Tocqueville insisted, "in the most compelling manner."[47]

What a turnaround from Savary's and Volney's dream of mutual sympathy and interaction, and what an (unfortunately) accurate blueprint for Algeria's future! How can we account for these strong differences of opinion? Was Tocqueville simply a racist? What had so changed in the intervening years? While there are no easy answers to the first of these questions, it is clear that the most important change occurring during this period was the enunciation and development of a new liberal, even at times revolutionary, nationalism, which was to color French republican politics from the first wars of the Revolution through the twentieth century.[48] Disappointment at the steady set of defeats at the hands of the English during the Napoleonic wars, combined with the lingering sense of *gloire* from France's aristocratic and monarchical past, colored Tocqueville's entire thinking about colonial and foreign affairs. Even Tocqueville's more noble work on behalf of the emancipation of French slaves was defended as a necessary part of the worldwide struggle against the English and for the retention of France's status as a leading world power. "I recognize . . . that the principal merit of our colonies is not in their markets, but in the position they occupy on the globe," wrote Tocqueville. "This makes several of them [i.e., the Caribbean] the most precious possessions France could have."[49]

Tocqueville went on to try to "prove that as long as slavery is not abolished in our colonies, our colonies will not, so to speak, belong to us. . . . The benefits will pass into other [i.e. English] hands the day they can be used" since the English, by abolishing slavery, had claimed the moral high ground in the Caribbean. Their free islands were a constant inducement for unrest on the remaining French slave islands.[50] Although Tocqueville made high-sounding declarations about the French invention of liberty and the necessity of abolishing slavery in French colonies, his insistence on both indemnification and forcibly stopping freed slaves in the French colonies from buying land upon emancipation—in order to keep them as virtual indentured laborers on the plantations—belied these humanitarian sentiments and betrayed their realpolitik intention.[51]

Most French republicans in the nineteenth century shared Tocqueville's conviction that colonial conquest in North Africa and the retention of France's earlier colonies in the New World were essential for maintaining French grandeur. There was opposition, but usually from small pockets in the extreme left and among intellectuals, particularly after the loss of Alsace-Lorraine. Nationalism twisted nineteenth-century French republicans and liberals into supporting the illiberal and racist policies of French imperialism in the colonial world, especially in North Africa, even if these policies were pursued mostly by monarchists, Bonapartists, aristocratic military men, and Catholic missionaries.

Why had nineteenth-century liberals forsaken the anti-imperialism of their philosophical forebears like Diderot and Volney? Sankar Muthu, in *Enlightenment Against Empire*, argues that whereas Volney's peers were deeply critical of Old Regime Europe for seeking to export its values to other parts of the world, liberals like Tocqueville and Mill, living after the triumph of the French Revolution, could more justly be proud of exporting European values.[52] Hence the expansion of the "civilizing mission" strain of imperialism so central in France under the Third Republic, but common as well to English Christian missionaries in the nineteenth century. Although Muthu may exaggerate the liberal character of nineteenth-century England and France and neglect the central role that technology played in instilling in Europeans a sense of superiority over others, his central insight is very useful. Clearly, once liberals took power and had to rule, they found the temptations of imperialism and colonialism hard to resist. The ideals of the French Revolution were readily invoked to justify practices that would have been anathema to men like Volney and Savary. Tocqueville's nationalism encouraged him to advocate if not racist, certainly insensitive policies toward both the native peoples of North Africa and the freed slaves of the French West Indies. An advocate of imperialism, he combined liberalism, nationalism, aristocratic pride, and monarchical *gloire* in a unique but enduring synthesis that presaged the *mission civilatrice* of the Third Republic.

While it is true that the knowledge Volney, Savary, and the philosophes obtained was far inferior to that of the travelers of the following century (e.g., Tocqueville), they were more open-minded toward exploration and more likely to celebrate cultural differences. To be sure, personal prejudices and racism were not entirely absent in their thinking.[53] But, despite these differences, travelers like Savary and Volney were careful to insist on the humanity of those who differed from them and the shortcomings of their own culture in ways that fostered a genuinely egalitarian humanism. Other enlightened thinkers thought likewise. Thus, for example, Diderot championed the Hottentots in the *Histoire des deux Indes* and insisted that Europeans could not judge that these people were more unhappy than themselves, unless they ignored European suffering in their own midst.[54] Herder, Kant, and Gibbon echoed many of these sentiments, and Herder summed up the late Enlightenment's cosmopolitanism thus: "There is no such thing as a specially favored nation on earth. . . . There cannot, therefore, be any order or rank. . . . Least of all must we think of European culture as a universal standard of human values. . . . The culture of man is not the culture of the Europeans; it manifests itself according to place and time in every people."[55] Bernardin de Saint-Pierre's frontispiece to his *Voyage à l'Isle de France* proudly displayed two babies, one black and the other white, both equally beautiful, nursing from the same "mother liberty," and Raynal and Diderot's *Histoire des deux Indes* was full of positive artistic portrayals of colonial peoples.[56] Savary praised the Arabs among whom he had lived: "This proud people are the only people on earth who have preserved the courage, generosity, and loyalty which bring honor to humanity. It is the Arabs whom the philosopher should study," he insisted, not those, like his European co-citizens, whose "spirit, heart, and affections" had become "corrupted" by "despotism and servitude."[57] Volney, although distinctly more negative in his depiction of both Arabs and Turks, agreed that, compared with Christians and Greeks in the Ottoman Empire, Muslims, "though haughty to the point of insolence, possess a sort of goodness of heart, humanity, and justice; and above all, [they] never fail to manifest great fortitude under misfortune and much firmness of character."[58]

Volney's universalism, however, lay elsewhere, namely, in the championing of a common social scientific method for all humankind. For Volney, man's education—including his religious instruction—and government were what determined the kind of society he lived in and his moral values.[59] Travel and the study of history were essential in teaching humankind the pitfalls of all societies.[60] Volney was not happy about what he found in Egypt and the Ottoman Empire—oppressed people, plague, a languishing civilization, famine, and incredible harshness. He wrote about these hardships, however, to alleviate them—both by encouraging a tolerant and enlightened foreign policy on the part of his own government toward these regions and decrying despotism and religious intolerance everywhere.

Global citizens and world historians before their time, these philosophes in many ways anticipated the new world history and globalism of the most recent generation of intellectuals in the twenty-first century—individuals like Kenneth Pomeranz, Amartya Sen, Kwame Appiah, Martin Bernal, Janet Abu-Lughod, and others—who have insisted that reason, toleration, freedom of thought, and democracy are not uniquely Western, and that European civilization itself has been part of a global exchange and interchange even before the Middle Ages.[61] Although the philosophes were often blind to the historical benefits of religion—which is understandable, perhaps, given their struggles against the church—most of them did not invoke their Enlightenment values to justify European intrusions in other parts of the world, and they took special care, unlike many contemporary political commentators on Islam, to insist that religion did not totally define the culture and habits of peoples and societies.[62] Most important, in the likes of Volney and Diderot, they spoke out strongly against the wars of conquest that would characterize the next century. In his *Les ruines*, written during the Revolution, Volney dispelled the notion that Europeans, even those experimenting with freedom—namely, Britain and France—were innocent in the world: "And those nations which call themselves polished, are they not the same ones that have filled the earth with their injustice for the last three centuries? Are they not those who, under the pretext of commerce, have desolated India, despoiled a new continent, and now subject Africa to the most barbarous slavery? Can liberty be born from the bosom of despots? And shall justice be rendered by the hands of piracy and extortion?"[63] This ominous warning against imperialism is as relevant today as it was when first issued two hundred years ago.

NOTES

1. Challenges to Enlightenment ideals, especially in the field of history, are traced in Joyce Appleby, Lynn Hunt, and Margaret Jacob, *Telling the Truth About History* (New York: W. W. Norton, 1994). Some of the chief works criticizing the Enlightenment from a left-wing perspective include Joan Landes, *Women and the Public Sphere in the Age of the French Revolution* (Ithaca: Cornell University Press, 1988); Joan Scott, *French Feminists Claim the Rights of "Man": Olympe de Gouges on the French Revolution* (St. Louis: Washington University Press, 1991); Emmanuel Eze, *Race and Enlightenment: A Reader* (Oxford: Blackwell, 1997); Michel Rolph Trouillot, *Silencing the Past: Power and the Production of History* (Boston: Beacon Press, 1995); Bhikhu Parekh, *Rethinking Multiculturalism: Cultural Diversity and Political Theory* (Houndmills, U.K.: Macmillan, 2000); and Edward Said, *Orientalism* (New York: Vintage, 1978). Recently, there has been an attempt to positively recapture the Enlightenment's left-wing and liberal legacy on the part of Stephen Eric Bronner, *Reclaiming the Enlightenment: Toward a Politics of Radical Engagement* (New York: Columbia University Press, 2004); and Ira Katznelson, *Desolation and Enlightenment: Political Knowledge After Total War, Totalitarianism, and the Holocaust* (New York: Columbia University Press, 2003).

2. See, for example, Harold Bloom, *The Western Canon: The Books and School of the Ages* (New York: Harcourt, Brace, 1994); Lynne Cheney, *Telling the Truth: Why Our Schools, Our Culture, and Our Country Have Stopped Making Sense, and What We Can Do About It* (New York: Simon & Schuster, 1995); and Alain Finkielkraut, *The Defeat of the Mind*, trans. and introd. Judith Friedlander (New York: Columbia University Press, 1995).

3. See especially Darrin McMahon, *Enemies of the Enlightenment: The French Counter-Enlightenment and the Making of Modernity* (New York: Oxford University Press, 2001).

4. Robert Darnton, *George Washington's False Teeth: An Unconventional Guide to the Eighteenth Century* (New York: W. W. Norton, 2003), 4.

5. See Tony Judt's "Israel: The Alternative," *New York Review of Books*, October 23, 2003, http://www.nybooks.com/articles/archives/2003/oct/23/israel-the-alternative/.

6. Interest in this area has increased in the last two decades due to the combination of the unraveling of the Algerian Revolution in the 1980s, the threat of Islamic militancy there and elsewhere in the Middle East, and the demands of Muslim immigrants in France for inclusion and better treatment. In France, this new work has been associated especially with Benjamin Stora and Mohammed Harbi, along with Louisette Ighilahiriz and Raphaelle Branche. See Benjamin Stora and Mohammed Harbi, eds., *La guerre d'Algérie, 1954–2004: La fin de l'amnésie* (Paris: Laffont, 2004). Alec G. Hargreave's many works, including his edited *Memory, Empire, and Postcolonialism: Legacies of French Colonialism* (Lanham, Md.: Lexington Books, 2005) and *Immigration, "Race," and Ethnicity in Contemporary France* (London: Routledge, 1995), have introduced the English-speaking public to these important contributions. Juan Cole's recent *Napoleon's Egypt: Invading the Middle East* (New York: Palgrave Macmillan, 2007), along with the translation of Alexis de Tocqueville's *Writings on Empire and Slavery* (Baltimore: Johns Hopkins University Press, 2001) by Jennifer Pitts, her book *A Turn to Empire: The Rise of Imperial Liberalism in Britain and France* (Princeton: Princeton University Press, 2005), and Sankar Muthu's *Enlightenment Against Empire* (Princeton:

Princeton University Press, 2003), are finally bringing these issues to the attention of English-speaking students of French history.

7. The first was the *Encyclopédie*; on the battle this work occasioned, see Robert Darnton, *The Business of Enlightenment: A Publishing History of the "Encyclopédie," 1775–1800* (Cambridge: Harvard University Press, 1979). On the second, see below. The full title was *Histoire philosophique et politique des établissements et du commerce des européens dans les deux Indes*.

8. On the court challenges and general attitudes toward race in eighteenth-century France, see Sue Peabody's *"There Are No Slaves in France": The Political Culture of Race and Slavery in the Ancien Régime* (New York: Oxford University Press, 1996).

9. Anthony Strugnell has compiled much scholarship on this seminal work in the journal *Studies on Voltaire and the Eighteenth Century*. See, for example, Anthony Strugnell, ed., *L'histoire des deux Indes et quelques débats du dix-huitième siècle* (Oxford: Voltaire Foundation, 2003); Gilles Bancarel and Gianluigi Goggi, eds., *Raynal, de la polémique à l'histoire* (Oxford: Voltaire Foundation, 2000); and Hans-Jurgen Lusebrink and Anthony Strugnell, eds., *L'histoire des deux Indes: Réécriture et polygraphie* (Oxford: Voltaire Foundation, 1995).

10. For circulation, see Robert Darnton, *The Forbidden Best-Sellers of Pre-Revolutionary France* (New York: W. W. Norton, 1995), 34–35.

11. I make this argument in my dissertation, "'A Conspiracy of Twenty Million Frenchmen': Public Opinion, Patriotism, and the Assault on Absolutism During the Maupeou Years, 1770–1775" (Ph.D. diss., Princeton University, 1991), 285–88. See also Durand Echeverria, *The Maupeou Revolution: A Study in the History of Libertarianism, France, 1770–1774* (Baton Rouge: Louisiana State University Press, 1985).

12. Guillaume-Thomas Raynal, *L'histoire philosophique et politique des établissements et du commerce des européens dans les deux Indes* (hereafter cited as *L'histoire des deux Indes*) (Geneva: Pellet, 1780), 10:477. On the pictures in this work, see Hugh Honour, *From the American Revolution to World War I: Slaves and Liberators*, vol. 4 of *The Image of the Black in Western Art* (Cambridge: Harvard University Press, 1989), esp. 54–56. For a somewhat contrary reading of these pictures, see Lise Andries, "Les illustrations dans *L'histoire des deux Indes*," *Studies on Voltaire and the Eighteenth Century* 333 (1995): 11–41, esp. 41.

13. For a brief biography of Savary, see J.-F. Michaud and L.-G. Michaud, *Biographie universelle ancienne et moderne*, 2nd ed. (Paris: Delegrave, 1870–73), 38:108–9.

14. For Volney's life, see Joan Leopold, "The Life and Work of Constantin-Francois Chasseboeuf, comte de Volney," in *The Prix Volney: Its History and Significance for the Development of Scientific Research*, ed. Joan Leopold (Boston: Kluwer, 1999), 1:8–31. See also "Volney," in Jules Barni, *Les moralistes français au dix-huitième siècle* (Geneva: Slatkine Reprints, 1970), 189–234; and Michaud, *Biographie universelle*, 44:64–72. For Volney and Savary, see Henry Laurens, *Les origines intellectuelles de l'expédition d'Égypte: L'orientalisme islamisant en France (1698–1798)* (Istanbul and Paris: Isis, 1987) and his *L'expédition d'Egypte, 1798–1801*, coauthored with Charles C. Gillispie, Jean-Claude Golvin, and Claude Traunecker (Paris: A. Colin, 1989); see also the introduction in C.-F. Volney, *Voyage en Egypte et en Syrie*, ed. Jean Gaulmier (Paris: Mouton, 1959). Gaulmier has written several other works on the subject. For a recent and useful bibliography of works on Volney, see Jean Nicole Hafid-Martin, *Volney*, vol. 17 of *Bibliographie des écrivains français* (Paris: Memini, 1999). On Volney's linguistic efforts, see Sophia Rosenfeld, *A Revolution in Language: The Problem of Signs in Late Eighteenth-Century France* (Stanford: Stanford University Press, 2001).

15. Savary, *Lettres sur l'Egypte* (Amsterdam: Libraires associés, 1787), 3:67.

16. Volney, *Travels Through Syria and Egypt* (London: G. G. J. and J. Robinson, 1788), 1:vi, 266–70.

17. Ibid., 2:463.

18. Savary, *Lettres*, 1:112.

19. For the reaction of civilian and military personnel on Napoleon's campaign to the two works, see Gaulmier's comments in his introduction to Volney, *Voyage en Egypte et en Syrie*, 16.

20. Said, *Orientalism*, 81.

21. See, for example, Volney's *Ruins; or, Meditation on the Revolution of Empires*, trans. Count Daru (New York: Vale, 1853), 183–84.

22. Said, *Orientalism*, 81.

23. Volney, *Travels*, 2:497. In like manner, Volney praised the Turkish people: "In many ways, the Turkish people are preferable, for legislators, than those of Europe, especially northern Europe. They are ignorant, it is true, but ignorance is better than being falsely knowledgeable. . . . They are neither brutes, nor stupid . . . and, unlike Europeans, disorder is never consecrated by their laws. They have never known, unlike us, the troublesome rights of the feudal system, nor the barbaric prejudice of birth which consecrates our tyrannical aristocratic system." Volney, *Considérations sur la guerre actuelle des Turcs* (London, 1788), 137.

24. Volney, *Travels*, 2:370. He goes on to detail the numerous ways local rulers spent all their time extracting revenue, often dishonestly, from their overburdened subjects.

25. Ibid., 1:197; 2:382–83.

26. Ibid., 2:382.

27. Ibid., 2:378, 385, 389–90.

28. These movements were also Pan-European; see R. R. Palmer's still-useful classic *The Age of the Democratic Revolutions: A Political History of Europe and America, 1760–1800*, 2 vols. (Princeton: Princeton University Press, 1954–64).

29. Volney, *Travels*, 2:481–89. Volney's ideas comparing the position of women in the East and the West are fairly balanced. Thus, while as a whole he considered French women to have greater equality and more interaction with men, he noted that French women, too, especially in the provinces, were sequestered like Oriental women; and, as a consequence of the severe restraints imposed on them, as well as male infidelity, gave themselves over to extramarital affairs (p. 485). He decried the frivolity of French sexual relations in ways that hardly favored Western values, and he noted how infrequent the actual practice of polygamy was (pp. 481, 486). Savary treats women in Egypt as suffering under much harsher conditions. See his *Lettres*, 1:130–43. A fairly recent book on the position of women in Egypt argues that Egyptian women were, in fact, relatively free in late eighteenth-century Egypt, but saw a narrowing of their rights as a backlash after the French left. See Afaf Lutfi al-Sayyid Marsot, *Women and Men in Late Eighteenth-Century Egypt* (Austin: University of Texas Press, 1995).

30. See *L'histoire des deux Indes*, 6:221; and C. L. R. James, *Black Jacobins: Toussaint L'Ouverture and the San Domingo Revolution* (1938; repr., New York: Vintage, 1989), 25. There has been considerable recent literature on the Haitian Revolution, including Carolyn Fick, *The Making of Haiti: The Saint Domingue Revolution from Below* (Knoxville: University of Tennessee Press, 1990); Laurent Dubois, *Avengers of the New World: The Story of the Haitian Revolution* (Cambridge: Harvard University Press, 2004); and John Garrigus, *Before Haiti: Race and Citizenship in French Saint-Domingue* (New York: Palgrave Macmillan, 2006).

31. Volney, *Travels*, 1:203–4. The language Volney used to describe the condition of the Egyptian and Syrian people was that of slavery. Influenced by Raynal and Diderot's *Histoire des deux Indes*, Volney compared Turkish rule over their empire with Caribbean sugar plantations, showing just how thoroughly the metaphor of New World slavery had penetrated French political discourse in the late eighteenth century (p. 2:373).

32. Volney, *Travels*, 1:196–97. That France was in the back of his mind is evident from his conclusion: "Then, remembering that the countries I had seen so desolate and barbarous, were once flourishing and populous, a second resolution succeeded almost involuntarily. 'If formerly,' said I, 'the states of Asia enjoyed this splendor, who can assure us that those of Europe will not one day experience the same reverse?'" Volney, *Travels*, 2:499.

33. On Volney's relationship to French-Turkish policy makers, see Tom Kaiser, "The Evil Empire? The Debate on Turkish Despotism in Eighteenth-Century French Political Culture," *Journal of Modern History* 72, no. 1 (March 2000): 6–34, esp. 26–27.

34. Volney, *Considérations*, 139.

35. Ibid., 125.

36. Juan Cole's recent work, *Napoleon's Egypt*, details the horrors and hypocrisies of Napoleon's venture. Napoleon, purportedly one of Volney's avid readers, helped precipitate the fall of Ottoman rule in Egypt precisely by using Volney's rhetoric, albeit hypocritically and with little genuine

interest in helping the Egyptian people, assuring Egyptian leaders and imams that he would help them break free of Mameluke and Ottoman overlordship. See Robert Tignor's introduction to *Napoleon in Egypt: Al-Jabarti's Chronicle of the French Occupation*, ed. Tignor and trans. Shmuel Moreh (1798; repr., New York: Markus Wiener, 1993), 8. See also Napoleon's proclamation, in *Napoleon in Egypt*, 24–27. It hardly seems fair, however, to blame Napoleon's imperialist venture in Egypt on Volney, as Said seems to do, even if he used Volney's *Voyage* and, more important, *Considérations* to gain knowledge of the region. Said, *Orientalism*, 81–89. As Juan Cole's recent work suggests, the willingness of Talleyrand and Napoleon to encourage and use religion for purposes of state stood in marked contrast to philosophes like Volney, who were determined to undermine the cultural and political power of religious authorities in the East and the West. See Cole, *Napoleon's Egypt: Invading the Middle East* (New York: Palgrave Macmillan, 2007), 18, 116.

37. See Benjamin Stora, *Algeria, 1830–2000: A Short History*, trans. Jane Marie Todd (Ithaca: Cornell University Press, 2001), 1–8. Ann Thompson argues that the call to intervene in Algeria was advocated by Raynal and other Enlightenment figures in the eighteenth century. See her "Arguments for the Conquest of Algiers in the Late Eighteenth and Early Nineteenth Centuries," *Maghreb Review* 14, nos. 1–2 (1989): 108–18.

38. For a recent and excellent biography of Tocqueville, see Hugh Brogan's *Alexis de Tocqueville: A Life* (New Haven: Yale University Press, 2006).

39. Although Tocqueville read Savary's Koran before going to Algeria, he bemoaned the length of time it would take to learn the native language. Tocqueville's very early notes on the Koran anticipate his later argument emphasizing the differences rather than potential similarities between Arabs and Frenchmen. See Tocqueville, "Notes on the Koran (March 1838)," in *Alexis de Tocqueville, Writings on Empire and Slavery*, ed. and trans. Jennifer Pitts (Baltimore: John Hopkins University Press, 2001), 27–35, esp. 32. See also his "Notes on the Voyage to Algeria in 1841," in *Writings on Empire and Slavery*, 49.

40. Tocqueville, "Second Letter on Algeria (22 August 1837)," in *Writings on Empire and Slavery*, 26.

41. See, for example, Matthew Mancini's interesting arguments to this effect in his *Alexis de Tocqueville* (New York: Twayne, 1994), 123–25.

42. Tocqueville, "Essay on Algeria (October 1841)," in *Writings on Empire and Slavery*, 59.

43. Ibid., 60.

44. See, for example, Tocqueville, "First Letter on Algeria (23 June 1837)," in *Writings on Empire and Slavery*, 6: "If Rousseau had known the Kabyles . . . he would not have uttered such nonsense about the Caribs. . . . He would have sought his model in the Atlas." See also his "First Report on Algeria (1847)," in *Writings on Empire and Slavery*, 172.

45. Tocqueville, "Essay on Algeria (October 1841)," 111

46. Ibid., 70.

47. Tocqueville, "First Report on Algeria (1847)," 167–68.

48. On Third Republican imperialism and colonial attitudes, see Alice Conklin, *A Mission to Civilize: The Republican Idea of Empire in France and West Africa, 1895–1930* (Stanford: Stanford University Press, 1997).

49. Tocqueville, "The Emancipation of Slaves (1843)," in *Writings on Empire and Slavery*, 204.

50. Ibid., 206–7.

51. Ibid., 219–21. Jennifer Pitt's important translation of Tocqueville's *Writings on Empire and Slavery*, along with other recent work, gives us a necessary corrective to the otherwise almost entirely hagiographical accounts of Tocqueville in the United States, which rarely mention Tocqueville's positions on either emancipation or Algeria.

52. Sankar Muthu, *Enlightenment Against Empire* (Princeton: Princeton University Press, 2003), 280.

53. For a balanced appraisal of Enlightenment attitudes toward non-Europeans, see Henry Vyverberg, *Human Nature, Cultural Diversity, and the French Enlightenment* (New York: Oxford University Press, 1989).

54. Cited in Muthu, *Enlightenment Against Empire*, 114–15.

55. Cited in ibid., 276.

56. Honour, *From the American Revolution to World War I*, 53.

57. Savary, *Lettres sur l'Egypte*, 3:32–33.

58. Volney, *Travels*, 2:489.

59. Ibid., 2:490.

60. Ibid., 2:499–500.

61. See the many works by Amartya Sen, especially *Identity and Violence: The Illusion of Destiny* (New York: W. W. Norton, 2006); Kenneth Pomeranz, *The Great Divergence: China, Europe, and the Making of the Modern World Economy* (Princeton: Princeton University Press, 2000); Janet Abu-Lughod, *Before European Hegemony: The World System A.D. 1250–1350* (New York: Oxford University Press, 1989); Martin Bernal, *The Fabrication of Ancient Greece, 1785–1985*, vol. 1 of *Black Athena: The Afroasiatic Roots of Classical Civilization* (New Brunswick: Rutgers University Press, 1991); and Kwame Anthony Appiah, *Cosmopolitanism: Ethics in a World of Strangers* (New York: W. W. Norton, 2006).

62. On the Enlightenment's blind spot toward religion, see Vyverberg, *Human Nature, Cultural Diversity, and the French Enlightenment*, 204.

63. Volney, *Ruins*, 72.

Robert Darnton, Carl H. Pforzheimer University Professor and Director
of the Harvard University Library. Photo: Justin Ide, Harvard University

APPENDIX:
PUBLICATIONS BY ROBERT DARNTON

BOOKS

Principal Works

Mesmerism and the End of the Enlightenment in France (Cambridge: Harvard University Press, 1968). Translations into German, French, Japanese, Dutch, Portuguese, Italian, Russian, and Chinese.

The Business of Enlightenment: A Publishing History of the "Encyclopédie," 1775–1800 (Cambridge: Harvard University Press, 1979). Translations into French, Italian, German, Portuguese, Spanish, and Chinese.

The Literary Underground of the Old Regime (Cambridge: Harvard University Press, 1982). Translations into Swedish, German, Dutch, Italian, Japanese, Portuguese, and Korean. A somewhat different work was published in French as *Bohème littéraire et révolution: Le monde des livres au XVIIIe siècle* (Paris: Gallimard and Le Seuil, 1983), and an expanded edition was published by Gallimard in 2010.

The Great Cat Massacre, and Other Episodes in French Cultural History (New York: Basic Books, 1984). Translations into French, German, Dutch, Swedish, Danish, Italian, Spanish, Catalan, Portuguese, Japanese, Hungarian, Russian, Korean, Chinese, Lithuanian, and Hebrew.

The Kiss of Lamourette: Reflections in Cultural History (New York: W. W. Norton, 1989). Translations into German, Dutch, Portuguese, Italian, and Japanese.

Revolution in Print: The Press in France, 1775–1800, coedited with Daniel Roche (Berkeley: University of California Press, 1989). Translation into Portuguese.

Édition et sédition: L'univers de la littérature clandestine au XVIIIe siècle (Paris: Gallimard, 1991). Translations into German, Italian, Dutch, Japanese, Spanish, and Portuguese.

Berlin Journal, 1989–1990 (New York: W. W. Norton, 1991). Translations into German, Dutch, French, and Italian.

Gens de lettres, gens du livre (Paris: Éditions Odile Jacob, 1992).

The Forbidden Best-Sellers of Pre-Revolutionary France (New York: W. W. Norton, 1995). Translations into Italian, Portuguese, Swedish, Japanese, German, Spanish, and Chinese.

The Corpus of Clandestine Literature in France, 1769–1789 (New York: W. W. Norton, 1995).

Démocratie, coedited with Olivier Duhamel (Paris: Éditions du Rocher, 1998). Based on a television series the editors jointly produced; see "Other" section, below.

J.-P. Brissot, His Career and Correspondence (1779–1787) (Oxford: Voltaire Foundation, 2001). An electronic book available only on the web.

George Washington's False Teeth: An Unconventional Guide to the Eighteenth Century (New York: W. W. Norton, 2003). Translations into German, Portuguese, Estonian, Spanish, Italian, and Hebrew.

Le rayonnement d'une maison d'édition dans l'Europe des Lumières: La Société typographique de Neuchâtel, 1769–1789, coedited with Michel Schlup (Neuchâtel: Éditions Gilles, 2005).

The Case for Books: Past, Present, and Future (New York: Public Affairs, 2009). Translations into French, Catalan, and Arabic.

The Devil in the Holy Water, or the Art of Slander in France from Louis XIV to Napoleon (Philadelphia: University of Pennsylvania Press, 2010). Translation into French and others pending.

Poetry and the Police: Communication Networks in Eighteenth-Century Paris (Cambridge: Harvard University Press, 2010).

Works Not Available in English

Drei Vorschläge: Rousseau zu lessen, essays by Ernst Cassirer, Jean Starobinski, and Robert Darnton (Frankfurt: Fischer Taschenbuch Verlag, 1989). Translations into Italian and Spanish.

Luz y contraluz de une historia antropológica (Buenos Aires: Editorial Biblos, 1995).

Denkende Wollust (Frankfurt: Eichborn Verlag, 1996).

Poesie und Polizei: Öffentliche Meinung und Kommunikationsnetzwerke im Paris des 18. Jahrhunderts (Frankfurt: Suhrkamp, 2002).

Pour les Lumières: Défense, illustration, méthode (Pessac: Presses universitaires de Bordeaux, 2002).

El coloquio de los lectores: Ensayos sobre autores, manuscritos, editores y lectores (Mexico City: Fonda de Cultura Económica, 2003).

Die Wissenschaft des Raubdrucks: Ein zentrales Element im Verlagswesen des 18. Jahrhunderts (Munich: Carl Friedrich von Siemens Stiftung, 2003).

Other

The Bohemians: A Novel, by Anne Gédéon La Fitte, marquis de Pelleport, introduced by Robert Darnton, translated by Vivian Folkenflik (Philadelphia: University of Pennsylvania Press, 2010). Translations into French and Dutch.

The Darnton Debate: Books and Revolution in the Eighteenth Century, ed. Haydn Mason (Oxford: Voltaire Foundation, 1998).

Démocratie (La Cinquième-Arte, 1998). A series of twenty-six half-hour telecasts cowritten and cohosted with Olivier Duhamel for French educational television.

What Was Revolutionary About the French Revolution? The Eleventh Charles Edmondson Historical Lectures (Waco: Baylor University Press, 1990).

Articles and Review Essays

"Marat n'a pas été un voleur: Une lettre inedited." *Annales historiques de la Révolution française* 185 (July–September 1966): 447–50.

"The Grub Street Style of Revolution: J.-P. Brissot, Police Spy." *Journal of Modern History* 40, no. 3 (September 1968): 301–27.

"Le lieutenant de police J. C. P. Lenoir, la Guerre des Farines, et l'approvisionnement de Paris à la veille de la Révolution." *Revue d'histoire moderne et contemporaine* 16, no. 4 (October–December 1969): 611–24.

"Une lettre inédite de Turgot." *Annales historiques de la Revolution française* 202 (October–December 1970): 657–61.

"The Memoirs of Lenoir, Lieutenant de Police of Paris, 1774–1785." *English Historical Review* 85, no. 336 (July 1970): 532–59.

"Les papiers du marquis de Sade et la prise de la Bastille." *Annales historiques de la Révolution française* 202 (October–December 1970): 666.

"The High Enlightenment and the Low-Life of Literature in Prerevolutionary France," *Past and Present* 51 (May 1971): 81–115. Reprinted as the first of the annual prize essays awarded by the American Society for Eighteenth-Century Studies in *Studies in Eighteenth-Century Culture* 3 (1973): 83–124.

"Reading, Writing, and Publishing in Eighteenth-Century France: A Case Study in the Sociology of Literature." *Daedalus* 100, no. 1 (Winter 1971): 214–56. Reprinted in *Historical Studies Today*, ed. Felix Gilbert and Stephen Graubard (New York: W. W. Norton, 1972).

"In Search of the Enlightenment: Recent Attempts to Create a Social History of Ideas." *Journal of Modern History* 43, no. 1 (March 1971): 113–32.

"The *Encyclopédie* Wars of Prerevolutionary France." *American Historical Review* 78, no. 5 (December 1973): 1331–52. Reprinted as the annual prize essay in *Studies in Eighteenth-Century Culture* 5 (1975).

"French History: The Case of the Wandering Eye." *New York Review of Books*, April 5, 1973, 25–30. An expanded version of this article appeared in French in *Minuit* 5 (September 1973): 48–64.

"Le livre français à la fin de l'Ancien Régime." *Annales: Économies, sociétés, civilisations* 28, no. 3 (May–June 1973): 735–44.

"Death's Checkered Past." *New York Review of Books*, June 13, 1974, 11–13.

"Giving New Life to Death." *New York Review of Books*, June 27, 1974, 30–32.

"Un commerce de livres 'sous le manteau' en province à la fin de l'Ancien Régime." *Revue française d'histoire du livre* 5, no. 9 (1975): 5–29. Reprinted in *Études sur le XVIIIe siècle*, ed. Roland Mortier and Hervé Hasquin (Brussels: Université libre de Bruxelles, 1976), 39–56.

"Franz Anton Mesmer." In *The Dictionary of Scientific Biography*, vol. 9, ed. Charles Coulston Gillispie (New York: Scribner's Sons, 1975).

"Poverty, Crime, and Revolution." *New York Review of Books*, October 3, 1975, 17–22.

"Writing News and Telling Stories." *Daedalus* 104, no. 2 (Spring 1975): 175–94.

"Trade in the Taboo: The Life of a Clandestine Bookdealer in Provincial France." The Rosenbach Lectures, University of Pennsylvania, published in *The Widening Circle: Essays on the Circulation of Literature in Eighteenth-Century Europe*, ed. Paul J. Korshin (Philadelphia: University of Pennsylvania Press, 1976), 11–83.

"The Life of a 'Poor Devil' in the Republic of Letters." In *Essays on the Age of Enlightenment in Honor of Ira O. Wade*, ed. Jean Macary (Geneva: Droz, 1977), 39–92.

"The History of *Mentalités*: Recent Writings on Revolution, Criminality, and Death in France." In *Structure, Consciousness, and History*, ed. Richard H. Brown and Stanford M. Lyman (Cambridge: Cambridge University Press, 1978), 106–36.

"The World of the Underground Booksellers in the Old Regime." In *Vom Ancien Regime zur Französischen Revolution: Forschungen und Perspecktiven*, ed. Ernest Hinrichs, Eberhard Schmitt, and Rudolf Vierhaus (Göttingen: Vandenhoeck & Ruprecht, 1978), 439–79.

"L'Atelier de Panckoucke en l'An II," *Revue française d'histoire du livre*, n.s., 23 (April–June 1979): 359–70.

"The Rise of the Writer." *New York Review of Books*, May 31, 1979, 26–29.

"Eighteenth-Century French Collections." *Acquisitions Newsletter* (National Library of Australia) 46 (October 1980): 35–38.

"Hunting for Humanity." *New York Review of Books*, May 15, 1980, 3–4.

"Intellectual and Cultural History." In *The Past Before Us: Contemporary Historical Writing in the United States*, ed. Michael Kammen (Ithaca: Cornell University Press, 1980), 327–54.

"What's New About the Old Regime?" *New York Review of Books*, April 3, 1980, 28–30.

"A Bibliographical Imbroglio: Hidden Editions of the *Encyclopédie*." In *Cinq siècles d'imprimerie genevoise*, ed. Jean-Daniel Candaux and Bernard Lescaze (Geneva: Société d'Histoire et d'Archéologie, 1981), 2:71–101.

"Neue Aspekte zur Geschichte der *Encyclopédie*." In *Sozialgeschichte der Aufklärung in Frankreich*, ed. Hans Ulrich Gumbrecht, Rolf Reichardt, and Thomas Schleich (Munich, 1981), 2:34–65.

"Poland Rewrites History." *New York Review of Books*, July 16, 1981, 6–10.

"The Art of Dying." *New York Review of Books*, May 13, 1982, 8–12.

"Work and Culture in an Eighteenth-Century Printing Shop." *Quarterly Journal* (Library of Congress) 39 (Winter 1982).

"The Epistemological Strategy of the *Encyclopédie*." In *Gelehrte Bücher von Humanismus bis zur Gegenwart*, ed. Bernhard Fabian and Paul Raabe (Wiesbaden: Harrassowitz, 1983), 119–34.

"A Survival Strategy for Academic Authors." *American Scholar* 52, no. 4 (Autumn 1983): 533–37.

"What Is the History of Books?" *Daedalus* 111, no. 3 (Summer 1982): 65–83. Reprinted in *Books and Society in History*, ed. Kenneth Carpenter (New York: R. R. Bowker, 1983), 3–26; and in several other works.

De Betekenis van moeder de Gans (the annual Huizinga Lecture at the University of Leyden) (Amsterdam: Athenaeum-Polak and Van Gennep, 1984).

"Les Contes de la mère L'Oye." *Lettre Internationale* 2 (Autumn 1984): 72–77.

"Danton and Double-Entendre." *New York Review of Books*, February 16, 1984, 19–24.

"Endpapers." *Los Angeles Times Book Review*, November 11, 1984, 15.

"The Great Cat Massacre, 1730." *History Today* 34, no. 8 (August 1984): 7–15.

"La Ilustración y los 'bajos fondos' de la literatura de la Francia prerrevolucionaria."
Revista de Occidente 41, no. 3 (October 1984): 7–46.

"Lesen im vorrevolutionären Frankreich." *Neue Rundschau* 95 (1984): 187–98.

"Le livre prohibé aux frontières: Neuchâtel." In *Le livre triomphant (1660–1830)*, ed.
Roger Chartier and Henri-Jean Martin, vol. 2 of *Histoire de l'édition française* (Paris,
1984), 342–59.

"The Meaning of Mother Goose." *New York Review of Books*, February 2, 1984, 41–47.

"The Origins of Modern Reading." *New Republic*, February 27, 1984, 26–32.

"Policing Writers in Paris Circa 1750." *Representations* 5 (Winter 1984): 1–31.
A somewhat different version published in French as "Dossiers secrets sur les
écrivains des Lumières," *L'Histoire* 64 (February 1984): 64–71.

"Scholarship and Readership: New Directions in the History of the Book." In *Books
and Prints, Past and Future: Papers Presented at the Grolier Club Centennial Convocation,
26–28 April 1984* (New York: Grolier Club, 1984), 33–51.

"Sounding the Literary Market in Prerevolutionary France." *Eighteenth-Century
Studies* 17, no. 23 (Summer 1984): 477–92.

"Working-Class Casanova." *New York Review of Books*, June 28, 1984, 32–37.

"Dialogue à propos de l'histoire culturelle" (with Pierre Bourdieu and Roger
Chartier). *Actes de la recherche en sciences sociales* 59 (September 1985): 86–93.

"La lecture rousseauiste et un lecteur 'ordinaire' au XVIIIe siècle." In *Pratiques de la
lecture*, ed. Roger Chartier (Marseille: Éditions Rivages, 1985), 125–55.

"Revolution sans Revolutionaries." *New York Review of Books*, January 31, 1985, 21–23.

"Rousseau und sein Leser." *Zeitschrift für Literaturwissenschaft und Linguistik* 15, nos.
57/58 (1985): 111–46.

"The Social Life of Rousseau: Anthropology and the Loss of Innocence." *Harper's
Magazine*, July 1985, 69–73.

"L'Anthropologie ou la perte de l'innocence." *Lettre internationale* 10 (1986): 36–38.

"Les Encyclopédistes et la police." *Recherches sur Diderot et sur l'Encyclopédie* 1, no. 1
(October 1986): 94–109.

"First Steps Toward a History of Reading." *Australian Journal of French Studies* 23
(1986): 5–30.

"The Forgotten Middlemen of Literature." *New Republic*, September 1986, 44–50.

"Geschäfte der Aufklärung." *Frankfurter Allgemeine Zeitung*, June 18, 1986, 33–34.

"Le marché littéraire français vu de Neuchâtel (1769–1789)." In *Aspects du livre neuchâtelois*, ed. Jacques Rychner and Michel Schlup (Neuchâtel: Bibliothèque publique et universitaire, 1986), 59–75.

"Pop Foucaultism." *New York Review of Books*, October 9, 1986, 15–16.

"The Symbolic Element in History." *Journal of Modern History* 58, no. 1 (March 1986): 218–34.

"Un colporteur sous l'Ancien Régime." In *Censures: De la bible aux larmes d'éros*, ed. Martine Poulain and Françoise Serre (Paris: Centre Georges Pompidou, Bibliothèque Publique d'Information, 1987), 130–39.

"The Facts of Literary Life in Eighteenth-Century France." In *The Political Culture of the Old Regime*, ed. Keith Baker (Oxford: Pergamon Press, 1987), 261–91.

"Histoire du livre: Geschichte des Buchwesens: An Agenda for Comparative History." *Publishing History* 22 (1987): 33–41.

"Literary History and the Library." *Princeton University Library Chronicle* 48, no. 2 (Winter 1987): 145–53.

"Robert Shackleton and a Vanishing Species of Dons." *American Oxonian* 54, no. 2 (Spring 1987): 90–93.

"*L'Encyclopédie*, an Eighteenth-Century Best-Seller." *The Courier*, July 1988, 28–31.

"The Heavenly City of the Eighteenth-Century Scholars." *ASECS News Circular* 70 (Fall 1988): 3.

"Livres philosophiques." In *Enlightenment Essays in Memory of Robert Shackleton*, ed. Giles Barber (Oxford: Voltaire Foundation, 1988), 89–107.

"A Star Is Born." *New York Review of Books*, October 27, 1988, 84–88.

"El beso de la fraternidad." *La Gageta del fondo de cultura económica*, June 1989, 20–27.

"Five Theses on Cultural Transmission." *Intellectual History Newsletter* 11 (June 1989): 3–4.

"Ideology on the Bourse." In *L'image de la Révolution française*, ed. Michel Vovelle (Paris: Pergamon Press, 1989), 124–39.

"An Open Letter to a TV Producer: Liberty, Equality, Absurdity." *New Republic*, April 3, 1989, 29–32.

"Toward a History of Reading." *Wilson Quarterly* 13, no. 4 (Autumn 1989): 87–102.

"Was war revolutionär an der Französischen Revolution?" *Neue Rundschau* 100, no. 3 (1989): 5–22.

"What Was Revolutionary About the French Revolution?" *New York Review of Books*, January 19, 1989, 3–10.

"Aus der Sicht des Zensors: Von der Uberwachung der Literatur." *Lettre Internationale* 10 (Autumn 1990): 6–9.

"The Brissot Dossier." *French Historical Studies* 17, no. 1 (Spring 1991): 191–205.

"Don Juanism from Below." In *Don Giovanni: Myths of Seduction and Betrayal*, ed. Jonathan Miller (New York: Schocken, 1990), 20–35.

"Écrit sur le mur." *Le Courrier de l'UNESCO*, June 1990, 12–17.

"Ein Zusammenbruch geborgter Legitimität: Die deutsche Revolution 1989 entsprach nicht den Handbüchern und Wünschen der intellektuellen." *Frankfurter Allgemeine Zeitung*, November 7, 1990, 3. Reprinted in the *German Tribune*, November 25, 1990, 5–7.

"Adventures of a Germanophobe." *Wilson Quarterly* 15, no. 3 (Summer 1991): 113–19.

"An Enlightened Revolution?" *New York Review of Books*, October 24, 1991, 33–36.

"The Fall of the House of Art." *New Republic*, May 6, 1991, 27–33.

"The Forbidden Books of Pre-Revolutionary France." In *Rewriting the French Revolution*, ed. Colin Lucas (Oxford: Clarendon Press, 1991), 1–32. Published in German as "Die verbotenen Bestseller in vorrevolutionären Frankreich," *Leipziger Jahrbuch zur Buchgeschichte* 1 (1991): 117–38.

"The Good Old Days." *New York Review of Books*, May 16, 1991, 44–48.

"The Literary Revolution of 1789." *Studies in Eighteenth-Century Culture* 21 (1992): 3–26.

"Runes of the New Revolutions." *Times Higher Education Supplement*, September 6, 1991, 16–17.

"Les métamorphoses de l'*Encyclopédie*." *Recherches sur Diderot et sur l'Encyclopédie*, April 1992, 21–23.

"Reading a Riot." *New York Review of Books*, October 22, 1992, 44–46.

"Die Republik des Geistes mit Blick nach Osten." In *Intellektuellendämmerung: Beiträge zur neuesten Zeit des Geistes*, ed. Martin Meyer (Munich: Carl Hanser Verlag, 1992), 226–48.

"O significado cultural da censura: A França de 1789 e a Alemanha oriental de 1989." *Revista Brasileira de Ciências Sociais* 7, no. 18 (February 1992): 5–17.

"'La France, ton café fout le camp!' De l'histoire du livre à l'histoire de la communication." *Actes de la recherche en sciences sociales* 100 (December 1993): 16–26.

"The Life Cycle of a Book: A Publishing History of d'Holbach's *Système de la nature*." In *Publishing and Readership in Revolutionary France and America*, ed. Carol Armbruster (Westport, Conn.: Greenwood Press, 1993), 15–43.

"Reviving the Republic of Letters." In *Transactions of the Eighth International Congress on the Enlightenment* (Oxford: Oxford University Press, 1993), 3–16.

"Seven Bad Reasons Not to Study Manuscripts." *Harvard Library Bulletin* 4, no. 4 (Winter 1993–94): 37–42.

"Book History, the State of Play." *Sharp News* 3 (Summer 1994): 2–4.

"Freed Between the Lines." *Times Higher Education Supplement*, February 18, 1994, 16–17.

"Last der Geschichte." *Frankfurter Allgemeine Zeitung*, April 16, 1994, 63.

"Robespierre—der Osten." *Frankfurter Allgemeine Zeitung*, November 12, 1994, 27.

"Rousseau in Gesellschaft: Anthropologie und der Verlust der Unschuld." In *Drei Vorschläge Rousseau zu lesen*, ed. Ernst Cassirer, Jean Starobinski, and Robert Darnton (Frankfurt: Fischer Taschenbuch Verlag, 1989), 104–14. Published in Italian as *Tre letture di Rousseau* (Rome: Editore Laterza, 1994).

"Sex for Thought." *New York Review of Books*, December 22, 1994, 65–74.

"Censorship, a Comparative View: France, 1789–East Germany, 1989." In *Historical Change and Human Rights: The Oxford Amnesty Lectures, 1994*, ed. Oliver Hufton (New York: Basic Books, 1995), 101–30.

"Cherchez la femme." *New York Review of Books*, August 10, 1995, 22–24.

"Diffusion vs. Discourse: Conceptual Shifts in Intellectual History and the Historiography of the French Revolution." In *Historia a debate*, ed. Carlos Barros (Santiago de Compostela, Spain: Historia a Debate, 1995), 3:179–92.

"An Exemplary Literary Career." In *André Morellet (1727–1819) in the Republic of Letters and the French Revolution*, ed. Jeffrey Merrick and Dorothy Medlin (New York: Peter Lang, 1995), 5–26.

"Fraternity: A Heretical View." *Odissei* (Moscow, 1994), 232–38.

"Histoire du livre—Geschichte des Buchwesens: An Agenda for Comparative History." In *Histoire du livre: Nouvelles orientations*, ed. Hans Erich Bödeker (Paris: Maison des sciences de l'homme, 1995), 451–58. Reprinted in *Studia Culturologica 3* (1995): 187–92.

"In der Medienfalle: Eine kleine Geschichte des Unflats." *Frankfurter Allgemeine Zeitung*, October 11, 1995, 5.

"Informo, dunque diffamo: Quando la stampa distorce la realtà." *Etruria Oggi* 38 (April 1995): 24–26.

"El libelo politico." *Nexos* 212 (August 1995): 37–45.

"A Philosophe Confronts the Terror." In *André Morellet (1727–1819) in the Republic of Letters and the French Revolution*, ed. Jeffrey Merrick and Dorothy Medlin (New York: Peter Lang, 1995), 27–38.

"The Pursuit of Happiness." *Wilson Quarterly* 19, no. 4 (Autumn 1995): 42–52.

"Sex ist gut fürs Denken! Vom emanzipatorischen Potentialen der Pornographie." *Lettre international* 28 (March 1995): 54–59.

"How to Read a Book." *New York Review of Books*, June 6, 1996, 52–57.

"Du Libertinage aux Lumières." *La Lettre clandestine* 5 (1996): 157–60.

"Nouvelles pistes en histoire du livre." *Revue française d'histoire du livre* 90/91 (1996): 173–80.

"Zur Bewegung geschrumpft: Was ist Aufklärung? Eine Antwort im Zeitalter der Inflationen." *Frankfurter Allgemeine Zeitung*, October 2, 1996, 6.

"Best-Sellers and Gossip-Mongers in Eighteenth-Century France." *UNESCO Courier*, June 1997, 14–18.

"Condorcet and the Craze for America in France." In *Franklin and Condorcet: Two Portraits from the American Philosophical Society*, ed. Jonathan Brown (Philadelphia: American Philosophical Society, 1997), 27–39.

"Fraternidade ou os periogs da história ethnográfica." *Folha de São Paulo*, June 6, 1997, 9–10.

"Free Spirit." *New York Review of Books*, June 26, 1997, 9–11.

"George Washington's False Teeth." *New York Review of Books*, March 27, 1997, 34–38.

"La Ilustración en el cadalso." *Crónica dominical*, May 18, 1997, 1–5.

"Shifting Symbolic Scenery in Berlin." *L'histoire grande ouverte: Hommages à Emmanuel Le Roy Ladurie*, ed. André Burguière, Joseph Goy, and Marie-Jeanne Tits-Dieuaide (Paris: Fayard, 1997), 133–38.

"Stratégies financières d'une maison d'édition au XVIIIe siècle." *Le livre et l'historien: Études offertes en l'honneur du Professeur Henri-Jean Martin*, ed. Frédéric Barbier et al. (Geneva: Droz, 1997), 519–26.

"The East-West Seminar in Eighteenth-Century Studies." In *La Recherche dix-huitiémiste: Objets, méthodes et institutions (1945–1995)*, ed. Michel Delon and Jochen Schlobach (Paris: Champion, 1998), 179–227.

"George Washington's False Teeth: A Civic Sermon." In *La Recherche dix-huitiémiste Objets, méthodes et institutions (1945–1995)*, ed. Michel Delon and Jochen Schlobach (Paris: Champion, 1998), 149–65. A reprint of an article published in 1997 (see above).

"Das amerikanische Jahrkundert." *Frankfurter Allgemeine Zeitung*, September 25 1999, 3.

"Lost and Found in Cyberspace." *Chronicle of Higher Education*, March 12, 1999, 134–35.

"New Life in e-books." *Times Higher Education Supplement*, March 5, 1999, 10. Reprint of the 1999 *New York Review of Books* article "The New Age of the Book" (see below).

"Le nouvel age du livre." *Le Débat* 105 (May–August 1999): 176–84. Reprint of the 1999 *New York Review of Books* article "The New Age of the Book" (see below).

"The New Age of the Book." *New York Review of Books*, March 18, 1999, 5–7.

"Poetry and the Police in Eighteenth-Century Paris." *Studies on Voltaire and the Eighteenth Century* 371 (1999): 1–22.

"The Real Marquis." *New York Review of Books*, January 14, 1999, 19–24.

"What American Century?" *European Review* 7, no. 4 (1999): 455–59.

"An Early Information Society: News and the Media in Eighteenth-Century Paris." *American Historical Review* 105, no. 1 (February 2000): 1–35. An expanded electronic version of this essay, Darnton's presidential address to the American Historical Association, was published online at http://www.historians.org/info/aha_history/rdarnton.htm. Reprinted in Portuguese in *Varia historia* 25 (July 2001): 9–51.

"Extraordinary Commonplaces." *New York Review of Books*, December 21, 2000, 82–87.

"Libraries: A Backward Look into Their Future." *Biblion: The Bulletin of the New York Public Library* 8, no. 2 (Spring 2000): 3–10.

"Looking the Devil in the Face." *New York Review of Books*, February 10, 2000, 14–16.

"'Philosophical Sex': Pornography in Old Regime France." In *Enlightenment, Passion, Modernity: Historical Essays in European Thought and Culture*, ed. Mark S. Micale and Robert L. Dietle (Stanford: Stanford University Press, 2000), 88–110.

Preface to Roland Mortier, *Les Combats des Lumières* (Ferney-Voltaire: Centre international d'étude du XVIIIe siècle, 2000), xxv–xxxi.

"Public Opinion and Communication Networks in Eighteenth-Century Paris." In *Opinion*, ed. Peter-Eckhard Knabe (Berlin: Spitz, 2000), 149–230.

"Robert Darnton." In *As muitas faces da história*, ed. Maria Lúcia Garcia Pallares-Burke (São Paolo, 2000), 233–68.

"Seeing and Hearing in the Age of Watteau." Published online by the American Federation of Arts at http://www.afaweb.org/education/watteau-transcripts.asp.

"Books in the British Raj: The Contradictions of Liberal Imperialism." In *Gutenberg-Jahrbuch, 2001*, ed. Stephan Füssel (Mainz: Gutenberg-Gesellschaft, 2001), 36–59. Another version appeared as "Literary Surveillance in the British Raj: The Contradictions of Liberal Imperialism," *Book History* 4 (2001): 133–76.

"Epistemological Angst: From Encyclopedism to Advertising." In *The Structure of Knowledge: Classifications of Science and Learning Since the Renaissance*, ed. Tore Frängsmyr (Berkeley: University of California Press, 2001), 53–75.

"The Great Book Massacre." *New York Review of Books*, April 26, 2001, 16–19.

"J.-P. Brissot and the Société typographique de Neuchâtel (1779–1787)." *Studies on Voltaire and the Eighteenth Century* 10 (2001): 5–47.

"Kleine Geschichte der *Encyclopédie*." In *Die Welt der Encyclopédie*, ed. Anette Selg and Rainer Wieland (Frankfurt: Eichborn, 2001), 454–64.

"Un-British Activities." *New York Review of Books*, April 12, 2001, 84–88.

"Book Production in British India, 1850–1900." *Book History* 5 (2002): 239–62.

"Entrevista." *Topoi: Revista de Historia*, September 2002, 389–97.

"A Euro State of Mind." *New York Review of Books*, February 28, 2002, 30–32. A somewhat different version appeared in German as "Das Glück der Gemeinschaft," *Der Spiegel*, January 7, 2002, 148–59, reprinted in *Experiment Europa: Ein Kontinent Macht Geschichte*, ed. Stefan Aust and Michael Schmidt-Klingenberg (Stuttgart: Deutsche Verlags-Anstalt, 2003), 125–43; in Portuguese as "Fronteiras imagininárias," *Folha de São Paulo*, July 21, 2002, 4–9; and in Spanish in *Lettra internacional* 75 (2002): 4–9.

"How Historians Play God." *Raritan: A Quarterly Review* 22, no. 1 (Summer 2002): 1–19. Reprinted in *European Review* 11, no. 3 (2003): 267–80; and in *Storia della Storiografia* 49 (2006): 3–15.

"Robert Darnton." In *The New History*, ed. Maria Lúcia G. Pallares-Burke (Cambridge: Polity, 2002), 158–83.

"La Société typographique et les batailles autour de *l'Encyclopédie*." In *L'édition neuchâteloise au siècle des Lumières: La Société typographique de Neuchâtel* (Neuchâtel: Bibliothèque publique et universitaire, 2002), 114–29.

"La Société typographique de Neuchâtel et la librairie française." In *L'édition neuchâteloise au siècle des Lumières: La Société typographique de Neuchâtel* (Neuchâtel: Bibliothèque publique et universitaire, 2002), 210–31.

"The Heresies of Bibliography." *New York Review of Books*, May 29, 2003, 43–45.

"History, Anthropology, and Journalism." In *Être dix-huitiémiste*, ed. Sergueï Karp (Ferney-Voltaire: Centre international d'étude du XVIIIe siècle, 2003), 259–77.

"I Like Contradictions." *Zeitenblicke* 2, no. 2 (2003), http://www.zeitenblicke.de/2002/02/index.html.

"Mlle Bonafon et *La vie privée de Louis XV*." *Dix-huitième siècle* 35 (2003): 369–91.

"The Science of Piracy: A Crucial Ingredient in Eighteenth-Century Publishing." *Studies on Voltaire and the Eighteenth Century* 12 (2003): 3–29. Reprinted in French as "La Science de la contrefaçon," *Revue Voltaire* 4 (2004): 253–70.

"Wielka rzez kotów." *Konteksty: Antropologia kultury, Etnografia Sztuka* 57, nos. 1–2 (2003): 83–97.

"All the News That's Fit to Sing." *Smithsonian* 35, no. 7 (October 2004): 110–19.

"Eine anstrengende Tour." *Frankfurter Allgemeine Zeitung*, July 7, 2004, 3.

"Il faut savoir compter." *French Historical Studies* 27 (Fall 2004): 725–31.

"It Happened One Night." *New York Review of Books*, June 24, 2004, 60–64. Portuguese version in *Folha de São Paulo*, June 13, 2004, 9–12; Spanish version in *Varia historia* 21 (July 2005): 290–304.

"Mlle Bonafon and *The Private Life of Louis XV*: Communication Circuits in Eighteenth-Century France." *Representations* 87, no. 1 (Summer 2004): 102–24. This is a much-revised version of an article originally written in French for *Dix-huitième siècle* and published in 2003 (see above). An enlarged version came out as a booklet in Spanish: *Mademoiselle Bonafon y la vida privada de Luis XV: Circuitos de communicación en la Francia del siglo XVIII*, Cuadernos de la Facultad de Letras y Ciencias Humanas, Pontificia Universidad Católica del Perú, March 2005. Also reprinted in *Media and Political Culture in the Eighteenth Century*, ed. Marie-Christine Skuncke (Kungl: Vitterhets Historie och Antikvitets Akademien, 2005), 21–54; in *Buchkulturen: Beiträge zur Geschichte der Literaturvermittlung*, ed. Monika Estermann, Ernst Fischer, and Ute

Schneider (Wiesbaden: Harrassowitz, 2005), 189–210; and in *Grands Articles: Sélections des meilleurs articles publiés par les revues françaises et internationales* 1 (Fall 2005): 66–77.

"Vies privées et affaires publiques sous l'Ancien Régime." *Actes de la recherche en sciences sociales* 154, 24–35.

"A cultura do boca a boca." *Folha de São Paulo*, February 6, 2005, 4.

"Collecting and Researching in the History of Books." *Princeton University Library Chronicle* 67, no. 1 (Autumn 2005): 49–55.

"Discourse and Diffusion." *Contributions to the History of Concepts* 1, no. 1 (March 2005): 21–28.

"Entre l'éditeur et le libraire: Les étapes des ventes." In *Le Rayonnement d'une maison d'édition dans l'Europe des Lumières: La Société typographique de Neuchâtel, 1769–1789*, ed. Robert Darnton and Michel Schlup (Neuchâtel: Éditions Gilles Attinger, 2005), 343–74.

"Old Books and e-books: The Gutenberg Prize Acceptance Speech of 2004." *Gutenberg-Jahrbuch* (Mainz: Gutenberg-Gesellschaft, 2005): 17–20.

Preface to *Le Rayonnement d'une maison d'édition dans l'Europe des Lumières: La Société typographique de Neuchâtel, 1769–1789*, ed. Robert Darnton and Michel Schlup (Neuchâtel: Éditions Gilles Attinger, 2005), 7–15.

"La Science de la contrefaçon." In *Le Rayonnement d'une maison d'édition dans l'Europe des Lumières: La Société typographique de Neuchâtel, 1769–1789*, ed. Robert Darnton and Michel Schlup (Neuchâtel: Éditions Gilles Attinger, 2005), 88–113. Also appeared in *Revue Voltaire* 4 (2004): 253–70; and translated into Portuguese as "A ciência da piratoaria: Um ingrediente crucial na edição do século XVIII," in *In si(s) tu: Revista de cultura urbana*, March 2005, 126–57.

Bohemians Before Bohemianism, KB Lecture, 2006, published as a pamphlet by the Netherlands Institute for Advanced Study (Wassenaar, 2006).

"Gamla böcker och e-böcker: Tal vid mottagandet av Gutenberg-priset, 2004." *Biblis* 36 (Winter 2006–7): 2–9.

Preface to François Moureau, *La plume et le plomb: Espaces de l'imprimé et du manuscrit au siècle des Lumières* (Paris: Presses de l'Université Paris-Sorbonne, 2006), 7–10.

"Anthropology, History, and Clifford Geertz." *Historically Speaking*, March–April 2007, 8, 33–34.

"The Devil in the Holy Water: Political Libel in Eighteenth-Century France." *Proceedings of the British Academy* 151 (2007): 387–422.

Foreword to Thierry Rigogne, *Between State and Market: Printing and Bookselling in Eighteenth-Century France* (Oxford: Voltaire Foundation, 2007), xv–xvii.

"Hvad er Boghistorie?" *Passage* 57, no. 2 (May 2007): 7–28.

"Old Books and e-books." *European Review* (2007), 15, 165–70.

"On Clifford Geertz: Field Notes from the Classroom." *New York Review of Books*, January 11, 2007, 32–33.

"'What Is the History of Books?' Revisited." *Modern Intellectual History* 4, no. 3 (November 2007): 495–508.

"Why Study the History of Books?" *Princeton University Library Chronicle* 67 (Spring 2007): 673–80.

"Finding a Lost Prince of Bohemia." *New York Review of Books*, April 3, 2008, 44–48.

"The Library in the New Age." *New York Review of Books*, June 12, 2008, 72–80.

"Google and the Future of Books." *New York Review of Books*, February 12, 2009, 9–11.

"Google and the New Digital Future." *New York Review of Books*, December 17, 2009, 82–84.

"On the Ropes?" *Publishers Weekly*, September 14, 2009.

"Reading, Now and Then." *Huffington Post*, October 5, 2009, http://www.huffington post.com/robert-darnton/reading-now-and-then_b_308767.html.

"Blogging, Now and Then." *New York Review of Books Blog*, March 18, 2010, http://www.nybooks.com/blogs/nyrblog/2010/mar/18/blogging-now-and-then/.

"The Grub Street Project. A Cautionary Tale." In *The Shape of Things to Come*, ed. Jerome McGann (Houston: Rice University Press, 2010), 59–63.

CONTRIBUTORS

David A. Bell is Sidney and Ruth Lapidus Professor in the Era of North Atlantic Revolutions at Princeton University. He is a historian of early modern France, and his most recent book is *The First Total War: Napoleon's Europe and the Birth of Warfare as We Know It* (2007). He has authored two other books and many articles. His scholarship has been recognized with the Gottschalk, Gershoy, and Pinkney book prizes, and with the Guggenheim and Burkhardt fellowships.

Roger Chartier is Professor at the Collège de France, Professor at the École des Hautes Études en Sciences Sociales, and Annenberg Visiting Professor at the University of Pennsylvania. He is a historian of written culture, publishing, and reading practices. His most recent book in English is *Inscription and Erasure: Literature and Written Culture from the Eleventh to the Eighteenth Century* (2007).

Tabetha Ewing is Associate Professor of History and Dean of Studies at Bard High School Early College. She specializes in the cultural history of mid-eighteenth-century France, focusing on Parisian public opinion.

Jeffrey Freedman is Associate Professor and Chair of the History Department at Yeshiva University in New York City. He is the author of two books: *A Poisoned Chalice* (2002) and *Books Without Borders: Cultural Intermediaries and Literary Markets in Enlightenment Europe* (forthcoming).

Carla Hesse is the Peder Sather Professor of History and Dean of Social Sciences at the University of California, Berkeley. She is the author and editor of several works, including *Publishing and Cultural Politics in Revolutionary France, 1789–1810* (1991) and *The Other Enlightenment: How French Women Became Modern* (2001). Currently, she is completing a manuscript titled "The Spirit of Revolutionary Law: Foundational Justice and the Politics of Legitimation in Republican France" and a series of studies of the afterlives of Jean-Jacques Rousseau. In 2007, she was the recipient of the Aby Warburg Prize and was inducted into the American Academy of Arts and Sciences in 2009.

Thomas M. Luckett chairs the History Department at Portland State University. He is the author of several articles and book chapters on the commercial history of eighteenth-century France. He is a member of the editorial board of the multivolume journal of the eighteenth-century Parisian observer Siméon-Prosper Hardy, *Mes loisirs, ou journal d'évènements tels qu'ils parviennent à ma connaissance (1753–1789)*, ed. Daniel Roche and Pascal Bastien (2008–). He is preparing a study of rioting in Paris during the pre-Revolution.

Sarah Maza is Jane Long Professor in the Arts and Sciences at Northwestern University and the author of three books on eighteenth- and nineteenth-century French social and cultural history. Her most recent book is *Violette Nozière: A Story of Murder in 1930s Paris* (2011).

Renato Pasta is Professor of Early Modern European History at the University of Florence. He specializes in the social and intellectual history of the Enlightenment, books and print, and institutions of learning. He is the author of *Scienza, politica e rivoluzione: L'opera di Giovanni Fabbroni (1752–1822), intellettuale e funzionario al servizio dei Lorena* (1989), *Editoria e cultura nel Settecento* (1997), and "The History of Books and Publishing in Eighteenth-Century Italy" (2005). He has edited a critical edition of Pietro Verri's late eighteenth-century history of Milan, *Storia di Milano* (2009).

Thierry Rigogne is Assistant Professor of History at Fordham University. His research explores the links between commerce, communication, and the culture and politics of early modern France. He is the author of *Between State and Market: Printing and Bookselling in Eighteenth-Century France* (2007). He is currently working on a book on the development of the French café from the introduction of coffee in the seventeenth century to the end of the French Revolution.

Leonard N. Rosenband is Professor of History at Utah State University. He is the author of *Papermaking in Eighteenth-Century France: Management, Labor, and Revolution at the Montgolfier Mill, 1761–1805* (2000), which appeared in a French translation in 2005. With Jeff Horn and Merritt Roe Smith, he co-edited *Reconceptualizing the Industrial Revolution* (2010).

Shanti Singham is Professor of History and Chair of the Africana Studies Program at Williams College. She specializes in eighteenth-century French political culture, with a focus on racism, imperialism, and resistance. Her publications include "Imbued with Patriotism: The Maupeou Crisis and the Politicization of the *Mémoires secrets*" (1998), "Betwixt Cattle and Men: Jews, Blacks, and Women and the Declaration of the Rights of Man" (1994), and "France, Algeria, Iraq: Teaching and Activism in a Time of War" (2006). She has been on the Steering Committee of Historians Against the War, where she spearheaded a Petition of Historians Against the War (2007), and is a political activist and community organizer in Chicago, Illinois, and Williamstown, Massachusetts.

Will Slauter is Maître de conférences at the University of Paris VIII–Saint-Denis, where he is a member of the Groupe de recherches en histoire intellectuelle. His essay in this volume was part of his dissertation research on international news in the age of the American Revolution. He is currently working on a history of intellectual property in journalism, focusing on English and American newspapers of the eighteenth and nineteenth centuries.

Charles Walton is Associate Professor of History at Yale University and specializes in the history of Old Regime, Enlightenment, and revolutionary France. His first book, *Policing Public Opinion in the French Revolution: The Culture of Calumny and the Problem of Free Speech* (2009), was awarded the Gaddis Smith International Book Prize by the MacMillan Center of Yale. He is currently writing a manuscript about cultural reciprocity and revolutionary politics titled "From Eden to the Terror: Reciprocity, Rights, and Free Market Politics in the French Revolution."

INDEX

Milton Keynes UK
Ingram Content Group UK Ltd.
UKHW010259220224
438247UK00001B/148